TOUCHING THE NEXT HORIZON

Other books by the author:

Experiences of Trance, Physical Mediumship and Associated Phenomena with the Stewart Alexander Circle Part One

Experiences of Trance, Physical Mediumship and Associated Phenomena with the Stewart Alexander Circle Part Two

Experiences of Trance, Physical Mediumship and Associated Phenomena with the Stewart Alexander Circle Part Three

Touching the Next Horizon

Experiences of Trance and Physical Mediumship
with the
Stewart Alexander Circle

the revised and updated version
of the original three books

Written and compiled by
Katie Halliwell

First edition 2021

Published by
Saturday Night Press Publications
England

snppbooks@gmail.com
www.snppbooks.com

ISBN 978-1-908421-47-0

www.snppbooks.com

DEDICATION

I dedicate this book to you all ~
to all those in both worlds
whom I have met on my journey ~
and to all of you who join me now.
May your journey be as enjoyable as mine.

ACKNOWLEDGEMENTS

I wish to thank Stewart and the Alexander Home Circle for their dedication and time in sitting over many decades, long before I became an honorary member.

Credit must of course be given to the Spirit Team for their continuous and everlasting patience in developing the medium and his home circle throughout these many years.

Also thank you to Tom and Ann Harrison for launching the original Trilogy; without their help, this publication would not have been born. And, an extra special thank you to Ann for all the time she spent on audio typing the transcripts incorporated here.

Gratitude must also go to the researchers and delegates of the Stewart Alexander and Friends seminars who contributed to the creation of the Trilogy.

And thank you to Warren James for setting up the on-line recordings for this edition. His computer knowledge truly helped an author who doesn't understand today's technology unless it works by steam.

I would also like thank Leslie Kean, the American journalist I met in 2015. Her invaluable contribution to this interesting subject is very much appreciated, along with her time in editing this new single volume.

For my updated photograph taken and donated by Philip Fearnley my grateful thanks, and also to Christine Turner for checking my ongoing work.

Finally, to my mentors Robert and Georgina Brake, words of thanks could never be enough. Without you, I would not have found my path to physical mediumship and a whole new world.

Wherever we walk, there will always be another horizon.

Such is the continuity of life.

I never thought that I would have to isolate and cut my own hair.

Many changes were forced upon us all during the Coronavirus Pandemic[1] and my heart went out to all those who suffered much during this difficult time.

Despite the isolation, in many ways the sudden experience did bring us closer together by thinking of others rather than ourselves.

I hope that this book will continue to play its part by offering food for thought, sustenance for the soul and comfort for the bereaved.

Katie Halliwell

1. The Coronavirus Pandemic shocked the human race in 2020 as it spread all over the world causing life to be put on hold. Government ordered lockdowns halted social mixing, masks had to be worn and many had to isolate to prevent the awful disease spreading. (Even the Alexander Circle had to stop sitting).

CONTENTS

Key:

The abbreviations of the main names in the verbatim accounts and recording transcripts.

The Spirit team

W.F. – White Feather.

W.   – Walter Stinson.

V.   – Vanguard – later known as Dr. Barnett.

Dr B. – Dr Barnett.

F.   – Freda Johnson.

Ch. – Christopher – speaks child-like.

Circle members and frequent visitors

S.   – Stewart Alexander, (the medium).

R.   – Ray Lister, (circle leader).

J.   – June Lister, (Ray's wife).

K.   – Katie Halliwell, (myself, hon. member).

G.   – Gaynor, (Stewart's sister).

M.   – Michael, (Stewart's brother).

L.   – Lindsey, (Gaynor's daughter).

C.   – Carol, (circle member).

T.   – Tom, (Harrison, honorary member).
              (*and in spirit after Oct 2010*)

A.   – Ann, (Tom's wife, honorary member).

Chris. – (circle member – not shortened).

Jane. – (circle member – not shortened to avoid confusion with June).

Chr. – Christine, (Katie's sister).

After showing the name of the person who is speaking it is usually shortened to an initial thereafter – unless there are two names similar.

Introduction

"A group of us, including a medium, were sitting in the living room in broad daylight just chatting away," my friend Ena told me, "when the medium happened to drift off to sleep. I suddenly heard my mother's voice speaking clearly from the middle of the ceiling and everyone else heard her too." Ena pointed upwards as she spoke. "Really?" was my reply, as I sat on her settee, quietly wondering how a deceased mother could possibly speak in mid air. Surely Ena must have had a vivid imagination, I mused, but then again she had said everyone who was there heard it. Puzzled, I continued to search for a rational explanation for this supposedly disembodied voice, but I failed to come to any conclusion.

I would often visit Robert and Georgina Brake, usually known as Bob and Ena, back in the 1990s to glean information about spirit communication. They had accumulated a vast amount of knowledge on extraordinary phenomena generated by physical mediums and had sat in 'séances' with many of them, including the famous Helen Duncan[1]. With great enthusiasm, Ena often described their experiences with Mrs Duncan. She told me that her first husband Ronald Hill, who was killed in World War II, materialised, stepped out of the cabinet (an enclosed space where

---

1. Helen Duncan was an outstanding physical medium in the 1930s to 50s. She was revered by many. Through Helen's wonderful mediumship, the so-called deceased and victims of World War II were able to materialise, walk around the room, and directly converse with their loved ones on the earth plane.

the medium sits), and then physically talked to her and Bob, giving his blessing on their marriage.

How could I possibly accept something so extraordinary, something that could not be possible? I remember tactfully leaning back on the settee, not knowing what to think, and when I glanced at Bob, he immediately sensed my doubts and confirmed that the phenomena Ena was describing *really* did happen.

Well, I was quite accustomed to clairvoyance and clairaudience through my own experiences, but this new information described by Ena was way off the scale. I trusted her, but it was mind boggling, and I felt I had every right to ask questions.

When I asked if such physical phenomena were happening now and if so, where would I find a genuine physical medium producing these things. It was then they told me about Stewart Alexander. Bob and Ena held him in high esteem, and they advised me to try out one of his guest séances. They had been to one in July 1995, and told me what happened while they sat in a completely blacked out room.

"WHAT! – Whoa! Hang on a minute." I exclaimed, "There is no way I can sit in the dark. I won't be able to hear."

I was born deaf and my parents were not aware of my disability at first because back in the early 1950s, doctors and nurses did not test a baby's hearing like they do now. Because I could not hear the spoken word, I was unable to talk properly, and as a child I had to have extensive speech therapy. Also in those days they had special schools for the deaf and dumb, but because my parents did not like the idea of sending me to a 'dumb' school, I spent my first two educational years (age 5 and 6) at the local ordinary school. Unfortunately, this failed to work because the school did not provide any teaching assistant support for disabled pupils, like most schools do now, and my education suffered tremendously.

At the same time, I was frequently sent to hearing aid technicians along with ear, nose and throat consultants (including a professor). I even had my tonsils and adenoids removed in the hope that this might help cure my deafness, which of course it didn't. After all that, at the age of seven, I did end up at a school for the deaf and dumb recommended by my speech therapist. Fortunately, as technology advanced, it became clear that deaf children were not dumb; they simply couldn't hear the words to talk. Much of our educational time in school was spent on speech lessons and this is why I can now speak very well. Because I can talk normally, people do not realise how deaf I am. I have to rely on the most powerful range of hearing aids and even with them, I find it hard to follow the flow of a group conversation. The delayed response in receiving the spoken word limits my ability to participate.

So, the very thought of sitting in the dark was a hurdle I was sure I could not overcome – I would not be able to lip–read, see any facial expressions, or look out for gestures. Goodness me, how on earth could a severely deaf person (even with hearing aids) participate under such conditions?

As regards to my deafness, even with hearing aids I find it hard to listen and do something else at the same time. I am unable to watch television without subtitles and I never listen to the radio. I can cope when one person speaks, but not in a group conversation, and when I do not wear my hearing aids, I hear almost nothing but the silence of my thoughts. In many cases, my deficiency also causes a delayed response during any conversation, particularly when my brain is preoccupied in guessing and trying to work out what has been said.

14

No – going to a séance was a definite impossibility and I totally dismissed the idea as completely out of the question.

But, in addition, I must admit that deep down I was actually quite apprehensive about attending such a séance because it was something that I had never experienced, and so out of the ordinary. But then again, I couldn't stop thinking about this as a rare opportunity, and as time went on, I developed an increasingly strong urge to go.

In January 1999 when I finally plucked up the courage to speak to Ray Lister, Stewart's home circle[2] leader. I explained my situation, telling him that I wasn't sure how I could cope in the dark. Ray booked me in for the 8th July that year and told me not to worry because he would sit next to me and would interpret anything I failed to hear.

So, with Ray's assistance, July 8th, 1999 was the day that changed my life. I was so moved and excited about what I had seen, that I wrote a report which was published in a spiritualist journal and I would like to share it with you here:

Hull Séance Report, 8th July, 1999

The time is 10am on 9th July 1999. I am sitting in a picnic area, glancing over the pond at Burton Agnes in East Yorkshire. To the left of me is Burton Agnes Hall around which I am going to venture later.

There is a lovely cool breeze and today is a day of my holidays, but today is very special. I write these notes with a feeling of elation and tears in my eyes, tears of happiness, that so many people deprive themselves of.

2. A home circle is a group of devoted people sitting regularly with the medium giving support and energy for the development of communication with spirit, and particularly for trance and physical phenomena.

For many years, I have had the sense of life after death. I have visited spiritualist churches, had private sittings with various mediums; I have often read about contact with spirit through direct voice and materialisation and many, many times have my dear friends Ena and Bob (Georgina and Robert Brake), told me of their wonderful experiences with direct voice and ectoplasm. I believed this was true and it was wonderful to believe, but now, there is no need to believe! I had actually seen and heard the real thing! Just as real as the pond and trees I am looking at now. What happened last night was something I will never forget!

Earlier this year, I had booked a place in a home circle through the Noah's Ark Society[3]. The medium was Mr Stewart Alexander. I had never been to a physical phenomena circle before but I knew I had to sit in the dark. I wasn't nervous, but quite apprehensive with a certain air of excitement. I had that urge to investigate something I had only read about in books and heard about through hearsay.

Now was the opportunity to experience it personally.

One point I would like to mention to whomever is reading this report is, that I am very hard of hearing and I was quite concerned about not being able to hear the spirit voices in the dark. I knew lip-reading would be totally impossible but really, I had nothing whatsoever to fear!!

Yesterday afternoon, I arrived at the hotel in Hull, and after a wash and something to eat I rang the circle leader, Ray Lister, to tell him I had arrived. Ray picked me up at 6.30pm, and his lovely, warm hearted, happy

---

3. Noah's Ark Society was founded in 1990 – to preserve, support and encourage the safe development of physical mediumship. It was active for around 13 years and had a monthly newsletter.

personality put me at ease straight away. I was taken to his house where the séance was to take place and I was introduced to the other circle members. We chatted for a while, but as I could not pick up group conversation, I was wondering how I would manage in the séance. I turned to Ray and said I was concerned about not being able to hear properly but Ray told me not to worry, as he would be sitting next to me and he would interpret for me if necessary.

Ray took me up the stairs into the séance room and showed me the corner where Stewart would be sitting. The room was painted black and chairs were positioned in a circle round a small table. On this table were two long, slim funnel-like objects with luminous tape stuck round the wider ends. Ray explained that these were the 'trumpets' our spirit friends might use. I also saw two drumsticks and a bell.

Ray explained that Stewart would be fastened to the chair with plastic cable ties which cannot be broken. While Ray was talking, I had hold of one of these cable ties and started to fumble with it, I formed a loop and it automatically locked itself, once I had done this, there was no way I could loosen it. I apologised to Ray as I knew the cable tie would be no use now. Ray said "That's no problem, we have plenty more." I now knew why we would have to cut the medium loose at the end of the séance.

Ray showed me where I would be sitting and he told me that if I did get frightened in the dark, I could grab his hand for reassurance. I went back downstairs and met Stewart who had a very loving and very warm personality.

At 8pm we all went up to the séance room. Stewart was strapped firmly to the chair and I noticed that two little luminous tabs were taped to his knees. The lights were switched off, but I wasn't really in total darkness

I could see the luminous paint on the edge of the trumpets and the two tabs on Stewart's knees. I concentrated on the luminous paint to eliminate the darkness, and I was entirely satisfied that no way could anyone move around without bumping into things.

Someone then opened the proceedings by asking for protection and soft music was played to lighten the atmosphere, then in just a few minutes, a North American Indian's voice came through, he seemed to be speaking from mid air, it was very clear and loud enough for me to hear. It was White Feather giving us his blessing and protection. I commented to Ray that I heard the spirit voice very clearly and I was amazed at how loud it came over. Ray replied, saying "He's the quiet one!"

Then a child's voice came through. This was Christopher, a loving, cheerful, laughing soul, who put us all at ease straight away. Tears of happiness started to form In my eyes as I actually heard a spirit voice and I now knew it was true. The atmosphere was filled with nothing but unconditional love. Christopher's job was to relax people, especially the new-comers, and what a good job he did too! He was excellent and all my apprehension just simply faded away.

Christopher asked to be introduced to everyone and Ray introduced me first as I was siting next to him. After Christopher, Freda, another spirit communicator, spent some time speaking to various people, then we were asked to play some music and one trumpet moved slowly into the air and then the other one moved as well. The two trumpets moved around above us and one reached up to the ceiling, the other made extremely quick rapid movements from one sitter to the next across the room.

One of the trumpets slowed down and came towards me. Ray remarked that it was looking at me and I said "Yes, it is." The trumpet then slowly and directly touched my left arm and began to very gently stroke my arm up and down. I also heard the drumsticks banging and the bell ringing.

Walter, another member of the spirit team, who is responsible for producing all the physical phenomena, was the next to speak and asked for the table to be moved up to the medium's knees. He then asked me to sit up to the table facing the medium. I couldn't see in the dark and Ray had to lead me up to the table and he brought my chair up to me. There was a red light shining through the table-top and Walter asked for the intensity of the light to be lowered.

I then saw what looked like some kind of thick paste or a kind of mist rolling on to the table – it was the ectoplasm – some of it was transparent. I was asked to place my right hand, palm down, on to the table and keep it there perfectly still. I felt very privileged to witness this ectoplasm, and when it stopped rolling towards my hand, I saw one finger form out of this somewhat transparent substance, then a thumb appeared and another finger, until there was a fully materialised hand on the table. It was Walter's hand and it moved until it was above my hand and then it touched my fingers and stroked the back of my hand and fingers. I expected the ectoplasm to be wet, cold and slimy, but to my surprise it wasn't, it felt like a real hand, it certainly looked like a real hand, and it felt warm, but solid to the touch – it was definitely a real 'human' hand.

I came away from that séance feeling wonderfully elated, to have actually experienced the physical phenomena Ena and Bob had so often talked about. I also felt very privileged to have been physically *touched by Walter's hand; to be touched by a soul from the spirit world.*

White Feather, Christopher, Freda and Walter were the main spirit contacts throughout the séance and a lot of interesting subjects were discussed.

I close this report emphasising the extreme love the spirit people expressed and the care and consideration they had for my hearing deficiency.

(end of report)

Even though the spirit communicators had clear, loud voices when speaking through Stewart in trance, I easily lost track of the conversation and could only pick up snippets of words, having to guess the rest. Ray would notice a bout of silence on my part, or seemed to sense when it might be difficult for me, and he would then step in to interpret. Even Freda, one of the spirit communicators would often say, "Has Katie heard me?" prompting the other circle members to help.

After that night, I began to contemplate on what Bob and Ena had been trying to tell me for such a long time. It was true, we do survive death, and the 'spirit people' from the other side do materialise. In 2002, after sitting as a guest with the circle for a few years, I was invited by Stewart's 'spirit team' – the group of communicators who work through him – to become an honorary member of the Stewart Alexander home circle. This opened the door to studying and writing more about the phenomena, supplemented by my own drawings, confirming what we all saw in the red light. It turned out that not everything was in the dark.

Little did I know that I would then spend the next decade writing reports on Stewart's physical phenomena, which, over time, I developed into three short volumes, with optional CD recordings of the séances. (My work has been purely voluntary and all profit above the cost of production has been donated to training Hearing Dogs for Deaf People.)

I witnessed many amazing events during my sittings with the small home circle. Not only did I experience direct voice independent of the medium – as Ena had described – and the materialisation of a living hand, I also encountered a plethora of other physical phenomena, such as:

❖ Trumpets[3] with illuminated bands on them levitating and gliding around the room, tapping on the ceiling and touching people's shoulders or gently stroking their faces at the far end of the room.

❖ Materialised spirit people physically walking around touching and talking to the sitters.

❖ A large orb of spirit light (the size of a small football) being carried round the séance room by a materialised form.

❖ Ectoplasm at various stages seen emanating from Stewart's mouth.

❖ A heavy low table being lifted up and turned without any visible support.

❖ Stewart (while strapped into his chair) being levitated a few feet up and held for a time in mid-air.

❖ Living matter passing through matter, such as Stewart's arm passing through a plastic cable tie – a restraint around the chair arm that can only be cut loose with a pair of strong cutters.

❖ Items moving around and drumsticks playing on the table.

❖ Healing direct from the spirit world, as Dr Barnett (a spirit visitor who was a doctor when on

3. Séance room trumpets are long tapered cones (simple megaphones) made out of lightweight material, usually metal. (Further details in Chapters 2 and 13).

earth) walked out of the cabinet and personally laid his hands on sitters needing attention.

There were also 'Book tests' where the spirit people would give a guest sitter information about certain words or a specific page in a particular book in a designated location, usually the sitter's own home. This was for the sitter to check the pertinence and accuracy later.

In the second volume of my trilogy I described the help and healing I received for my deafness. Dr Barnett materialised by using the ectoplasm and walked out of the cabinet to give me healing direct from the spirit world. As strange as this may seem, one of his experiments was to attach ectoplasmic tubes from the medium in the cabinet to each of my ears. This usually happened when Dr Barnett was developing independent direct voice so the voice was heard away from the medium.

Gaynor, Stewart's sister who sat to the medium's left, was always the first to hear a faint voice between herself and Stewart. This independent voice would slowly build in volume and clarity until everyone in the circle could hear it—except me. Gaynor would then have to interpret Dr Barnett's words.

That was until I felt a heavy pressure on and around my head (particularly above my ears), as if I was wearing some sort of hat. I was then surprised to find myself engaged in conversation with Dr Barnett directly, without Gaynor's help. Whenever he did this, I found I had less difficulty in hearing, even in the pitch dark, with none of my usual visual clues. You can read more about this fantastic experiment in Chapter 8.

The third book, with reports of further experiences and more of my illustrations, was published in 2011. All three books contained several accounts of strong personal evidence of survival provided by loved ones who had passed through the transition we call death and could speak to us through Stewart's mediumship.

With the success of the trilogy, providing a window into the séance room for people who may never be able to experience it for themselves, I decided in 2019 that the time had come to condense all three books into one volume. This decision was made in cooperation with the current members of the circle. Instead of separate companion CD recordings, these, at the time of going to press, are now available online enabling readers to listen to the voices of the spirit team as we heard them within the séance room. Although transcripts of the recordings are provided in the book, I would highly recommend that readers listen to these remarkable voices, so that they can appreciate the very individual characters of the spirit people who have been speaking through Stewart for decades, some of them in independent voice.

And, you—the reader and listener—may now be able to understand what Ena encountered and how she must have felt when she heard her deceased mother's voice speaking in mid air, although nothing can compare to being in the room when it happens. But believe me; if you have not personally experienced the phenomena and find it hard to accept, like I did before sitting with Stewart, I understand completely. That is exactly how I felt back then when Bob sensed my doubts and had to confirm to me that it really did happen.

Now, having had the experience of witnessing the astounding physical phenomena for almost two decades, I can tell you with total certainty that *it really did happen.*

Listening to the Recordings:

Before you start on your journey of discovery I think it will be helpful if I say how you are able to listen to the tracks detailed within this book.

On the internet go to:
   https://alexanderproject.bandcamp.com

Make sure the word 'audio' at the top left of the webpage is selected (in black) and not the word 'community'.

When the screen shows all the tracks- (beginning with – "Stewart Alexander's natural voice.") click on the play button (▶) (a right facing triangle) and if the 'buy track' pop up shows, ignore it.
   (You don't have to buy them unless you wish to)

Wait a few seconds and the track will play.
        (Check your speakers are turned on.)
To pause, simply touch the play button again now showing pause (❙❙).
Then touch the play (▶) button again and wait a few seconds for it to start.
You can skip to any track you wish to hear by repeating this.
If you should wish to buy any or all the tracks just follow the instructions.

Part One

My first-hand experiences of
trance and physical phenomena
with the
Stewart Alexander Circle
during the years 1999 to 2001.

For Part 1 recordings listen to Sections 1 to 18 on
www.alexanderproject.bandcamp.com

Chapter One

A Brief Explanation

Since genuine physical mediumship is so hard to come by these days, the least I can do is share my experiences by telling you what really happened.

Unlike clairaudience and clairvoyance where the medium has to relay the message to the recipient, trance and physical phenomena offer direct communication between every sitter in the room and the spirit people. Yes – you, the sitter, can actually talk to the spirit people themselves.

Trance and the manifestation of physical phenomena are two completely different techniques, but are in many ways connected. The medium often has to go into a deep trance before producing any type of physical phenomena and when this happens, every precaution is taken for the safety of the medium. There is a danger of the medium being harmed due to inappropriate behaviour of inexperienced sitters, and this is why many home circles are 'closed circles', not allowing any visitors who are not connected to the sitters into the séance room.

It would be extremely risky to grab a materialised form without permission from the spirit team, or to introduce any sudden light into the séance room because the ectoplasm would shoot straight back to the medium. This can cause a haemorrhage or damage to internal organs (and in some cases, result in death as it did with Helen Duncan). This is one of the reasons why genuine physical phenomena séances are rarely demonstrated in public. However, trance without physical is a much safer procedure. For those who are unfamiliar with the mechanics of trance, I offer this brief explanation.

Usually the condition is achieved through meditation or deep relaxation and results in a disconnection or dissociation of the mind (spiritual), from the brain (physical). This allows an external consciousness (spirit) to take control of the medium's brain and therefore organs of speech. However, this temporary connection may vary enormously from a light overshadowing which exerts influence upon the medium's thoughts, to a deep state of absolute unconsciousness during which he/she is unaware of all that takes place. Although Stewart's mediumship is of the latter kind, we know from spirit that the level of control achieved is never absolute. Transmissions can be influenced by the medium's own subconscious in a manner that we are unable to understand, but, in spite of that, the spirit people generally achieve between 75 and 90% accuracy with their communications.

As already stated, the physical phenomena take place when Stewart has reached that deep state of trance, but there have been occasions when the spirit team have woken Stewart up to witness the trumpet phenomenon for himself. It was interesting to hear Stewart speaking from the cabinet in the corner at the same time both trumpets were moving around at a fair distance, even touching the ceiling at the other end of the room.

The séances were often held in complete darkness at the request of the spirit team.

Séances for guests were conducted under the following conditions:

Stewart always recognised the fact that people taking part in his public séances understandably needed the reassurance that the phenomena which developed owed nothing to his own conscious or unconscious actions. As a result he never sat for the public unless the following controls etc. were applied:

Immediately prior to a public séance he was often bodily searched to ensure that he took nothing into the room that could be used to create fraudulent activity.

He sat in his own high backed chair with wooden arms, and this was often closely examined by guest sitters to ensure that there was nothing hidden within it which could be used to produce phenomena fraudulently.

When the medium took his place his ankles, thighs and chest were all roped tightly to the chair and luminous tape was secured to his knees so that his exact position in the darkness of the séance room could be determined at all times. Needless to say – he never left his chair.

Strong cable ties were then used as straps to tightly secure his arms directly to the arms of the chair. Since these were self–locking, they could only be removed at the conclusion of the séance by the use of wire cutters.

Once secured a representative of the sitters, selected for the task came forward and checked all ties. He/she repeated this at the conclusion of the séance to ensure that all was as before.

Since Stewart always sat as a part of the circle his hands were often held by the sitters who occupied the seats at either side of him.

(On one occasion the sitter who was occupying the seat on his left was asked to reach out and hold his hand. As she took hold, a fully materialised form was, *in that moment*, standing directly in front of her, with two hands resting lightly upon her head.)

It is worth noting here that Stewart occasionally came out of trance when the phenomena were in progress, and could observe what was taking place at a distance from him. Occasionally this also extended to him actually hearing the direct voices which spoke independently of him.

It is important to realise that the mindset of the sitters is crucial to a successful séance. Those with closed-minds, and fixed ideas that the spirit people do not exist, will unknowingly create a barrier and, in so doing, adversely affect the delicate emotional balance of the séance room. Under these conditions, the manifestation of physical phenomena and evidential communication often proves impossible.

The spirit people live in the world of thought, occupying the same space but in a different dimension, and are therefore aware of our thoughts. As like attracts like, the spirit people will only come if they are invited to do so, and patience, along with an open mind, is also very important.

When the conditions are good within the séance room, the manifesting phenomena become tangible, so much so that we can all hear, see and witness the same thing. Only a happy, lively atmosphere will create such conditions and we do this by playing music, singing, or engaging ourselves in a jovial conversation – and there have been times when the spirit people have happily joined in.

Stewart's home circle would often sit twice a week, one being a private development meeting and the other, a guest séance like the one I first attended. It was a delight to hear Freda—a spirit communicator who was a teacher of small children when she lived on the earth—speaking in a school ma'amish voice so completely different from Walter's smooth Canadian accent and Christopher's cheeky child–like banter.

Ena would often tell me that the spirit people talked in a manner just as natural as we do on this earth plane and as a result of visiting Stewart's séances, I was to find out how right she was – such was the clarity and definition of the communication that everybody in the room could hear. Well, after all, it has taken Stewart at least forty years of continuous sitting to develop into such an extraordinary physical medium.

Stewart Alexander,
trance and physical medium.

If you would like to know how Stewart became a physical medium, you can find out more in the revised and updated version of his autobiography – *An Extraordinary Journey: The Memoirs of a Physical Medium.*[1]

---

1. *An Extraordinary Journey: The Memoirs of a Physical Medium*
ISBN 9781786771377 (White Crow Books 2020)

Chapter Two

RAY AND JUNE'S SÉANCE ROOM

Who would think that one simple room measuring 10ft 6ins (3.2m) x 9ft 3ins (2.8m) could be profoundly special to so many people?

It was definitely unique, as I was to find out.

The séance room

When I entered this room for the first time in July 1999, I was astonished to find the four walls painted black. Despite this unusual decor, there was a wonderful feeling of love, peace and harmony within that space and the aura of the room radiated a beautiful sense of belonging. At that time I was oblivious to the important role it would play in my life for the next sixteen years.

Allow me to take you on a little tour.

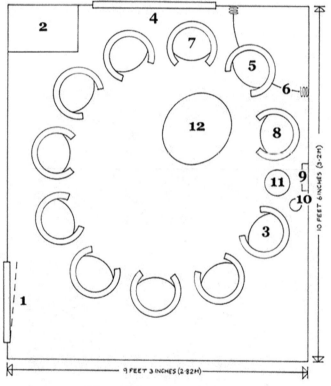

Plan of the séance room

As we enter through the door **(1)** and sit down on one of the chairs, we see a shelf high up in a corner **(2)**; this is where the CD player is located and it is operated by a remote control from where Ray sits (3). The CD player is to provide soft music at the start of each sitting as Stewart goes into trance.

To the right of this shelf there is a permanently boarded up window (4) covered by a curtain.

In the next corner is Stewart's chair (5) situated below a curved curtain rail (6). The curtains hanging down from the rail are sometimes closed by the spirit people to form a sort of cabinet to help build up energy within the area (particularly for the production of ectoplasm). We could always tell what was happening in the dark by watching the luminous tabs permanently fixed on the top and bottom of each curtain.

The two chairs to the left and right of Stewart's (7 & 8) are normally occupied by the same two home circle members. When I first visited the home circle, June (7) and Gaynor, (Stewart's sister) (8), sat on those chairs and after Gaynor's transition to the spirit world in February 2009, Lindsey, (Gaynor's daughter) took her place. After Lindsey emigrated to Australia in February 2012, Carol took over the position.

Our circle leader Ray sits at (3) to have access to the power points (9). The power points are operated at the request of spirit friends and it is Ray's responsibility to disconnect the electricity, particularly at the start of any manifestation of physical phenomena.

During the sittings, our spirit friends sometimes ask a sitter to get up and sit next to Stewart. Since the room is in total darkness, Ray operates a red torch (flashlight) (10) so that the invited person can be guided when swopping places with June for the duration of the demonstration.

A dimmable LED red light (11) can be adjusted for shining on to the ceiling or on to Stewart. At the spirit people's request, this LED light is sometimes switched on for a minute or two during transfiguration[1], allowing sitters to watch Stewart's face change.

Returning to the door (1), this is closed prior to the séance when all the sitters were comfortably settled inside the room. A curtain is pulled across the closed door and fastened in place with tacks to ensure no speck of light can seep through any possible gaps.

The walls are painted black, the floor is carpeted and the ceiling is white.

The low table (12) usually positioned in front of Stewart is lit by a dimmable light from beneath a glass top, covered by a red fabric material.

Ray Lister (the circle leader) and his wife June had dedicated this room for the exclusive use of the Alexander home circle in 1995. Equipped with chairs and a small table as shown, the séance room could comfortably seat around eleven people. This customised interior must have greeted hundreds of guests from both the spirit world and the earth plane.

There are a number of small and not so small items of equipment used during a séance which need an explanation before I introduce you to the sittings. They are labelled in the photograph overleaf to help you link them to their use.

Table (A): This table is used for a variety of physical phenomena. As mentioned earlier, it has a glass surface over a light bulb which can be dimmed to the required intensity. The whole of the table top is covered with a red cloth secured in place by high strength adhesive black tape.

The Chair (B): The more comfortable the medium feels when sitting, the sooner he can go into trance, so

---

1. Transfiguration is a phenomenon of the spirit person's face appearing in front of the medium's face. (see page 170)

whenever possible the chair travels with Stewart and has been in constant use over the years. It has been carefully inspected by guest sitters (carpenters in particular) prior to a séance to confirm that nothing has been or can be hidden within the chair itself. (The arms of the chair are fixed into the back of the chair and to the seat, so no bindings can be slipped off it.)

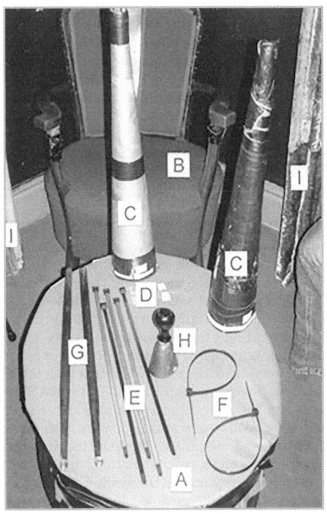

Some of the equipment used in the séance room

The Trumpets (C): Not musical trumpets, but simple megaphone–like cones made out of light metallic material. The two trumpets are often levitated and sail around the room. Sitters can watch their graceful movements in the darkness by observing the luminous tabs taped to the broader ends. Further details about the trumpet phenomena will be explained later in this book.

Luminous Tabs (D): These are secured to Stewart's knees and he is unable to remove them himself because his wrists are securely fastened to the chair arms by means of plastic cable ties. With the help of the luminous knee tabs, sitters were able to observe the medium's position at all times. I found it was helpful to focus my eyes on these knee tabs especially when sitting in inky black darkness and the only time the tabs would disappear and come back again was when a materialised spirit form walked in front of them (or the cabinet curtains were drawn across them).

Cable Ties (E): The cable ties are heavy-duty, secure and self–locking. They are used to fasten Stewart's wrists to the chair arms until, at the conclusion of a séance, a member of the circle cuts him free using a pair of strong cutters. Walter (in spirit) often likes to offer a gift to a sitter after the living matter through matter demonstrations (see Chapter 12) and this is usually the same cable tie which has been dematerialised and passed through both the chair arm and the medium's arm. To make sure that Stewart remains firmly fastened to the chair for the remainder of the séance, Walter then takes a spare cable tie from the table top and uses it to secure the medium's wrist once again to the chair arm. When this happens, we can hear a slow clicking noise as the spare cable tie is being pulled tight – yes – the spirit people do this themselves.

Looped Cable Ties (F): Prior to the start of a

séance, two separate looped cable ties are often placed on the table for the spirit people to use should they wish to demonstrate the matter–through–matter experiment by linking the two together (See Chapter 12).

Drumsticks (G): The drumsticks are used by the spirit people to tap away on the table top, (often to the rhythm of our singing).

The Bell (H): As he often chooses to play with the drumsticks, little Christopher (in spirit) also likes to ring the bell, sometimes making musical tunes or just to let us know he is there.

The Curtains (I): These are closed and opened by the spirit people whenever they wish to build up energy within the enclosed space we call 'the cabinet'.

The other pieces of equipment used and not shown on this photograph are a **red light** suspended from the ceiling above the small table; a **pencil** and a **pad of paper** for the spirit people to write messages and a **digital voice recorder** to record the whole of the séance.

As mentioned before, this room was often used twice a week, one evening for home circle development and another evening for guest sitters. If you are wondering why I have written about it in its past tense, it is because we no longer use it. Thursday 15th October 2015 was to be the last time I would set foot in it. This was because Ray and June have since sold their house, meaning the séance room had to be repainted and converted back into an ordinary bedroom before they could put it on the market.

Ray and June are the only two original circle members who have remained with Stewart and have supported him for more than thirty years with fierce loyalty.

A circle leader's role is a multiple task with a lot of

responsibility. Ray's main job was (and still is) to protect the medium by making sure the guest sitters do not do anything irresponsible, especially during a demonstration of physical phenomena. As mentioned in the previous chapter, any sudden artificial light or movement like the unauthorised grabbing of a materialised form will send the ectoplasm shooting straight back to the medium and this can cause serious bodily harm. Ray calls attention to this as he determines the trust, honesty and reliability of any new guest hoping to sit for the first time.

June and Ray Lister

Ray and June have worked non–stop for as long as I have known them, as well as working full-time, they have spent many hours on the telephone making arrangements for people wanting a place in the guest meetings, sorting out the equipment and recording all the séance sittings. They are, in my opinion, the unsung heroes who have devoted a great deal of time looking after the medium, the circle, guest sitters and the spirit people. As well as being hosts to the home circle meetings and the guest séances they always provided refreshments.

Not only did they offer the séance room and such excellent provisions within their home, they have also travelled with Stewart all over the country, setting up large meetings at various venues. Driving a van full of black-out materials, they would set off and rig up temporary séance rooms, often in large halls with very high ceilings where a ladder was required to cover up the windows.

Ray and June have also been of great assistance with the distribution of my original trilogy with the accompanying CDs and they looked after me during my researching days. In the early years, I could only visit the circle on an average of four times a year because it was difficult for me to get time off work, and I live 80 miles away (129km). Whenever I could visit, they would provide me with accommodation for the night, which I greatly appreciated.

Since the closing of the Lister séance room in December 2015, the home circle members have continued to meet at another venue.

Chapter Three

THE SPIRIT TEAM

Before the clock struck 8pm, we would enter the séance room and close the door on all our worries and a much-troubled world outside. It was a time when we were about to enter into our heaven on earth and meet our loved ones residing in the spirit world – a world each and every one of us are destined to go to when the time comes, a world the physical eye cannot see, even though it occupies the same space. It is always close by, but in a different dimension.

We would always experience a wonderful feeling of gathering together and a sense of belonging as we took our seats while engaging in jovial and cheerful chat.

Our circle leader, whom we affectionately call Raymondo, would suggest we should begin and the chatting would stop before he uttered an opening "invocation" – asking for protection for us all, especially for the medium. He would then go on to state that our purpose is to help, heal and serve others in need; to assist our spirit friends in spreading the word that there is life after death, and ask for the unconditional love to be expanded around our lives for the greater good.

We then listened to the regular séance music until a slow deep breathing sound was heard from the medium. That was when we started to encourage and welcome the first visiting spirit person as he tried to speak using the medium's vocal cords. Slowly the words came out loud and clear, "White – Feather – come – speak – with his – brothers – and – sisters."

White Feather, the Spirit Guide, who is Stewart's principal guide and door-keeper, then opened the séance with his blessing and returned later to close the two-hour-long meeting.

White Feather

(psychic artist's impression)

As a North American Indian when he lived on earth, he would have been aware of the forces of nature which included an understanding of both the psychic and spiritual senses. His connection with Stewart is invaluable, and you may be interested to know that when he spoke through Stewart in trance in the early days of development, the circle members noticed the medium's left hand always appeared deformed.

To clarify this, Stewart was once a guest sitter at a Leslie Flint[1] séance. Much to Stewart's surprise, White Feather came through and spoke independently. At this point, Stewart took the opportunity to ask him if he had a physical deformity during his earthly life. The guide immediately replied, "Do you mean my left hand?" thereby confirming his identity. We have been told that White Feather was born with a deformed hand; therefore, it would appear that the spirit people often come back as they were when on earth.

---

1. Leslie Flint was an exceptional direct voice medium.
   See https://www.leslieflint.com

After White Feather completed his blessing, he then "popped out" to allow Christopher to step into the medium's aura. Christopher came in with his high-pitched child-like banter full of laughter, and we heard a completely different character and tone of voice. Christopher remembers his life on earth as a child because he died when he was 6½ years old. His main role is to help first time nervous guest sitters to relax and to lighten to mood, bringing more positive energy into the room.

Christopher

(psychic artist's impression)

This is an important job as the spirit people are very sensitive to the atmosphere, and it is essential that the conditions are good to be able to generate a successful sitting. I have sat next to Stewart when Christopher is in control, and I have noticed how the medium's body physically doubles up like a child and there is a lot of rocking and wriggling about in his chair. This is why Ray fondly calls him 'Wrigglebottom'.

The visiting spirit child would often tell us that he is "half in and half out", meaning that he didn't quite have full control of the medium.

It is not easy for the spirit people to project their own personality when the medium's brain (akin to a natural computer) has been programmed by Stewart during his earthly life. The non regular spirit people, when they come through for the first time, occasionally remark how strange and difficult it is to control the human instrument. But when Christopher was fully settled in, his character and cheerful personality were projected loud and clear.

> Author's note:
>
> We are told that when people die of old age, they may in the spirit world return to their prime. A lot will depend on the way they died but when they recover their health they rejuvenate. This is because it is the physical body that ages and decays, not the spirit. In Christopher's case, he passed as a child, but was able to grow up in the spirit world. He loves his job and it is his own choice to speak to us as a child, which he prefers to do, especially when newcomers are visiting the circle. Occasionally in the home circle, we have heard Christopher speaking to us as a grown man.

The next person to be introduced was Freda Johnson who made her transition to the spirit world in the late 1950s. She died of old age. When Freda communicates with us, she doesn't come back as an elderly lady but as herself in her prime. Freda was a teacher of small children when she lived on the earth plane and when she communicates through Stewart in trance, she often comments about the strangeness of speaking through a male organism. The timbre of the voice we hear portrays male characteristics simply because she is speaking through the medium's own vocal cords, but she still sounds feminine. Freda is excellent at explaining and answering questions, and, like a good teacher, she makes herself very clear by rephrasing and repeating anything we do not understand. She also has the patience of a wonderful tutor and I am sure that every sitter loves her personality and character, as do I.

Freda tells us that before she can communicate

through Stewart she must first draw close to him, so that her energy and aura effectively fuses with his before she can activate and control his brain. Then, and only then, can she transmit her thoughts and those of other spirit friends directly to the circle sitters. However, since the level and degree of trance attained tends to vary, the purity of any communication must, of course, vary also. When the level of control is good, and there is very little unconscious interference from the medium's brain, communication is untainted, and that is when we enjoy the most wonderful meetings with our friends from the spirit world.

The spirit world is one of thought, where the etheric (spirit) body is free from the heavy and slow vibrations of our earth plane. Freda once explained how she can travel from A to B in the blink of an eye; apparently she has only to think of a place, or a person, and she is there, or she is with them. Time and distance as we understand it, does not exist in the spirit world. Freda knows about any event taking place simply through the attraction of thought.

Author's note:

Have you ever wondered about 'thought'?

What is it? And where does it come from?

If you sit back and really think about this, it might help to know that thought has no language. For example, if you wanted to pick up a piece of paper, do you actually think in WORDS, I ... am ... going ... to ... pick ... up ... the ... paper? Or – do you just do it?

You just do it of course; it is the natural motive of your consciousness, the same consciousness that lives on after so–called death.

Everything in the spirit world is instant with no need for language, therefore not only do the spirit people have to slow down to our vibrations, they also have to use the

> *spoken word to communicate with us, a procedure which is not a necessity in their world.*
>
> *The spirit world communicates through the power of thought.*
>
> *So when you suddenly, for no reason at all, think of a deceased loved one, it is likely that the consciousness of that soul has blended in with your aura attracted by your love, and that is how, in some ways, your loved ones can get closer to you now than they could when they were on the earth plane.*
>
> *Always remember that they are only a thought away and like–attracts–like plays a big role in the acceptance of unconditional love.*

When Stewart eventually developed a deep trance state, physical phenomena began to take place, and this was generally orchestrated, created and controlled by Walter Stinson, whose Canadian personality came over extremely well when he spoke. He is a charming gentleman, as the ladies are quick to discover.

Walter's sister, Mina Crandon, was a famous physical medium, in the 1920–30s, and known to the world as 'Margery the medium'. Throughout her mediumistic career she underwent a considerable number of scientific tests. Walter was killed in a railway accident in 1911, and as Mina's mediumship developed he worked through her, specialising in ectoplasmic phenomena. For many years he continued to demonstrate life after death this way, and now resumes this task through Stewart. With countless demonstrations using ectoplasm, he describes the experience of materialising and walking out of the cabinet thus:

1) Like walking through thick mud.

2) Like a strong elastic band pulling him back to the medium.

3) Like wearing a very heavy wet overcoat.

Walter Stuart Stinson
sketched by the author
from a photograph

It is no easy task for them to utilise the ectoplasmic energy, but our spirit friends persevere with a strong determination to prove the reality of their own survival.

You will be reading more about Walter's experiments later in this book.

There is also another spirit person in the team who for a time was simply known to us as 'The Voice', or the 'Vanguard'. We did not know his name until he identified himself as Dr Barnett at a séance I attended on 22nd February 2005. He is a spirit gentleman who specialises in the production of the independent direct voice – an audible communication using a speaking mechanism known as a 'voice box', created out of ectoplasmic energy. In simple terms, ectoplasm is produced from the medium and fashioned into the mechanism which our spirit friends use in order to speak directly to us. This means Dr Barnett does not speak directly through Stewart, but from another location in the room using only the ectoplasmic voice box. Over time he attained a voice level which is easily audible within the séance room when the energy is at its peak, and it is then that other spirit people are invited to communicate using the same mechanism. (More about this is explained by Vanguard himself in Chapter 9).

Having introduced the main five members of the spirit team who come to speak with us, we must not forget the abundance of help they get from the spirit scientists working in the background. Without them, the physical phenomena would not be possible. Sitters often hear the main spirit communicators break off during our discussions as they pause to listen and talk to the workers on their side of life.

Here are the first five recorded sections of this book. I invite you to listen and appreciate the different voices and characters of each spirit person compared to Stewart's own persona. There is nothing frightening about these recordings as some people seem to imagine, for example, one lady enjoyed reading my reports but didn't want to hear dead people. Well – I have to say that these people are not dead, they are very much alive in the spirit world. Another lady was worried about listening to Christopher, but after she heard him, she was so relieved and amazed to hear a normal child's voice without the ghostly groans and eerie noises she expected to hear. I am aware that people without our knowledge may be uneasy and frightened by the word 'spirit', but please be assured, they are not ghosts. So, try not to let an overactive imagination override the truth. Our spirit friends' voices are so natural, loving and caring, so much so, that to me they are one big, united family as we all are within the circle, and I am sure you will feel the same after reading this book. It is highly recommended that you listen to these voices, but if you are unable to use the computer links via the website, the notes and transcripts are provided in this book.

Section 1

Stewart Alexander's natural voice.

Private sitting – 25th May 2000. (41seconds).

The first voice you will hear is that of our medium Stewart Alexander immediately upon his return to consciousness following a private trance sitting I had with him in May 2000. It is important that you become familiar with his voice, and that you appreciate his personality. You can then compare this with the various spirit people who make use of his physical body. I would remind you that whilst he is in that state of deep trance, he is totally unaware of all that takes place through and around him. To all intents and purposes, he is in a state of deep sleep, and he remembers nothing when he wakes up.

Stewart. Right, Katie   **Katie**. Ok?

S. Yes, fine.   **K.** You Ok?

S. Yes, thank you.   **K.** I thank you.

S. No June? ... June's gone?*   **K.** Er, Yes.

S. Oh God, Oh dear. *(Stewart sighs and stretches after waking up from trance).*

K. Thank you, Stewart.   **S.** That's alright, Katie.

K. It was a very good experience.

S. Was it Ok?   **K.** Yes, yes.

S. Lovely. Lovely.   **K.** It was very interesting.

S. Who came? ... Freda?   **K.** Pardon?

S. Who came?   **K.** Walter and Freda.

S. Oh – right, right.

K. We had a little scientific discussion.

S. Oh, did you.

K. Yes, very good, very interesting.

S. Oh, did you. Well, it's not very often Walter comes you know, in an afternoon.

(end of section 1)

Circle member, June Lister sat with me until Stewart went into trance. She then left the room, as instructed by Freda, so that we could proceed with the private sitting.

Section 2

White Feather speaks.

Guest séance – 8th July 1999. (2min. 02seconds).

The voice you are now going to hear is through Stewart's vocal cords, but White Feather has taken over Stewart's brain and physical body.

White Feather. White Feather come speak with his brothers and sisters.

All. Good evening, White Feather, / Welcome.

W.F. Once again White Feather is delighted that we have come together in this place of love.

Ray. Yes, very nice, White Feather.

W.F. Once again, White Feather wants you all to know that for a short time we shall remove the barrier between our world and yours so that we can come together in love.

All. Thank you, White Feather.

W.F. White Feather as always speak very good England.

June. Very good, absolutely yes. Doing well.

(other sitters laugh gently at his joke).

W.F. There is much to be done (**Ray.** That's good.) – and White Feather know that you all bring with you such great love and we return that manyfold.

All. Thank you.

W.F. There are many souls in my world who have gathered here tonight all hoping to make contact with you. (**Various voices.** Good. / That's nice./ Thank you.) – White Feather know that we shall enjoy and share in a wonderful meeting of souls within this room. There is much to be done. White Feather will pop out now.

All. Thank you, White Feather.

(end of section 2)

Section 3

Christopher's cheerful banter.

Guest séance – 8th July 1999. (1min. 32seconds).

Notice the big difference in voice and personalities as you listen to Christopher and remember – it is Stewart's body that is being borrowed all the time.

Christopher. *(shouting)* Katie!

Katie. I can hear you.

Ch. Are you sure? **K.** Yes I can.

Ch. Bloody 'ell, I can't keep this up all night!

(All in the circle laugh).

Ch. *(laughs)* She's lovely isn't she? Yeah. I like you Katie.

K. I like you too. You're really happy.

Ch. Well I always try to be. 'Ere, Katie if I can explain. When people come to sit with old Stewart – Don't tell 'im I called 'im 'old Stewart'. (**K.** No, I won't.) No.

When people come to sit with old Stewart sometimes they are very, very nervous – so it is my job to relax everybody.

K. Right, and you are doing a good job too.

Ch. Am I?   **K.** Yes. Yes. *(others join in with yeses)*

Ch. Yes, yes, no wonder I like my job. (**K.** That's why.) – I'm the best, mate. I've got qualifications in relaxation. *(laughs)* Sabine, I've been told I've got to try and speak a little slower; so you can understand. (**Sabine.** Yes, I speak German.) – Yes, well I can't speak German. Yes, sometimes people over 'ere say I sound as though I am speaking German!

June. Double–dutch!

Ch. Yes, yes but I do my best, Sabine. If you don't understand what I'm talking about, just stop me and I'll repeat it. (S. Thank you, thank you.) – Yes, yes, it's alright. But don't stop me too often or we'll be here until two in the morning. *(laughter)*. Heh, hee! I love mi job!

All. We know.

(end of section 3)

Section 4

Freda Johnson introduces herself to the guest circle.

Guest séance – 8th July 1999. (2min. 13seconds).

Stewart's mind is still disconnected from his brain as Freda takes her turn in controlling the human instrument. This lovely lady in spirit sounds like a man and explains the reason why she does so and how 'limiting' she finds it.

Freda. A wonderful coming together. A wonderful

meeting between our two worlds... *(sounds of everyone agreeing.)* – Now I'd like to begin, if I may, by explaining something to those people who've not sat with Stewart before, or rarely sat with Stewart before. May I first of all introduce myself to those souls. My name is Freda Johnson. Now let me say this, that it has been commented upon that my voice... has all the... shall we say, suggests that it is in reality the voice of a male rather than a female but I'm always at pains to point out, forgive me if you have heard me say this before but I do feel that it is important.

June. It is important.

F. What is all important is not the way that I sound but what I have to say. That is all that is important and also of course that I'm able to project, that I'm able to transmit, that I'm able to present my personality, loud and clear to you all.

June. That's important. *(agreement from all.)*

F. Of course my voice tends to be male-like, simply because I'm speaking through a male organism. I'm surrounded by all this maleness, dears. Ladies here this evening will be interested to hear that it is not very pleasant! *(laughter from all)* – but I have to do the best and work with what I have. *(more laughter from another sitter)* – So this evening I'm delighted to say that I'm quite content with the control, with the quality of control that I have upon the medium.

Man's voice. You're doing very well.

(end of section 4)

Section 5

Walter Stinson says a few words.

Guest séance – 8th July 1999. (2min. 39seconds).

Once again, we hear a completely different personality. Walter's Canadian accent is quite noticeable as he emphasises the reason for physical phenomena, to show you the reality of his world and that man is eternal.

Walter. Ok, Folks.   **All.** Ok, Walter.

W. You can all hear my voice?   **All.** Yes, Walter.

W. In that case I begin as always by saying – Good evening folks.

All. Good evening Walter. / Welcome.

W. What a truly wonderful response as always.

All. Thank you Walter / Ok, Walter.

W. It is a wonderful delight to see you all here this evening.

All. We enjoy it tremendously.

W. Folks, we know that many of you have travelled a great distance to be here. (**Man's voice.** We have indeed.) We know. But we are so delighted (**Man.** Oh good.) – that you have all joined together. (**Voices.** Yes, yes) – Our purpose in returning, our sole purpose in communicating with your world in this manner is not so folks can witness those things which people in ignorance within your world would consider to be miracles. Hmm? It is not that, folks. It is simply to show you what we can achieve, what we can do, how we can reach out to you all when we have love and harmony. From that, we hope that each of you will leave this room and have confirmed within your mind that man truly is eternal. That communication between our two worlds is a wondrous reality, folks. (**All.** Yes.) – People say – but why party tricks, why move illuminated trumpets, why do this and why do that – Hmm? but it is only to show you – it is no party trick; it is only to show you the reality of our world; it is to show you the reality of ourselves; to show you that man is eternal; that our world for a short time can join with yours; that we can come together as one; this is the sole purpose of our return folks. **All.** Yes, yes.

(end of Section 5)

Section 6

The Vanguard speaking in independent direct voice.

Guest séance – 31st August 2000. (2min. 37seconds).

The Vanguard, (later to be identified as Dr Barnett) experiments in one of his early attempts at independent voice. This voice is not coming from Stewart's vocal cords as it does when he is speaking in trance; it is coming from a voice box made of ectoplasm emanating from the medium's body.

In this section we hear the spirit person struggling to speak, but you will be able to appreciate how Dr Barnett (through constant practice) advanced this technique over a period of time if you listen to Section 19 recorded four years later. This is one of the reasons why patience and consistency is so important when sitting in a circle.

June. You'll get there.
Ray. We'll let you know how you are doing.
Katie. Is this independent voice?

R. It sounds like it Katie. / **J.** Come on, that's it.

R. I can hear the breath now my friend, I can hear your breath. Yes this is good, this is. Yes that's right. I can hear the volume now, yes, that's it, keep going.

J. Keep going, friend.

R. Once we've got the volume, then we get the clarity of the words my friend, come on.

Voice. I do hope that my......(*more indistinguishable words are heard*)

J. It is getting there. / **R.** We can hear your voice and it is getting clearer. / **J.** It is; it's nice.

Voice. ....difficult to speak.

R. I didn't quite catch that, my friend.

Gaynor. He's endeavouring to speak. It's right next to my cheek. It's right near to me.

Voice. ...speaking mechanism, as always is so unstable...

G. Yes, the speaking mechanism...

V. (*louder*) ...I do hope that you are all able to hear my voice.

G./ R. Yes, you are getting clearer now, my friend, yes.

V. I must say that in a sense I find this to be most frustrating.

R. Oh yes, you must do. / **J.** You must do friend.

G. You're doing well, very well.

R. But you do get better each week, you know that.

V. Well, it is very generous of you to say that.

Circle. Well you do. / You do, you do./ Really do./ It's true.

V. I often feel that perhaps...well it would make the process just a little simpler if I were...if I were able to hear my own voice. (**Ray.** Yes, of course, yes) – It is the fact that I'm unable to do so which I suppose contributes largely to the fact that I'm never quite certain if I'm meeting with any particular level of success.

Circle. Yes, you are, you are doing very well.

V. You can all hear? (**R.** Yes) – Then my friends I would like to say this. (**R.** Yes.) – That although I am quite aware and conscious of the fact, I'm aware of the fact, that so many who come here would expect that a visitor from my world would be able to speak in his own voice and in this way to transmit his own thoughts without the burden of the interference, no matter how small, of......

(end of section 6)

Chapter Four

WALTER'S MATERIALISED HAND

As already mentioned in my Report in the Introduction, at my very first séance in July 1999, I was invited to sit at a small, low table facing Stewart. I had no idea what to expect when Walter asked me to change seats. I thought I could hear quite well with my hearing aids when the spirit team spoke through Stewart in trance, although, having said that, you will notice here how the circle members had to speak on my behalf and repeat certain words for me. I may not have the ears to hear, but I certainly have eyes to see, and this allowed me, as an artist, to illustrate what I saw, giving you a better idea of what happened.

Section 7

Walter materialises his own hand.

Guest séance 8th July 1999. (4min. 22seconds).

Walter. You folks who are sitting a long way from the table, if you wish to stand, you may.

Man's Voice. Ok, thank you, Walter.

W. Katie, ma'am

Ray. *(speaking to the sitters)* Just so you can see what is going on, that's all.

W. All you folks here, I tell you what I hope to be able to do.

58

R. Ok, Walter. / **Katie.** Thank you.

W. In a moment I shall produce the energy you have heard referred to as ectoplasm. (**K.** Yes I have.) – This I hope to be able to show you upon the table-top and from that energy I hope to be able to create, to mould, my own hand folks, but you must tell me if I am meeting with success, for I depend and rely upon you. Ok, Ok. Raymondo, may we have the music very quietly. **R.** Yes, yes, yes

Music plays and Circle hums along with it.

June. Can you see something coming across the table? Can you Katie?

R. Something moving, yes.

(*Special note!: I was so amazed at what I was seeing, I was absolutely speechless.*)

J. Something coming across the table-top.

R. It's just sort of spreading. Some of it is spreading; some of it is see–through isn't it?

Others. Yeah, yeah there it is.

R. There's like fingers coming out of it 1, 2, 3, 4. I can see 4, well done friends.

K. Fantastic!

R. You can see where it is transparent in places. Well done, Walter.

J. Well done, Walter. That was successful Walter.

W. Ok, Ok. (**J.** That was successful, Walter) – You could see? (**All.** Yes) Then Katie ma'am you must do something for me. Can you hear my voice ma'am.

R. Katie can you hear him. **K.** Yes I can.

W. Ma'am, I would like you to place your right hand upon the table with your palm downwards. That is fine ma'am. I ask you to keep your hand perfectly still. Hmm? **K.** Right.

Katie places her right hand upon the table.

W. I want you to tell the folks exactly what you can feel. Hmm? **K.** Yes.

R. What you can see, what you can feel. **K.** Right.

J. Just keep your hand perfectly still Katie.

R. What it is like – warm, cold, hot anything and everything about it, just keep your hand perfectly still. (**K.** Yes.) – Now there's the lump, shall we say, coming forward, onto the table, reaching towards Katie's hand.

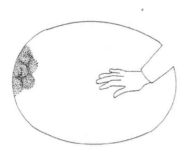

A lump of ectoplasm comes forward on to the table.

K. It's nearly there but not quite.

R. But the hand hasn't formed yet.

K. But the hand is coming.

The hand is forming.

R. The hand is forming, can you see it now it's forming. Can you see the fingers now? The fingers are coming towards Katie's hand.

(Katie quietly confirms each statement with a 'yes'.)

J. Keep it down now.

Some of the ectoplasm is transparent as it stretches between the fingers.

K. Yes! Oh I can touch it. Oh! I can. Oh! It's like a real hand!

R. Are they touching you?

J. It's a real hand! It's a real hand!

K. Oh! It's warm, it is warm!

R. Yes. Well, that is what they do ... they come back as they are.   **K.** Oh! It's lovely!

R. Are they touching your hand now? That's good, Walter. *(June chips in 'yes he is').*   **K.** Yes, yes!

There is now a solid hand, touching
and stroking Katie's hand.

R. That's wonderful that, Walter. Touching your fingers, still touching your fingers? Is it going back now?

J & K. Yes. It is going back.

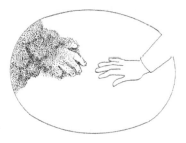

The hand returns to being an ectoplasmic
blob as it moves back to the medium

R. It is going back towards the medium. Well done, friends that was ... / **J.** Well done Walter.

K. That was an experience!

R. That was wonderful, Katie.

W. Ma'am, I hope that it will be an experience that you will never forget.

K. I certainly won't!

W. Of course it is warm and of course it is real, for it is my hand ma'am!

R. Yes, that's right Walter.

W. Ok, Ok. Ma'am I ask if you would remove your hand and return to your seat.

K. Thank you.

(end of section 7)

It was definitely an experience I would not forget. It was an astonishing demonstration. When the hand touched mine, I was so dumbfounded, I couldn't even get my words right! I didn't mean to say, "I can touch it" I should have said, "I can feel it!"

The ectoplasmic mass had weight and solidity to it— a blob which crept out on to the table to the rhythm of Stewart's breathing. As you can see in my illustrations, the substance is not flimsy, wispy or ghostly, it is a solid, physical mass.

After the séance, I was so overjoyed to know that it was true; we do survive after death and the spirit people do return and materialise just as Bob and Ena told me. I was so elated, I couldn't get to sleep that night!

Chapter Five

ECTOPLASM

Having seen how real and tangible ectoplasm is, I needed to know more about it. I put the question to Freda when she spoke to me through Stewart in trance on 25th May 2000, at a private sitting in the afternoon. I found Freda to be very helpful as she explained what she knew about the substance, without being too scientific.

Section 8

Freda explains ectoplasm.

Private sitting – 25th May 2000. (7min. 57seconds).

Katie. ... so many questions that they asked as well. They asked me, 'What is ectoplasm made of?'

Freda. Oh I'll tell you dear. I'll tell you. I think,. . . I wish that you'd asked this question of Walter because his understanding is far greater than mine but I will do my best for you dear. (**K.** Thank you.) – Life itself is a trinity, dear. There is the physical, there is the spiritual body and then there is the mind. (**K.** Yes.) – The physical body is that which you inhabit as you proceed along through life upon the earthly path. But the life of the physical body is merely temporary, dear.

K. Yes.

F. When you pass from the earth plane then your

physical body returns to the earth but your spiritual body is an exact replica of your physical body. Within your spiritual body is your mind. I'm uncertain whether you have heard me say this before, Katie, but the mind is all that you are; all that you were and all that you will be. It is your personality; it is your complete memory. It is...it is you in totality, dear, but it is the eternal aspect of yourself, for your spiritual body together with your mind will proceed on into eternity. It is indestructible, dear. Your physical brain is merely an instrument of the mind; that is all. It is nothing in itself. But it gives physical expression to your mind, dear, the eternal aspect of yourself.

You will therefore understand that there is physical matter and there is spiritual matter... (**K.** Right, yes.) – Between the two is a form of dynamic energy which we often refer to as ectoplasm for it is neither physical nor spiritual in nature; it is the only substance or energy which lies between the two states of existence. It is both spiritual and it is physical. (**K.** Yes.) – You understand what I am saying dear? (**K.** I think I do.)

F. When you take part in a physical séance and we attempt to manifest in a physical manner – then we must take from the medium the energy, the vital energy, the substance, ectoplasm, and it is upon this that all physical phenomena rests and depends; without that there would be no physical contacts. It is between the two states of existence, unique to neither but common to both. You understand what I am saying, Katie? (**K.** I think so, yes.) – Ectoplasm can be manipulated by the –er–scientific people in my world in such a manner that its very nature can be changed. Its molecular structure can be changed from something that is almost smoke-like in appearance to something which is solid to the touch. (**K.** Right) – It can be changed; it can be manipulated to something which is filmy, which is unsubstantial to something which is very substantial, that is solid to the touch. (**K.** Right.) – From the ectoplasm the scientific people are able to create what we often refer to as either pseudopods[1] or ectoplasmic arms. It is these that are connecting themselves to the trumpets, dear. But the other end of the arm or the pseudopod must remain in contact with the medium for it is truly a part of the medium. It is a vital form of energy. We are then able to create... *(intake of breath)* – We are then able to change the structure of the arm from something which is invisible to something, on occasions, which is visible and it is this which will support and manipulate the trumpets. You understand, Katie? (**K.** Yes I do, yes.) – I think that you have seen photographs? (**K.** I have, yes.) – That is all it is, dear, I make it sound very simple... 'that is all that it is' – it's very complex.

K. Yes. It's just when you are trying to talk to other people, trying to explain to them.

F. I know dear, but that's understandable, that's understandable, and that is precisely why ectoplasm is extremely sensitive to any form of light – it is rather like the photographer trying to develop his photographs in light – it cannot be done, dear. It has to be done – the whole process within the darkroom. Life itself cannot be generated within light. It generates within darkness, within the womb of the mother, dear, and it is like an accelerated form of life itself. It is the birth of this form of energy but what takes nine months ...what takes nine months to reach fruition is created in seconds within the séance room. You understand what I'm saying? (**K.** I understand, yes, I understand.) – I know it is a great deal for you to understand, dear, and I'm doing the best that I can in the time that I have.

---

1. For information on pseudopods (ectoplasmic rods) and trumpets – see Chapter 13

K. It does help. It will help me to explain it to other people.

F. Yes. And I say that if suddenly light is introduced within the séance room then the ectoplasm would return extremely quickly to the medium and this could create a haemorrhage, dear. (**K.** Right, yes.) – That is why it is dangerous. Physical mediumship, the exercising of physical mediumship is always dangerous. It has the danger – it has danger connected with it at all times and for precisely that reason most of the physical mediums in the past have chosen to work within the safety of their own séance rooms. (**K.** I can understand that.) – within the safety of their own closed circles, where outsiders, where strangers have not been allowed within.

K. Yes. So in a way this explains why only the few people know and see the ectoplasm.[2]

F. Of course, of course dear. We hope that this evening we shall be able to show…Have you seen ectoplasm, dear?

K. I have, yes I have. Walter.. er ..developed his hand.

F. But you have not seen it within the red light as it leaves Stewart? (**K.** No.) – We hope that we shall be able to show you this evening, dear.

K. I've just seen it on top of the table.

F. Yes, where Walter was able to create his hand. What we hope to be able to show you this evening you will see, will be unaffected by the red light, that it will appear as white – snow white. (**K.** Yes) – That'll be a wonderful treat, dear. (**K.** Yes, that'll be lovely because....)... Something else for you to see.

K. Yes, thank you, yes.

(end of section 8)

---

2. What I really meant to say was "... only a few people get to know about and see the ectoplasm."

As Freda explained, ectoplasm is part of Stewart's vital energy and it can flow from any orifice of his body, (his mouth, nose, ears etc.).

The promise which was made here was fulfilled at a séance held in the evening of that same day. This time, Walter let us see the ectoplasm emanate from Stewart's mouth in the shape of what looked like candy floss – or a very large white beard.

Section 9

Walter demonstrates ectoplasm in the light.

Guest séance – 25th May 2000. (3min. 37seconds).

Walter. Ok, Ok. We shall try to fulfil a promise which we made earlier today.

Voices of circle. Oh yes / Good /Ok, Walter./ The curtains are moving./ Yes/ Yes/ They are open again.

W. Folks, we shall endeavour to extract from the medium the energy ectoplasm. (**Ray.** Ok, my friend, yes.) – In doing so we hope that we can make it visible to you.

Mixed voices. Thank you, Walter. / Oh, wonderful!

W. .. As it moves, ... as it passes from the invisible to the visible state, then you should be able to clearly hear the transformation as it takes place.

Circle. Right, Walter/ Yes Ok, Walter.

W. Ok, Ok.

R. We shall be listening intently, yes.

(sounds of laboured breathing)

Women's voices. I can hear a crackling noise./ You can hear it now. /A crackling noise. / Yes.

('static' crackling sound heard)

R. We did ask him once whether that was the energy

actually coming out, you know, of the body of the medium and he said no, it was actually transforming it from invisible to visible. Sort of like a charge within the particles.

Man's voice. It sounds like a trapped butterfly.

R. That's the first time I heard that one. (*Laughter*)

Various voices. Sounds like bubbles in the bath/or Rice Crispies.

R. Yes. Now you don't want me to do anything at the moment, do you Walter?

W. No.

R. You'll give me instructions, won't you?

Mike (*guest sitter*). I feel a lot of coldness.

Circle. Yes, / You can, yes.

W. Michael, sir, you will indeed continue to feel a lowering of the temperature. Raymondo – (**R.** Yes, sir.) – When we are able to give the signal, we want your light for a period of two seconds only and then off.

R. Ok, my friend.

Woman's voice. Where shall we look?

Gaynor. Into the cabinet.

R. Into the cabinet towards Stewart. Now, I won't move forward.

June & Gaynor. And I won't. I'll sit back / and I'll sit back.

R. So what you want to be doing is looking at Stewart's face in the cabinet. Usually it comes from the nose or the mouth.

J&G. And I'm sitting right back

R. And I've got to concentrate. (*A tap is heard.*)

J. There you are, Ray. (*There is a swishing of the curtain.*) – See it?

Circle. WOW! / It's wonderful, Wow!

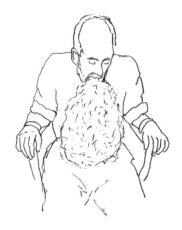

This illustration shows what we saw as the ectoplasm flowed from his mouth.

J. See. That light's bright, isn't it, Ray?   **G.** Yeah.
(There is a choking sound)
Woman's voice. W–ow!   **J.** Ok, friend.
R. Are you alright there now, Walter?
G. Raymondo! / **R.** Ok.
W. Yes, The light is too bright.   **R.** Ok, Walter.
W. Were you all able to see?
Circle. Oh yeah / Yes / Beautiful. / Awesome/ Like a great white beard/ It's fantastic, yes / Like candy floss.
J. The light is bright isn't it, Ray?
R. I've turned it right down now.
J. You've turned it right down? *(A tap is heard)*
J. There you are Ray. *(The light is put on again)* – There you are, look! (**Circle.** Oh! Wow!)
R. I could still see it the second time; it was still there; it is just a question of getting this....
W. Then let us see what else we can do.
All. Ok, Walter.

(end of section 9)

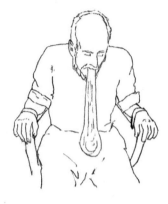

Left: And this is what I saw at a séance a few years later. This time it is in a different form, more solid, showing the shape of a heavy ball.

Section 10

Walter picks up a pen and writes.

Guest séance – 31st August 2000. (2min. 11seconds).

In this experiment, Walter did not develop the ectoplasm into a fully formed hand because he needed to save energy for more physical phenomena later on. Here, he used enough energy to divide the ectoplasm into two – a pincer shape to pick up the pen and the other 'blob' solid enough to pull the pad towards him and hold it in place.

Walter. June, I want the pad and the pen upon the table. (**June.** Right, Walter.) – Let me see what else I can do. Hmm? Raymondo, switch up your light slightly.

R. Switch it down a bit? **J.** Up a bit he said.

Gaynor. Down.

J. No, up a little bit he said. **G.** Sorry.

W. That is fine. That is fine.

J. I've put the pad on the table for you, Walter, and the pen.

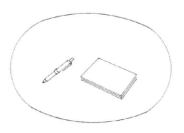

The pen and pad are placed on to the table.

G. The light went up and down a little bit.

R. No, just the light went on an off a little bit.

J. Yes it did.   **R.** Short connection somewhere.

J. Yes it's been travelling around a bit, hasn't it Ray? *(A long yawn is heard)* **G.** Good Heavens!

J. It's been travelling around. Can you see the mass coming out – coming towards the pad?

The mass begins to flow on to the table.

G. Are they going to write something?

The mass splits in two

J. Yes, yes. They are picking up the pen.

(clicking noises are heard as the tape recorder changes sides)

G. I can see the pen moving.

J. It is, yeah, it is, yeah. Well done. Walter. You are doing all right there.

G. I think he is going to write. Who's doing that? *(referring to the clicks)*

The pincers pick up the pen and write.

W. Ma'am, tell me how do I spell Katie?

K. Oh! – K. **(W.** Yes) – A. **(W.** Yes) – T. **(W.** Yes) – I. **(W.** yes) – E. **(W.** Yes)

J. Is that how you have spelt it, Walter?

W. That is fine. *(laughter from June).*

J. Well done, Walter.

K. I think it's marvellous, that.

J. It certainly is.

(Sounds of tearing and paper being crumpled hide Katie's comment)

J. Makes you wonder how they tear it off with one hand, doesn't it?

W. Katie, ma'am, reach out, that is for you to keep.

K. Thank you. **(J.** Have you got it Katie?) – Thank you very much, thank you.

W. It is my pleasure.

J. Well done Walter, well done.

W. It is a small memento for you to keep forever, ma'am.

K. Thank you, Walter, I shall treasure this.

Walter's handwritten message.

J. You certainly will, won't you. Well done.

(end of section 10)

On this occasion Walter had not formed a complete hand but this is what he had to say at a sitting held on 28th June 2005, where he explained what happens when ectoplasm forms into a solid hand:

> *"I extract from the medium a considerable quantity of ectoplasm. It is neither spiritual nor physical in make–up. It exists between the two states, common to both, unique to neither. When the energy has been converted into a form visible to you, when it becomes pliable, when I know that it is of a molecular state which will allow me to work further upon it, I then dip my etheric hand into the energy, into the ectoplasm which I find clings to my etheric hand. This organised mass from which I create my etheric hand – has weight.*

It is the weight that creates the problem. It is difficult for us to manipulate physical weight, physical mass, because I come from a world as you know which exists on a finer vibrational level than your own. So I have to slow down my vibrations. I have to catch the moment. I have to submerge my own etheric hand into this mass of energy.

Sometimes if you listen carefully when I perform the experiment, you may hear the sound of the energy as it passes from the invisible to the visible state, not always but often. So it has weight, the energy has weight and it must be of a particular state which lends itself to manipulation."

Ectoplasm is also used to create partial or full materialisations.

When the energy reaches its peak, our spirit friends can then fully materialise; by this I mean they can actually walk among us in the darkness of the séance room. We can hear them walk and they are for a short time solid to the touch.

Author's note:

Many people make the big mistake of thinking we sit in a séance to communicate with ghosts; this is absolutely not true. The spirit people are not ghostly apparitions. They are solid in their own world but not so in ours, so they cover themselves in a material substance extracted from the medium known as ectoplasm, and are solid and real to the touch, even when they walk around the séance room.

At a séance held on 25th May 2000, a materialised form walked round the room and two hands physically touched the top of my head, while at the same time, Mike (another guest sitter) who sat next to me confirmed that two hands were touching his head. This meant that two spirit people had materialised and walked round the room that night. One of the materialised forms, known as 'The Voice' stood right in front of me and I could hear him speak quite well.

Section 11

A materialised form walks round the room.

Guest séance – 25th May 2000. (3min. 29seconds).

This excerpt opens with indecipherable comments by the Circle.

Ray. He's come back out now.

June. Listen, someone's walking.

Katie. I can hear them!   **J.** Oh, wonderful.

Gaynor. Oh bless you, friend. You are so welcome.

Materialised Form. My friends...

R. It's our friend again, 'The Voice'.

M.F. I must ask that you should all remain perfectly still.

Circle. We certainly will / There's a tapping. / **R.** Yes.

K. Oh, someone is touching my head.

Various voices. Ohh,Lovely, Katie

Ray. When you say...

K. Two hands on my head.

R. Two hands on your head.

K. Oh, Thank you very much.

M.F. Bless you, my child.

K. Thank you, thank you very much.

(other comments not decipherable)

J. Have you got them on yours, Mike?

Mike. Touching my hair.

R. One or two? One or two, Mike?

M. I'm not sure I think two. Yes, two.

K. Two are still on my head.

R. Are they still on your head?

K. Yes they are still on my head.

R. And are they on yours Mike?

M. They are still on my head, yes.

R./J. & others. That's superb. Bless you friends. / Two people? / Yes. God bless you friends.

M.F. I would like you all to understand (**R.** Yes, we're listening.) – that what we are doing here within this meeting place between our worlds now is but nothing to what we know we shall be able to do in time. (**Circle.** Yes, yes etc.) – It is our intention my friends, that soon we shall be able to walk amongst you within the light.

Circle. Oh superb, that would be wonderful. etc.

M.F. – We hope that we shall achieve this. *(Indistinct comments follow)* – My friends, all that we have done here this evening we could not have done without the love that you have brought here.

All. Thank you. / **R.** You can take it all home with you.

J. He's still walking about.

K. Hands on my head again. Thank you.

M.F. Oh my child there is so much to be done. (**K.** Yes, I understand.) – You know… (**K.** I do. I'll do all I can.) – You know, my love and all the love of all those in my world involved in this wonderful work, shall always be with you. (**K.** Thank you, thank you. I shall do all I can.) – We know and we understand.

K. Yes. Thank you.

(Circle chatter make the comments undecipherable)

K. Thank you.   **J.** Wonderful, friends, as always.

M.F. ...I find as always that the weight ... It is so difficult ....

(Circle comments drown out the last words)

G. You've done well, friend. / **J.** We appreciate that.

G. You've done exceptionally well. He's got stronger.

(end of section 11)

Although I have so far been telling you of my experiences recorded during the years 1999 to 2001, I thought, at this stage, while we are on the subject of ectoplasm, I would add some more reports outside this timescale.

On 16th November 2004, Walter invited me to feel the ectoplasm in its different stages of manifestation. I was sitting in the dark, next to Stewart, when Walter (speaking through Stewart in trance), asked for my right hand. He held my wrist near to the medium's chest and asked me to keep my hand open with my palm upwards. He also asked me to keep my hand perfectly still. To start with, I could feel a very cold draft of air on my palm before feeling something like warm snowflakes. After that, I felt the ectoplasm in various forms:

Like thin crinkly paper;

Like soft material draped over my hand;

Like the bottom of a ball with some weight to it,

Like a hard solid texture, similar to rough cloth.

Previously, in February 2004, I was sitting next to Stewart on his right when Walter materialised and walked out of the cabinet with the intention of reaching the other end of the room. As he set off, I felt a very soft silky drape of ectoplasm over my left hand.

To save energy, the spirit people do not always cover their feet (or full bodies) in ectoplasm when walking round the room and the ectoplasm drapes over the materialised top of the form. This would be what I felt when Walter walked out.

At another home circle séance on 17th November 2011, Walter asked Ray to switch on the red light for a few seconds. When he did so, we clearly saw a solid state of ectoplasm developed under Stewart's chin, shown here.

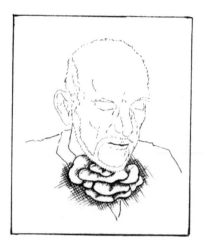

I would describe it like fungus on a tree and it looked like solid rubber, which goes to show how ectoplasm can change and appear—and be used in different forms.

Chapter Six

PERSONAL EVIDENCE

So far I have concentrated on the phenomena and techniques of trance and physical mediumship, but amongst my reports during that period, there were also some personal connections with my loved ones in spirit.

I have included five of these here.

Section 12

Katie's Dad speaks.

Private sitting – 25th May 2000. (1min. 20seconds).

Here is my Dad speaking through Stewart in trance for the first time. At the time of this sitting, Stewart had no idea that both my parents were in the spirit world.

Dad tried very hard to speak and found some difficulty in controlling the medium's brain and vocal organs. The mention of Mum being with him was an evidential point, because I never called my Mum 'Mother'. I always called her 'Mum', but Dad used to say 'Mother' quite often, in fact, I do remember him using this phrase. He would often say 'Mother' as an announcement, for example– "Mother has cleaned the floor, so don't walk on it." The way he said 'Mother' convinced me that it was Dad speaking through Stewart.

Dad. Ohh! Yes... Kate!

Katie. Come on Dad you're doing very well –

Dad. Kate, is that you?   **K.** It is indeed.

D. Oh, I say this is so wonderful.

K. It's nice to talk to you again.

D. I don't know if you can hear everything that I'm trying to say. (**K.** I can, yes.) – It's rather like trying to speak to you through a fog. I know that I'm doing what I was told to do but at the same time my mind, I find, is so confused. Oh...Kate!

K. You're doing very well I can hear you very well

D. Oh...Mother's here, we're both together, we're both together...but...I...oh

K. Keep trying.   **D.** I'm trying so very hard

K. It must be very difficult.

D. Oh I can't begin to tell you how difficult this is... Give our love to them all...give our love to them all...

K. Yes, I will.

(end of section 12)

Section 13

Walter delivers evidence to Katie and Christine.

Guest séance – 4th May 2000. (1min. 38seconds).

A loved one in spirit often connects with your thought energy, especially when you are feeling happy and the atmosphere is in complete harmony. My sister, Christine, often thought of Mum when she did the ironing. When Mum was on the earth plane, she was very particular about her ironing. Christine now lives on a narrow boat and because a proper ironing board cannot be put up in the confined cabin space, the ironing is never done as Mum would have liked it. Christine often wondered what Mum would think of this.

Here Walter relates Mum's thoughts on the subject of ironing to us. I didn't know what Walter was talking about until Christine told me after the séance. This evidence tells us how our loved ones in spirit are much closer to us than we realise, and they know what we are thinking.

Walter. Ok. Ok. Ok. Your mother brings her love to you both.

Christine. Oh, thank you, Mum love.

W. Ok. Ok. Tell me something – Did she... What is this regarding ironing? Hmmm? (**Katie.** Ironing?) – Yes, was she particularly...(**Chr.** Yes) – careful? (**Chr.** Yes, yes.) – You know what I'm saying here? (**Chr.** Yes, she was, yes.) – She says she's trying to bring some evidence to you of her presence here this evening. She's saying that I must mention this to you both. Hmmm?

Chr. I've been thinking of her while I've been ironing. Yes.

W. I hope therefore that this proves to you, Chris, how close your loved ones who are now in my world are – how close they are to you all.

Chr. Oh bless them, I know.

W. You send out a thought and they receive, hmmm?

Chr. Thank you. Mum. / **K.** Thank you.

W. Ok, Ok, Ok. She's saying if only once again she could hold you both.

K. That'd be nice. / **Chr.** That would be lovely.

W. But you know... but you know that she still loves you in the way that she always did.   **Chr.** Bless her.

K. She's always in our thoughts.

W. And you in hers ma'am. This is a time to rejoice!
Everyone. Yes. Yes.

(end of section 13)

The next two sections relate to Bob and Ena, and as you already know a little about them from the Introduction, the evidence speaks for itself.

Section 14

Christopher introduces a visitor.

Guest séance – 31st August 2000. (54seconds).

You will hear Christopher's chirpy voice at the beginning of the séance announcing that a "Ronald Hill" is here, (and he can't spell!). When I heard the name, it didn't register at first, then I eventually realised that this soul was linking with me because of my connection to Ena.

Christopher. All right. We've got somebody here as well by the name of Hill. H.–I.–L. – Hill. Is there somebody here who recognises the name of Hill, H–I–L?
Man's voice. It could be .... *(unrecognisable)*
Ch. Does somebody recognise the name of Ronald Hill. H–I–L?
K. Ronald Hill? It wouldn't be to do with Ena's? ...er...
Ch. I don't know who it's got to do with. There's a gentleman here this evening **(K.** Ena's first husband) – who's expressing some concern for his wife, and he is telling me his name is Ronald Hill. **(K.** Yes.) – You know what this is about? **(K.** I do, yes.) – Bloody 'ell I'm good tonight, ain't I?
Gaynor. You are, aren't you!

Ch. I'm surprising myself. (laughs) We're going to have a good night tonight!

(end of section 14)

I was to find out what was going to happen later that night. It was such a delightful surprise to actually speak to Ronald Hill himself as you will hear in this next section.

Section 15

Freda helps a spirit communicator.

Guest séance – 31st August 2000. (7min. 49seconds).

Ronald was the first husband of my friend Ena. He was killed in action during World War II. He gave his blessing to Bob and Ena on their marriage when he materialised at a Helen Duncan séance in 1941 and asked Bob to take care of her until she should join him in the spirit world.

Ena's health by now was deteriorating and Ronald was concerned for his once–wife. This conversation took place on 31st August 2000; my last visit to the séance room in Hull before Ena passed to the higher life on 5th February 2001. Ronald knew what was going to happen and got this message through while he could. "Chiefy" is Ena's spirit friend.

You will also hear Mum trying to talk to me, but as it was very difficult for her to control the medium, Freda stepped in to help get her message across.

Freda. The gentleman who comes here this evening is telling me that his name is Ronald Hill dear. Now, he is connected with a lady friend of yours.

Katie. Yes, Georgina Brake.

84

F. Yes. Now he's saying this: that he has tried for some time to reach her dear, and this he has particularly done during her sleep state. He has tried to reach out to her – and you must know dear, that he has been a little concerned in regard to her health dear. Now he's saying this… and I'm not quite certain why, Ronald, will you not come and say this for yourself dear? I find this, Katie dear, to be such a nuisance. I would rather they come and speak for themselves. So I shall now allow him to come and speak dear – I must ask you to encourage him as much as you can and I'm sure that you will, dear.

K. Yes of course.

F. Wait a moment.

K. Yes. Hello Ronald, Ron, come on Ron, *(wheezy breathing is heard)* – Come and tell us what you have to say to Georgina.

Others. Come on friend/ Come on, you can do it.

K. What have you got to say to Georgina?

Ron. *(rasping intake of breath)* Oh, can (**K.** Hello.) – you hear my voice? (**All.** We can hear you.) – I'm not certain whether…how much I shall be able to do. I never knew you when I was on your side, but I do so want to take this opportunity to come here this evening…Halliwell, Halliwell.

K. Halliwell, Yes, Katie.

Ron. …want to take this opportunity to come here this evening to thank you for all that you have done for my wife.

K. Ah, I thank you for what you have done, and for what your wife has done. Is there anything I can pass on to her?

Ron. Yes of course, of course. I want you to first of all to begin by telling her that I have taken this opportunity this evening to come to send my love, to send my love. (**K.** I'll tell her, I'll tell her.) – You must also pass my love—my regards to Bob, (**K.** Yes, I will.) – my dear friend, my dear friend. Tell him also that I am so delighted and so pleased and I have been for so many years now at the way in which – er–er – the life which they have been able to lead. You understand these words? (**K.** Yes, yes.) – I'm er – er–, what she has done, my darling, ... what my darling has done. She must know that I have been trying so hard to influence her from my side. (**K.** Yes. She'll understand.) – At last she has done it. She has put it down. She has left a record. That's all that really matters, (**K.** Yes. That's important.) – she's left a record[1]. Yes. Tell her that I am here with Chiefy. (**K.** Ohh, yes,yes, I will./ **Ray.** Chiefy? / **K.** Chiefy, yes.) – There's so many here ... there's so many here but tell her, tell her, that when the time comes I will be waiting. (**K.** I'll tell her, yes.) – It will be the three musketeers. (**Ray.** *(chuckles)* It'll be the three musketeers.) – united at last. **K.** Yes, that's lovely.

Ron. All my love. *(intake of struggling breath)*

June/Gaynor. Ok/Ok, friend./ **Ray.** Cheers Ron.

Ron. I can't manage any more.

Gaynor. You've done very well, very well.

K. Thank you Ron. I'll tell Ena and she'll listen to the tapes. *(sounds of kisses 'blown')*

G. Kisses. That's lovely. / **Ray.** That was nice.

J. That's nice. **G.** Well done.

K. Wonderful, lovely to help Ena.

Ray. It must be love. /

J. Yes, it will do her the world of good.

All. Ok, friend,....come on, come on / You can do it / You're welcome. *(a new visitor is heard trying to speak)*

---

1. Ena's record of their story is available in *Of Love Between Two Worlds.* (available from Saturday Night Press www.snppbooks.com)

Voice. I want ooo...   **Ray.** You want...?

Voice. I want to speak with my daughter. I want to speak with...

J&G. Who's your daughter, friend?

Voice. It's Mum.

J&G. It's Mum. Hello, love.   **K.** Hello.

Voice. It's Mum, Oooh yes!

Sitter. Who's Mum are you? Katie's?   **K.** Yes?

Voice. Oh. Aye. Oh, this is so wonderful, wonderful.

J. Wonderful, Katie.

K. Wonderful yes. I'm having a bit of difficulty hearing you

Voice. Oh I know, oh, I know oh, oh, oh...

K. Lovely to hear you, lovely to hear you...

Voice. My love, my love. (*choking gurgle*)

J. All my love, Katie, she said.   **K.** Well done.

Freda. Katie dear, (**K.** Yes Freda.) – I have your mother here. She's sending her love to you. (**K.** She did very well.) – Oh she did, dear. Considering it's her first time. She was shouting so loudly... (**K.** Yes. I know it is difficult with my hearing.) – That does not matter dear. Raymond...(**Ray.** Yes) – This meeting, dear, everything we are saying...

Ladies, you'll be interested to hear this. I've said this to you before, Katie, but the ladies will be interested to hear that Raymond has a machine dears, and everything that we say within this room, it goes within the machine so that at some time in the future, in many years from now, you will be able to hear my voice revolving around and around within the machine dears, (*chuckles from the circle*). It's very technical and I'm not certain that I understand this myself but it goes round, dears. That's all that you need to know so you'll be able to listen to your mother's voice dear. (**K.** Yes. I will, thank you.) – She's sending her love to everyone. (**K.** Thank you.) – I find that I'm shouting, dears.

All. You are!

Ray. We do agree with you tonight, HaHa!

J. Is that 'cos it's breezy outside?

F. It's for Katie, dear. It's for Katie. (**J.** I know, I know.) – We are well aware of everything that you have done, dear. (**K.** Thank you.) – We are well aware of everything that you have done. (**K.** Right. Thank you.) – and you'll be surprised at the outcome. (**K.** Right.) – you understand what I am saying? (**K.** I do.) – you'll be surprised at the outcome. (**K.** Yes.)

J. That'll be nice.

(end of section 15)

The next section was recorded in the year 2002, but I thought it appropriate to include it here, as I have referred in the previous section to Ena's passing in 2001.

Section 16

Georgina Brake (Ena) communicates for the first time.

Home Circle Séance – 15th October 2002. (3min. 23seconds)

In this section, you will hear Ena (now in spirit) talking to the members of the home circle for the first time. I was not present at this particular meeting and Ray kindly recorded the message and posted the cassette tape to me. In the recording you will hear Ena saying, "I have met with Medi." The circle members did not have a clue what Ena was talking about. If I had been there, I would have responded directly because I know who 'Medi' is. Many years ago Ena often sat with

Mrs MacHattie, a medium who was fondly known as 'Medi' and it was through Mrs McHattie that Ena came to know 'Chiefy', a wise North American Indian spirit guide who often spoke in that circle sixty years ago. Ena had told me of him many times, so this was wonderful evidence for me when Ron said he was with 'Chiefy' as no-one in the circle that night had ever heard of him.

Happily, Ena is now meeting many people and having a wonderful time in the spirit world. The recording is very quiet and breathy but worth listening to.

Michael. *(Stewart's brother).* Come on friend... Yes... We can hear you. **Ray.** Come on, friend.

M. We can hear you, come on. / **R.** This is good, yes.

M. Well done. / **R.** This is good, my friend.

(a whispering voice is heard)

June. So strange – yes.   **M.** It is isn't it.

R. Is that what they said – so strange.

M. It's very hard to do, isn't it?

Spirit Voice. *(whispers)* Yes... You... can... hear...

J. Yes, sweetheart.

R. We can hear you. /   **M.** You are doing very well.

Gaynor. You are doing very well.

(Breathy sounds are heard as the spirit tries to speak.)

M. That's it, come on.

R. That's it. You're getting stronger.

G. Keep going.

Spt. V. I... didn't... quite.. imagine... that ... the ... day ... would ... come ... when... I ... was ... communicating... in ... this... way...

M. Glad you are.

Spt. V. Yes, yes. Can…you…pass…on ..my love…to… Bob.

June. Bob, Yes

Spt.V. and … to… my… Katie.

J. Katie? Of course we can.

Spt. V. It's Ena.   **R.** It's Ena.

J. I'll do that, Ena. Bless you, we'll do that.

R. We'll let them know you've been.

M. Well done, Ena.

R. It's nice of you to come, as well.

Spt. Ena. I…have..wanted..to..do..this..for..a..long… time.

R. Oh, you're welcome.

Spt.Ena. Never… thought… that… I … would… be … able… to… manage… before… this… evening… yes.

J. That's wonderful; you're doing a good job.

Spt.Ena. Give… my… love… to…

J. We certainly will.

Spt.Ena. … I… have… settled… down… where…. it… is… all… that… we… could… possibly… have … imagined… Much… much…more.

J. Brilliant / **M.** That's wonderful.

Spt. Ena. Oh! I … have… met… so…many… people.

R. You've met so many people?

Spt. Ena. Oh yes! I'm… having… a… wonderful… time.

R. Good. Oh, She's having a wonderful time?

M. That's good.

Spt.Ena. I.. have… met… so… many…. people. 'Medi', yes. I… have…met with…'Medi.'

Gaynor. 'Meeni'?

J. With whom Ena? Who have you met with, Ena?

Spt.Ena. So… many… people..I've…been… speaking…

to...Mrs...Duncan.

G. Mrs Duncan, Excellent

R. Mrs Duncan, that's good!

J. That's wonderful.

Spt.Ena. Yes. I'll... try... again.

J. Oh you must! / **G.** All right, all right, Ena.

R. You please come again.

J. You must come again.

G. Bye, bye now.

M. Well done! That was very well done.

J. Well done, sweetheart. Thank you, bless you.

(end of section 16)

Chapter Seven

FREDA AND WALTER TALK TO KATIE

To conclude Part One, here is what Freda and Walter said to me during a private sitting in May 2000.

Section 17

Freda speaks about the acceptance of 'Truth'.

Private sitting – 25th May 2000. (4min. 30seconds).

Freda explains how no amount, or quality, of communicated evidence will appeal to the closed mind and informs me of people who think they are mediums when they are not.

Katie. One of the questions that people ask is 'why isn't this general knowledge, why is it only a few that know about the spirit and the afterlife?'

Freda. I think Katie that the best way that I can answer that is in this manner: that there are only a very small percentage of the population of the earth who express an intelligent interest in these things, but is it not strange that most of the population of your earth even though they will speak in ignorance, with a total lack of knowledge or understanding, will proffer opinions which they cast in stone as great truths, when really they are merely speaking with a total lack of understanding or knowledge. For you who have taken the time, for you who have taken the trouble, to investigate for yourself, for you who know the truth then it is not, I would say – it will never be fruitful to speak to those who have already made up their minds and based their understanding and opinions upon nothing but biased personal beliefs. What other subject upon the earth would someone chose to elaborate upon if they had no understanding? There is none dear. Only on this matter of the nature of life that everyone suddenly has a wonderful opinion.

Katie. Yes. It is interesting to hear your point of view because I'm trying to help these people and there is so much magic happening that they think 'Oh there must be ways of doing this, because magicians are so clever and do all sorts.'

Freda. Oh yes, dear, we have heard this.

K. And you hear all sorts of that, what they're thinking of, (**F.** Oh yes, dear.) – and it is difficult to express the truth.

F. And of course one has to bear in mind also that in the past there have been so many, what Walter often refers to as 'pseudo–mediums', those who profess to be mediums who are nothing of the sort. Many of these are deceiving themselves. You understand what I'm saying, Katie? Many believe themselves to have the gift when in reality they have merely – they will be exercising an overactive imagination – that is all. Then we have those mediums, who have perpetrated, and I use this word because there is none other that will express what I am trying to say here; there are those who have operated in a fraudulent sense. We all know of these. We know their history, dear, but there are always and have always been quite excellent mediums and it's these that you hear so little about. People forget them. People say all Spiritualists are frauds, all mediums are frauds. Well, that is rather like saying that because there is one bad apple in a basket, dear, that all the apples must be bad. There are within your – there are within your police force those, from time to time, who behave in a dishonest manner, but that does not mean to say that all of your police force are dishonest. It merely means that a very small percentage are. And so it is within Spiritualism and within Mediumship, there will always be those who produce fraud in an unconscious or in a conscious sense but then equally there will always be those who are quite genuine. (**K.** Yes, yes.) – There is so much ignorance, Katie.

(end of section 17)

Section 18

Walter talks to Katie.

Private sitting – 25th May 2000. (4min. 11seconds).

Walter points out that the spirit people are simply fellow human beings who have gone before us and try regularly to make contact because death is not the end.

Walter. I would like to begin today by saying something which I believe is extremely important, hmm?

Katie. Yes.

Walter. If I at any time I should say anything that you are unable to hear then I would like you to stop me, ma'am. (**K.** I will, yes.) – Ok, Ok. Did you know … may I call you Katie? (**K.** Katie, yes.) – Fine, you may call me Walter, ma'am. (**K.** Ok, Walter, thank you.) – Did you know that there are many souls in your world, particularly those who call themselves Spiritualists, who believe that we who choose to return and work in this manner are in some way elevated spiritual souls?

They believe that we are filled with great spirituality –
I can tell you, ma'am, that this is poppycock. Hmm?

I want you to clearly understand, for this is
important, whilst there are indeed those who return in
this way; who choose to return in this way; who enjoy
opportunities *(heavy breath)* – to instruct, to advise, to
inform, to educate people as to the true nature of life;
there are those who do return so that they may fill
those who come here with great spirituality; those who
will share their spiritual knowledge. There are those
who will do so, visitors from my world, workers from
my world, but that is not the purpose of our work
through Stewart, Hmm. It is merely so that we can
share with you the wonderful truth, the wonderful
reality of life beyond death and of communication
between our two states that we should from time to
time be able to reunite those who come here, with their
loved ones who now reside in my world. That is the
nature and the purpose of the work that we undertake
through Stewart, Hmm? Ok, Ok, It is important, Katie,
that all who come here should understand. So we want
you today to think of us not as some great spiritual
souls but as fellow human beings, for that is what we
are ma'am. We are a little further along the path of
life but we still occupy, we all occupy, the whole of
mankind; we all occupy the same path of life. Only we
have progressed a little further upon that road than
what you have and that is the only difference, ma'am.
Perhaps, because we have passed through the change
called death our perspective on life is a little larger, a
little broader than what yours might be, but other than
that, that is all, ma'am.

Ok, I'm delighted that you are here today. You are a
kindly soul and you have great work to do on behalf of
my world, ma'am. Hmm.   **K.** Thank you, yes.

(end of section 18)

Part Two

My experiences of trance and
physical phenomena in the
Stewart Alexander Circle
from the year 2002.

For Part 2 recordings listen to Sections 19 to 25 on
www.alexanderproject.bandcamp.com

In 2002, Freda invited me to become an honorary member of the home circle. This was indeed a privilege giving me the opportunity to write further reports on physical phenomena not often demonstrated in a guest séance.

In case you are wondering why a guest séance is different from a home circle, perhaps this brief explanation might help.

In a guest séance, newcomers are bound to be nervous and apprehensive, just as I was on my first visit. Young Christopher (in spirit) is needed to play his role in relaxing the sitters by using his cheeky banter to lighten the atmosphere. Then the spirit people have to use up time and energy introducing themselves along with explaining the physical phenomena about to be demonstrated. On top of all that, they have to work with different energies brought in by the guest sitters.

In a home circle, the spirit people have the opportunity to work with the energies they are accustomed to and are able to try out new experiments without having to make sure the medium is safe. This is because every circle member is aware of the important do's and don'ts in a physical phenomena sitting.

To put it simply:

A guest séance takes energy from spirit.

A home circle gives energy to spirit.

The Stewart Alexander Home Circle 2003

Taken on the launch of Part One of the Trilogy.

From the left: Tom (now an honorary member), Katie, (honorary member), Stewart (physical medium), Gaynor (Stewart's sister), Ray (circle leader), June (Ray's wife), Mike (Stewart's brother) and Ann (Tom's wife, honorary member).

Tom and Ann were full members of Stewart's home circle for six years, from the mid-nineties, until they moved to Spain in January 2000. At their last sitting before they left, the spirit team made them honorary members so that whenever they returned to the UK for holidays they were able to sit with the circle.

Chapter Eight

Help from the Spirit World

Due to the intensive therapy I had as a child, my speech is now quite normal. As I have already mentioned, this can disguise the fact that I am severely deaf. Because of the deafness I have developed the habit of picking up snippets of conversation and guessing the rest of the words. Often I am so preoccupied with this, I lose track of what has been said. The spirit people were well aware of what was happening and understood the difficulty I was experiencing.

Little did I realise then, the amount of help and healing I would receive.

The following are some of the experiences I had in the séance room.

4th May 2000 (Guest séance)

Walter. Ma'am – you may feel on occasions that you are a voice in the wilderness. But I tell you this ma'am – that you are beloved of my world.

Katie. Yes ... thank you.

W. Your words ma'am, whether spoken or written, they will carry such import and will affect the minds and hearts of more people than you can begin to imagine.

K. Oh! That's lovely thank you.

W. If it was not so ma'am, then I would not say so.

K. Yes.

W. Your love for our world is recognised by us.

K. Yes, I love you all very much.

W. Ma'am, I will tell you something else – we do understand your hearing impediment. (**K.** Yes.) – I will tell you this also, that we in our world would like nothing better than that we should be able to cure that which is wrong. (**K.** Yes, Thank you.) – But I tell you that it is not possible ma'am, we can do what we can do, but where you have lost in one direction, you have gained so much in another. (**All.** Yes.) – You are a dear soul, ma'am.

After this conversation so early in my connection with the circle, I realised that I would never be cured, but when Walter assured me that they would do what they could, I thought this meant that the spirit people would speak slower, along with asking the circle members to interpret if necessary. Little did I know then what unusual preparations were being made to enable me to hear spirits speaking by direct and independent voice.

<u>9th April 2002 (Home circle)</u>

Vanguard.[1] My voice is still audible?

All. Yes – very much / Very clear.

V. The speaking mechanism has been well established and constructed.

All. Yes – very good.

V. You will notice how we have contained the energy within the confined space.

Ray. Yes – within the cabinet.

V. It is strengthened.

---

1. Vanguard is part of the spirit team – later known as Dr Barnett.

K. It is a lot better; I have been able to hear you tonight.

V. We are aware of your hearing impediment Katie, may I call you Katie?

K. You can – yes – thank you.

V. And for that reason, we have done all that we can to construct the speaking tubes from the cabinet to your left and right ears.

K. Thank you.

V. We hope that this is why hearing within this room is now so much simpler for you.

K. It is yes, it is a lot easier tonight.

V. We are uncertain how long we shall be able to maintain the speaking tubes, we shall do our best.

K. Thank you very much for your help.

Quite often, while sitting in the darkness of the séance room, especially during the voice box phenomena, I had noticed a strong sensation of pressure on and around the back of my head. It felt as if I was wearing a hat. This sensation was so heavy that my instinct was to place my hand on my head to check if there was anything there, but I knew I could not make such a move when ectoplasmic energy was expanded across the séance room.

Author's Note:

When I meditate at home, I sometimes sense a tingling around my head and a very light feeling as though wearing a hat, which I know has been experienced by others. I have been told that this is spirit energy entering my aura. The sensation during Dr Barnett's experiment was entirely different because there was an element of extreme heaviness and a feeling of weight around my head, particularly just above the ears.

However, whenever I had this sensation, everyone noticed that my hearing inexplicably improved within the séance room to such an extent that I was able to converse with the spirit people speaking via direct voice without any further help or interpretation from the circle members.

13th May 2003 (Home circle)

Walter. Katie ma'am, can you hear my voice?

Katie. I can hear you Walter.

W. That is fine – is it not remarkable that whenever you come here and sit in our midst, you encounter no great difficulty in hearing our words? (**K.** It is.) – You must understand that whenever we know that you are to join with us, throughout the day we are extremely busy, creating special conditions within the room that we know will help you to hear all that is said

K. Thank you very much.

W. If you could only spend your entire life within this room, you would have no problem with your hearing at all!

(Much laughter and various comments from the circle).

At a home circle séance held on 19th August 2003, Walter made a special request to Tom and Ann Harrison to include his words in the book Tom was writing on his experiences. I enclose this excerpt from Tom's book, *Life after Death: Living Proof.*[2.]

> "On 19th August 2003, when we were again sitting with them, Walter Stinson made a special request concerning Katie's situation. Quote: 'Tom, Ann – it may be of interest to point out to you both, that which is so obvious but which you may have failed to

2. ISBN 9780955705014. Saturday Night Press Publications (2008)

appreciate. We say this because, in the work you are involved in at present – your memoirs, Tom, this will, deservedly so, demand a place within.

'You know that our friend Katie is in many ways profoundly deaf. When she comes within this room, where our two worlds meet and blend together, then – because of the work she has done and will perform, it is vitally important and necessary to ensure that the lady would be able to hear all that transpires. For that reason, the scientific people in my world connected with this Circle, began to work upon a method by which, once she was here within, and the light had been extinguished, arrangements could be made so that she would miss nothing and would be able to hear. Is that not so Katie? (K: It is Walter).

'That in itself again demonstrates quite clearly the power of the Spirit. Do you understand, Tom?' (T: I do) 'The power of the Spirit – so we say to all those folks who may have impediments of hearing, that within our room, arrangements will always be made to try to ensure that those who are so afflicted will be able to appreciate and understand and hear for themselves.

'We know that there are so many within your world with no understanding of our work, who will always advance theories, no matter how ridiculous they may be, no matter how inappropriate, to account for what takes place here. But let them explain that Tom. Hmm?"

Whatever little hearing I do have fluctuates, especially when I suffer from a head cold, which has a considerable effect on my ears. When this happens and I am not able to hear as well as I should, it is hard to tell of any absolute improvement. Sometimes I am unable to hear clearly because I am tired. At other times I think that I can hear better, but how much of it is wishful thinking and hopeful imagination, I do not know. One thing is certain: possible outside evidence appears to indicate that something happened and that my hearing has benefited as a result of spiritual healing.

Evidence of Possible Healing 1

In February 2004, I needed a new ear-mould and it is customary for the audiology nurse to look inside the ear before doing an impression inside the ear canal. There were two nurses treating me during this particular appointment, so I guess the first nurse must have been a trainee. The first nurse looked in my left ear and asked the other nurse for a second opinion because she could see something black which she wasn't sure about. The other nurse took a look and told her that the black she detected was a perfectly clean, clear eardrum. It would appear that the first nurse had never seen such a clean ear drum and with it being so clear of any wax which can muffle the clarity of hearing, I did wonder if this might be the work of spirit, doing as much as they can to help my hearing.

Evidence of Possible Healing 2

My right hearing aid is a digital aid, and the level of sound frequency had been set by the computer at the audiology department about three years prior. In June/July 2004 the output of this hearing aid became uncomfortably loud, creating a terrible distortion, and because it was a digital aid without a volume control, I could not turn the sound down. As a result I had to occasionally remove the aid from my ear. The only solution was to have the aid checked on the audio computer. The audiologist gave me a hearing test first and then compared the frequencies of the hearing aid, which proved not adaptable to the frequencies of my hearing test.

It was definitely too loud. There was no malfunction of the aid and the puzzled audiologist could not understand why the aid had been set too loud in the first place. Certain frequencies on the aid had to be altered and reduced. Again, I am bound to wonder if this situation has developed as a result of spirit healing.

I am not a person who reaches conclusions immediately. I accept the fact that I am still deaf, and always will be, but I certainly cannot discard the external evidence indicating definite improvement.

On November 16th 2004, the spirit person we now know as Dr Barnett, (known then as the Vanguard) materialised and gave me healing, bringing energies direct from the spirit world.

Walter. There is one thing which we would like to do before we bid you goodnight. There is a soul here who you know of as the 'Vanguard' or 'the Voice'.

All. Yes

W. He would like to try and do something for Katie.

Katie. Oh! Right. Thank you.

W. Raymondo, switch on your overhead light – you may remove the table.

(Ray moves the table, and Walter asks everybody to move back).

W. Raymondo, would you, yourself, help Katie to move her chair so that its back is to the cabinet? Place it three to four feet in front of the cabinet. Katie ma'am – you will kindly take your seat again. Raymondo, when you are ready, if you could please disconnect all your lights.   *(Ray as requested, disconnects them).*

W. That is fine, That is fine. Katie let me hear your voice.

K. I can hear you Walter. I'll keep talking.

Ray. Are you alright there, Walter sir? Is there anything you'd like us to do? Would you like a little music?

W. Quietly. *(Ray plays music on the cassette player).*

K. I'll just keep talking.

R. Well, if you just keep talking, they will get the vibration, then they will come out towards you.

(Stewart coughs). **K.** Stewart is still with us.

R. Aye, he's come back, are you in the cabinet Stewart?

Stewart. Curtains are closing.

June. Yes they are.

S. It's freezing in here. *(referring to the cabinet).*

J. Yes, its freezing cold. **S.** Curtains are wafting.

J. Yes they are. *(Stewart gives a big yawn and talks to June).* Oh! The curtains are wafting frantically. *(Stewart and June are still talking and Katie joins in).*

R. Are you alright Stewart? *(silence from Stewart).* Oh! he's gone again......Come on friend.

J. You are very welcome.

R. Come and do what you need to do Vanguard with our friend Katie.

K. Oh! His hands are on my shoulders, and now his hands are on my head. **J.** Oh – lovely.

K. Hands still on my head.

J. I can hear the breathing. **K.** Yes.

J. Yes – Well done friend.

K. You are very welcome. ...Hands still on my head.

R. Hello, my friend, nice to have you with us. Thank you for helping Katie. **All.** You're welcome.

Vanguard. Miss Halliwell. (**K.** Yes) – You can hear my words? (**K.** I can, Yes.) – Then I wonder? Would you most kindly remove your spectacles?

K. Oh, Yes – I'll remove them now. *(Katie hands spectacles to Ray).* – Hands still on my head.

V. Miss Halliwell. (**K.** Yes.) – I wonder, would you most kindly with your right hand, take my hand.

K. Yes, I've got it. – Yes, I've got his hand. He's got one hand on my head and put my hand on my shoulder.

V. Would you most kindly take my left hand?

K. Yes, I've got his hand – he has put my left hand on my shoulder.

R. So both your hands are now on your shoulders?

K. Both my hands are on my shoulders and he has put his hands on my head – both hands – Yes, there is vibration, a lot of vibration. . . . Certainly a lot of vibration, Gosh! Yes, Oh Gosh, I can feel the energy coming through. Yes ... feels a bit warm. He's gone to the back of my neck ... hands on my head and back of my neck. *(a whistling is heard)* – That is my hearing-aid whistling.

V. Yes, we are transferring spiritual energy from our world through into yours so that you may benefit. Do not expect wondrous results, it will take time. (**K.** Thank you.) – But you may look forward to a gradual improvement. With your love for my world, we return your love.

R. That's nice.

K. Oh! Very nice that's wonderful.

V. God bless you, my child.

K. God bless you too – Oh! my head is tingling now.

J. Well done friend.

(Vanguard retreats and Stewart starts coughing as he comes out of trance.)

All. Look after Stewart, friends, please.

Freda. Now we feel that we have had a most successful evening. (**All.** Wonderful – Yes.) – Katie dear. (**K.** Yes Freda?) –The gentleman who has administered healing to you. (**K.** Yes.) – He wants me to speak to you for a moment so that he may be quite certain that you understand what he expects. (**K.** Right, Ok, Freda.) – He has taken energy from my world and he has channelled it into yourself dear. (**K.** Yes, thank you.) – You cannot look for immediate results, immediate improvement, but Oh! my goodness, he fully expects that improvement will take place over a short period of time. (**K.** Thank you.) – And on each occasion that you come here dear, he tells me that he will administer a little more healing, and we do feel that your hearing is much improved to what it was when you first came here. (**K.** Yes, it is. Yes.) – He is extremely pleased dear, extremely pleased.

I am not the only one who has had this unique kind of help with healing direct from the spirit world. There are more testimonies from other sitters in Chapter 25.

Chapter Nine

Dr Barnett and Direct Voice

On 22nd February 2005 the Vanguard identified himself as Dr Barnett, a valuable member of the spirit team specialising in speaking in the independent direct voice. As I wrote earlier, this is another form of audible communication using a speaking mechanism created out of ectoplasmic energy, which usually developed somewhere to Stewart's left, between himself and Gaynor.

When the scientists in the spirit world have fashioned the ectoplasm into the voice box, Dr Barnett has to convert his thoughts into audible sounds so that they can be heard within the séance room. If you are able to listen to the recordings you will notice how well he speaks in Section 19, compared to the earlier experiment in Section 6, as he explains the techniques of the artificial 'voice box'.

Section 19

Vanguard speaks through and about the independent voice box.

Home Circle – 16th November 2004. (14min. 11seconds).

On the original tape, this recording had an interfering shushing noise which we have not been able to remove. If you have difficulty hearing this section, the transcript follows here. Gaynor wasn't present at this particular séance and I took her place next to Stewart.

Vanguard. *(via Independent Voice).* It is not that we shall in any way, endeavour to place you in an altered state of consciousness.

All. We know

V. It is merely if you are able to relax that we can take a little more energy from you...

June. No problem, friend.

Katie. Take as much energy as you like.

V. We thought you ought to be aware of what is taking place here this evening.

Circle. Yes/ Thank you friend / You're very welcome friend.

Ray. It is very nice to have you with us.

K. Yes, He spoke very clearly. He seemed to be speaking from my right.

V. I believe that it is the first occasion that we have commenced our meeting by speaking with our own independent voice. (**Circle.** Yes, yes.) – When we found that conditions were just quite exquisite this evening we decided to make the effort to open proceedings in this manner. (**R.** Thank you.) – I hope that my words are a little clearer now. (**J.** Yes. / **R.** Nice and clear.) – You can hear well? (**All.** Yes we can.) – I thought that just for a few moments I may explain to you the way in which we in our world have been able to make arrangements for this communication to take place, the method involved.

R. That would be interesting. / **K.** Very interesting.

V. As you are no doubt aware, the artificial voice box, for that indeed is what it is, quite artificial. It has been created by, both through, means of the energy which we have been able to extract from the medium and then the scientific people in my world have been able to take that energy and to mix it with a kind of energy from my world, a kind of chemical, if you wish, – and these are mixed together in such a way that we find then that it becomes quite malleable that we can create from it what we wish and we have been able to mould, we have been able to fashion, a replica of the human voice box. – and it is by means of this temporary structure that we are able to vibrate your atmosphere and convert our thoughts into audible sounds. (**R.** Sounds? ...) – Well, perhaps you will appreciate, understand, just how difficult this is if it is not... it may appear to be simple, simply because you can hear my words, but it is exceedingly difficult.

R. Yes. It is very hard for us to understand how you do it. / **K.** Yes.

V. Allow me to say, it is exceedingly hard for ME to understand.

R. For you to understand as well? Oh yes.

V. ...My responsibility is merely to vibrate the atmosphere converting my thoughts into audible sounds that you may hear them, you may hear...

R. So that we may hear them.

V. It is not my responsibility to create the speaking mechanism that is others, other souls in my world, scientific people... (**R.** That's correct.) – who have that responsibility.

K. The thoughts are being spoken?

V. Yes, yes, but you will understand that this temporary structure is so unstable that under the finest of circumstances even under the very best conditions it is so unstable that it is in a constant state of movement, it fluctuates such a great deal that one must use all one's powers of concentration to send thoughts into the mechanism. These are then converted into audible sounds.

K. I see.

R. Well, you are doing very well, friend.

J. Very, very well.

K. Because we speak through our brains, our brain works out the sounds.

V. Exactly. We too are speaking to you by our thoughts. Our minds ... our minds are the spiritual equivalent of your physical brains. There is a great parallel between the two. I hope I have explained that.

K. I think I understand now. (**V.** Yes, yes.) – Your thoughts are being transferred into this speaking mechanism and ... I don't know if I am right or not ... and the speaking mechanism is changing it into... audible sounds.

V. Precisely so.

K. You would wonder how they could do it.

V. With a great deal of difficulty, I may say!

K. That's very interesting.

V. I suppose in a manner of speaking it may sound quite complex to you but I've tried to make it simple... but I know the explanation of itself leaves a great deal to be desired but I am unable to think at present in what manner I can present the information to you in a more simplistic manner. It would not be possible. Allow me to say that when you wish to speak then you... what you have to say... it begins life within your brain and your speaking mechanism, in a manner of speaking, it converts your thoughts into audible sound.

R. That's correct.

V. Then try to imagine that the speaking mechanism that we have created, the temporary physical structure if you will, that is the equivalent of your speaking mechanism. You understand, your vocal cords, your vocal organs, your vocal... voice box, your speaking mechanism and so therefore, thoughts originate within my mind as I speak to you now and these thoughts are then converted into audible sounds in exactly the same way as your physical voice box converts your thoughts, which originate in your brain, into audible sounds. There is little difference between the two.

K. Yes. I can see that now. It is like speaking without the brain. (**V.** Oh no!) – Isn't it?

V. ...Oh no. You see my mind is the equivalent of your physical brain. (**K.** Oh right, right.) – You understand? (**K.** Yes, I do.) – Forget the brain for the moment and substitute the mind, (**K.** Right. I think I've got you.) – the mind. The mind, to a spiritual being, to those who reside in my world, is the equivalent of the brain to your physical world. You understand? There is very little difference. The only principle difference is that your brain is a temporary structure, the mind is eternal. That is all.

K. That's interesting, isn't it?

R. Yes. The mind tells the brain and the brain converts it into voice. / **K.** Yes, I think I've got you there.

V. When death occurs the brain dies away. It belongs only here as it is a physical structure but it has no existence in my world. In your world the mind uses the brain as an aid that speaks directly to the voice box. In my world the brain does not exist so the mind speaks directly to the temporary speaking likeness. It converts thoughts into audible sounds. (**Ray & Katie.** We understand now.) – I do hope so.

R. Yes. You have explained yourself very well.

K. You have done marvellously well. / **J.** Very well.

V. Thank you and I have perhaps spoken longer this evening than I have ever been able to do so before.

R. That's correct my friend. Is that may be because you spoke first?

V. Not exactly so. But we determined that tonight we would sacrifice all other methods of communication and concentrate singly upon what you know as the independent voice and that is what we have done.

R. Well that's excellent.

J. You have done very well, friend.

K. Yes that was very interesting. That is a good one for the book.

V. We know such a great deal about your work. Yes, it is well known in my world...You see... to work upon this is so very important.

K. Yes. I'll try to do my best to spread your word that you are trying to explain (**V.** Oh yes, yes) – and it is good to hear your voice direct so that people can listen to you.

V. Well, I hope that in listening to my voice, in listening to my words, it will, I hope, convey a little reassurance to all those who listen and hear what I have to say; reassurance that as they listen to my words they are listening to the words of a soul who exists beyond death and I, my friends, I am one of so many others who have all resided upon the earth and survived death. Death which in reality is such a small thing, assuming considerable...(**R.** Mmm, very interesting. / **K.** Yes. Smashing. Good. It's very intuitive.) – such extraordinary significance that because, you see, the nature of life and death is largely unknown in your world and if only if it was widely accepted that man is a spiritual being that he cannot die, that there is eternal life for all souls, if only that was established upon your earth then you see that death indeed would be seen, not as something to be afeared, but something, in many ways, to be welcomed. (**All.** Yes.) – A time of

rejoicements. Sadly so misunderstood in your world...
so misunderstood in your world...

K. It is just that people can't see... the reality of it all
can they?   **R.** No, they can't, no.

V. Perhaps one day they may, perhaps one day they
may.

K. Yes I'm sure we will. We are going to grow a bit. We
are doing all we can.

V. We are all doing precisely that. We are all working
so tremendously hard. Both in your world and mine, we
are all working so tremendously hard so that we may
eventually show to Man, demonstrate to Man, this
wonderful reality.   **J.** Team work.

V. God Bless you all, my friends.

J. Oh, God Bless you. Thank you for coming.

All. Thank you.

(end of section 19)

Section 20

Vanguard identifies himself to Katie.

Home Circle – 22nd February 2005. (6min. 35seconds).

To my surprise, at this sitting 'The Voice' or 'the
Vanguard' identified himself as Dr Barnett. This was
yet another exciting development, and I thought it
fitting to include this recording so that you will be able
to share my delight as you hear him speak once more
by independent voice.

Christine (Katie's sister). Oh,I can just about hear...
Ray. Yes we can hear you now. We look forward to this
part of the night.

Dr Barnett. I hope that you are able to hear my words.

All. Yes we can.

Ray. Yes, I'm at this side Dr Barnett and I can hear you.

Chr. And I'm over here and I can hear you.

Katie. And I'm at the end of the room.

Dr B. Well, my friends, allow me to say that I am, as I always am, quite delighted to have this opportunity to converse with you all. (**All.** Thank you.) – May I say that it gives me particular pleasure to... to welcome into our gathering this evening all our lady visitors.

All. Thank you / Pleasure to be here.

Dr B. It is a great pleasure for me also. I do hope that you can hear my voice.

Chr. I can. Can you Katie?   **K.** Yes, I can.

Chr. Yes we can. Thank you.

Dr B. I ought to introduce myself to the lady who is working so hard on a journal of her experiences here in this circle of friends. (**Chr.** That's Katie.) (**K.** Yes.)

Dr B. I know that you will know me as the Vanguard. (**K.** Yes I do.) – which is a name which has been created over a long period of time by many people who come here, but a short while ago I was able to reveal that my true name is Dr Barnett.

K. Wonderful to hear that, Dr Barnett.

Chr. Yes, it is. Thank you.

Dr B. I worked from my side of life, the spiritual aspect of life, many, many years ago, via what you know of as the direct voice through the mediumship of a gentleman who you may have heard spoken of in the past, his name, George Valiantine. He was an American gentleman with great physical power for the manifestation of the independent direct voice, but now, in common with Walter, I have, myself, chosen to return once again to take up the work which he, and which I, commenced at approximately the same period of time, working through our individual channels of communication. It is with the greatest of anticipation, it is with the greatest enthusiasm, it is with the greatest of aspiration that we feel that together we possess the most formidable team.

All. Yes, yes exactly.

K. Yes. We will work together, Dr Barnett. I am very pleased and very privileged to do so, to work to help you.

Dr B. The pleasure, madam, is mine entirely. (**Chr.** How very nice. / **K.** Thank you.) – There is so much that we will be able to accomplish (**K.** Yes, I hope to do so.) – ... My friends, I am losing control of the speaking mechanism.

Chr. You're very good, considering the energy had gone.

Dr B. We will do much in the future, together.

R. Yes we can.   **Dr B**. Goodnight, my friends.

All. Good night, Dr Barnett. Thank you.

Gaynor. That voice was getting lower and lower and lower. It was dropping right down. It was right near the floor.

Chr. He was very clear though wasn't he, when he was strong.

G. All the times he has talked and he has never told us who he was, did he?   **Others.** No, no

G. He must have decided the time is right to tell us.

Chr. It's lovely to give the gentleman a name isn't it?

G. Yes, yes.

(end of section 20)

Chapter Ten

FREDA JOHNSON TALKS ABOUT HER LIFE

Before we continue with the phenomena I think it is time to let the lady member of the spirit team say a few more words. I was not present at the two séances which follow but I'm sure you will enjoy Freda's words as much as I did.

Here Freda Johnson talks about her life on the earth plane, a time when she thought of Spiritualism as total nonsense. You can imagine the shock she would have experienced when she passed to the spirit world, only to find out that she was indeed very much alive after her physical death.

Freda talked of her family both on the earth plane and in the afterlife. Even though the family know they have survived 'so-called death', they do not realise (along with many other people in the spirit world) that they can communicate with their loved ones still upon the earth.

Section 21

Freda talks about attaching herself to the spirit team.

Norfolk – July 2003. (7min. 55seconds).

June and Alf Winchester live in Norfolk and are long-standing friends of Stewart. One day, during a sitting in their home, Freda spoke through Stewart in

118

trance and chatted with June and her friend, Julie Wright.

Freda. It's rather remarkable, this is all rather remarkable. You see, Julie dear, the truth is when I was on your earth I had not the least interest in Spiritualism. Well, I must tell you I had heard of it but I was not really interested in it. I thought it was all nonsense, I have to tell you dear, nonsense and it wasn't until I passed that I realised it was anything but.

There was survival and I can tell you it was a tremendous shock, – a tremendous shock. Can you imagine one moment being on the earth and the next moment opening my eyes to see, greeting me, people who I had loved upon the earth, who had long since preceded me into the spirit world? I thought I was in the middle of a dream. And I have to tell you that my life, within what you call the spirit world, was one of great interest. I was always a person and I am still a person with an enquiring mind. I always had and still have this enquiring mind. I need to know, I want to know and I have to tell you that someone told me, several people told me, as time passed that it was indeed possible for time to time to make contact with loved ones who were still upon the earth.

Well, me being me, June, I thought that was a lot of nonsense. But then one day I was walking along and I noticed a group of people and I went and stood just on the periphery and I was listening to someone speaking and I heard…I heard something, which I have to say, surprised me…a great deal because these people were talking about the possibility, not just the possibility, but making plans for the further development of a particular circle and a particular medium that they had been working with for many, many years in order as they said to refine the mediumship, to refine the channel of communication. Well, of course my ears pricked up – of course they would, dear, yours would also – and I stood and I listened very carefully to what was being said, and then I heard that they would come together each week immediately before a circle, which was to take place. Of course, I now know that this was Stewart's circle but then I didn't, and I understood that immediately prior to each circle that they would gather together to discuss further developments, to exchange ideas. And I have to say that on the following occasion when they met, I made it my business to be there and I was sitting there also listening, very intently, but the extraordinary thing was that no-one seemed to take any notice, no one seemed to ask well, who is she.

No one said a thing, dear. It was as if I was being accepted and I thought that was rather wonderful. There were many people there, not just simply those who you have heard speaking here this evening but many people.

And then the time came many, many weeks later when someone was standing saying something – and I...if I say that I interrupted, that sounds rather rude. I would not say that I interrupted so much as when he stopped to draw breath so I began to speak and everyone turned towards me and listened and I was merely saying, I was making observations on what I had noticed and several people began to nod in agreement, dear.

It was extraordinary because here was this old lady who in truth knew very little about this 'business' who suddenly commanded the ear of everyone there who, I'm sure, were far more... were vastly more experienced than what I was, but there they all were listening patiently to what I was saying and several began to nod their heads in agreement, dear. I was most surprised. And then suddenly one of them said 'But who is she?'

and then it was as if there was a dawning of realisation on the faces of all those souls who were there because suddenly sweeping across them all was this, what I can only describe as puzzlement, dear. 'But who is she?' And everyone began to ask, but who are you? And that was the beginning of my involvement in this work.

So I have to tell you, Julie, that I entered the spirit world knowing nothing about these possibilities and I ended up in this rather, what I have always regarded to be a privileged situation, a privileged position, highly privileged, because it is not given to many and I feel so grateful and so very privileged.

The greatest difficulty that we have in our world is trying to convey to people who come and sit, the enormous difficulties in communication. What you have witnessed here this evening may appear to have been simplicity. It was not, dear. Tremendous work and a great many years of constant effort went to produce what you have witnessed here. It is difficult – communication. If we are able to communicate on any level, even one word or two words or to make the slightest rap or tap or to move a trumpet perhaps only one quarter of an inch, that is a miracle in itself because you are of a different level of consciousness, a different level of existence. We are separated not only by time and space we are separated by much more than that, dear, and to be able to try to weld, to blend the two worlds together is far from simple, it is a miracle, dear... It is a miracle. But sometimes... sometimes, seemingly without effort, we are able to communicate in a manner that fills us with satisfaction. But rarely, but rarely.

(end of section 21)

Section 22

Freda talks about her life on the earth.

Home Circle – 3rd August 2004 (15min. 13seconds).

Freda. So, dears, what can I tell you? I lived upon the earth as you well know, quite a number of years ago now and I was for a long time a teacher of children, a school teacher. I must say I did not have a large family, a small family, a very close family, but not an extensive family. You understand, dears, not an extensive family but we enjoyed our lives upon the earth. We always felt we needed little company outside the family group, we were happy and content within our own company, dears, so we tended to live together a great deal, to be in each other's company a great deal, to socialise together, never really feeling the need to extend beyond the family group. Of course my work as a school teacher that was something quite different, I worked with children, I worked with children, but that did not in any way infringe itself on my private life.

I had several aunts. I had several uncles. I had a boy of my own. I had a husband who we shall not speak of, you understand, and of course, grandparents and mother and father but they passed into the world of spirit early within my earthly life. They were not there for long. I was but a young woman when they left. My mother's name was Alice and my father's name was John. His second name was Edward, John Edward, and I was extremely close as indeed we were all extremely close to one another. I can tell you it was a most difficult time when my parents... and they left the earth within a matter of months of each other and I can tell you it was most distressing. Most distressing. Because as you well know I have said many times to you that I had no knowledge of Spiritualism and certainly no knowledge of even a possibility of an afterlife. I had heard of Spiritualism but that is all, I took no interest. As Walter would often say – he uses the word 'Poppycock' – well that is the way, I suppose, I thought of Spiritualism.

So we were a very close and intimate family and I have to say I'm sure you've heard how, many years ago, families, whole families would come together on a weekend to socialise within the home and how they would all gather together round the piano. Someone could always play the piano, dears. Someone could always do so and it was no different in our home. My aunt, my aunt Mabel, she played the piano and we would all stand around and we would all sing, very often harmonise, dears, harmonise. Of course we did not drink. Father used to drink a little but of course he left the earth when I was but a young woman, but my aunts most certainly would not drink anyway, so it was buns, it was cakes... and it was light refreshments...light refreshments. So we enjoyed ourselves, we enjoyed our lives.

Gaynor. It sounds very good.

F. I suppose it was very, very ordinary. It was nothing startling or surprising, nothing notable concerning our existences upon the earth. We were just very ordinary people living very ordinary lives. We were not notable in any way. Of course, I did what I could in order to pass my knowledge to the children, to the younger generation and I suppose in a way... I would not in any way... er... I do not think that I would exaggerate... I am not being presumptuous in saying to you that I think that I was rather good at what I did. I helped... I hope that I helped. Is there anything that you would like to ask?

G. Freda, you said that you have a boy... you had a boy on the earth. He is with you now, is he?

F. He is now dear, but not so many years ago – when I first began to communicate...

June. He was still on the earth?

F. ... he was still upon the earth (**G.** Oh! Was he?) – but he came a number of years ago now, very recently. He came into my world. So that the family group is now once again complete.

G. So you are with all your family?

F. Oh yes, we are all together.

G. So you still socialise very closely with each other like you did on earth?

F. Oh yes, but of course let us say that my own particular circle of friends has in many ways, I suppose, increased a great deal in more recent times. I've seen a different world, I've seen different possibilities, I've seen ways in which I could be of more help, to be of service to my fellow man both in my world and in your world so that my circle of associates has increased quite dramatically in recent years. I am no longer as insular as I was when I was upon the earth or indeed as I was when I first came here. So all kinds of possibilities have been opened to me. You see we continue to learn, dears.

J. All the time. We do, don't we, Freda?

F. Oh yes, but you will learn. You will find that when you come into my world that you will really begin to learn. You will really begin to learn. You may feel that you are learning a great deal when you are upon the earth and of course that is true in many ways but much of what you learn is of no...(**G.** ...consequence, is it?) – ...in my world. Precisely so, Gaynor. ...is of little consequence in my world. You see life itself it is all about service. It is all about refinement of the spirit. It is spirituality. It is to be of service to one another; to help in whatever way that we can; to touch the souls, in a very kindly way, of all those people that we... that we contact in life, both sides of the Great Divide. It is to be of service; it is to be of help; it is to infuse upon others that which we know...

G. Is that everyone on your side then, Freda? You know. You like... 'cos we sit in circle every week and to communicate with yourselves so you have your family there with you and you communicate with us but do your family do that kind of thing as well?

F. Oh no, dear! You mean working with spiritual groups? (**G.** That's right.) – Oh no, indeed there are many people in my world who have very little, if any knowledge at all, that such things as these are possible, that they actually take place. Of course, my people know but only because of their association with me, you see. But there are many, many souls in my world, ... of course they know that they have survived death, quite evidently they do, but they ... many do not realise that they can communicate with their loved ones still upon the earth.

Human beings, I suppose, irrespective of which side of the Great Divide they are, we are very much alike, we are very much alike and a great deal depends on our own individual knowledge. And a great deal therefore depends upon circumstance, what life itself...what has been exper...what we have been exposed to throughout our lives, on both sides. If you have had no exposure, if you had no experience of, if you have no knowledge of, if you have not been in a position whereby you have learned of these things, or been touched by souls who know of these things, then it is not surprising that you will have no knowledge concerning them.

It is tragic. It is one of the tragedies of life that there is such grief and such a lack of knowledge concerning survival, concerning the nature of life. It is so very sad. That is why I always say that we are all, and I include myself in this, that while we are all so very privileged and so very fortunate...

G. Absolutely.

J. Oh, we are very privileged, Freda, we are, we really are.

F. Oh, dears, yes, oh yes. I always bless the day that I took the time and the trouble to ingratiate myself with that little group of souls that I observed all those years ago on my side of life, discussing what they were going to do with this circle discussing and exploring the possible progress for the future. And I never cease to bless my good fortune, for now I know.

J. You get great pleasure out of it.

F. Oh, I get tremendous pleasure out of it, June. (J. We all do)... Tremendous pleasure. I particularly enjoy the occasions when I am able to bring about reunions.

All. We all do/ Wonderful/ Yes that's right.

F. If you could see sometimes the grief that exists and see how peoples' very lives can be changed in but a few moments, in the exchange of a few words and a few sentiments...

Ray. That's right friend.

F. ...then you will... and I know you have observed this yourself but I see it from both sides, then of course it is wonderful. That is the great reward for my work for all our work... (**R.** That's right.) –... for make no mistake, we all play an essential role.

J. We certainly do all of us.

R. We all get pleasure out of helping other people.

F. And let me tell you, as you are able to help, it may only be in a small way, it may be in a large way, as you are able to help, to be of service to people, as you go along through your life so you are accumulating the credits to your souls, dears. Do you see? You are accumulating the credits which belong to you and as you do so your souls, so your spiritual selves, will continue to refine so that when the day comes for you to leave the earth and come into my world you will find that you will be well advanced. You understand? It will be like going home.

J. Going home. I was just going to say the same.

F. ... and you will arrive in my world with a great deal of credits, you see... a great deal of credits... and of course there will be many people in my world waiting to greet you; people who owe you such a great deal, such great gratitude.

R. Well, that would be very nice when we come over to meet our friends, or people like yourself who we've spoken with over the years, Freda.

F. Oh, we will have a wonderful time, I can promise you that, a wonderful coming together, a wonderful time to rejoice. Can you imagine? You see the two circles my side and your side, the day will come, of course it will, when little by little your circle begins to diminish in size and mine, ours, in my world will begin to expand,

G. I was thinking that, Freda.

F. ... to grow to increase and when the final one from your world, from your circle, leaves and comes into my world then we will be a united whole. It is a wonderful way to think.

G. I was thinking that when we pass over we could join the circle on that side.

F. Oh yes, oh yes. We are waiting for you all to come. But of course it will not be for a long time yet so you will be relieved to hear that. *(much laughter)* It will be a long time yet. It will be a long time yet. There is so much for you all to do, so much for you all to do. So many people in your world that we must reach, must reach, and we welcome these opportunities that enable us to do precisely that. And Walter is so busy, busy,

busy. He's working away. There are a group of people. There is one standing by your left shoulder, Gaynor. He is trying to touch your left shoulder.

G. Is he? That's nice.

F. You must speak up if you feel...

G. I will

F. ... he is trying to touch your left side as I am speaking to you. These souls are working now but what they are doing will be revealed to you all in time to come, time to come, but now dears, I think I ought to return.

(end of section 22)

Chapter Eleven

MATERIALISATION

When the energy is at its peak, ectoplasm builds up within the cabinet and materialisations can then start to manifest. The spirit people use this substance to transform their etheric bodies into physical matter, so that they are then able to physically draw back the cabinet curtains, walk out and circulate while actually touching and talking to the sitters.

Some people, in error, often think that we have ghosts walking around the room, which is definitely not so. We are not talking about a wispy, transparent image of a ghost; we are talking about a solid materialisation of a spirit which is entirely different. There are no ghosts in a physical séance. In fact, Christopher once joked that if he saw a ghost, he would be the first to run out of the room!

Materialised spirit people are absolutely real and solid to the touch, with the ability to move around and speak through their temporary form.

Ectoplasm is extracted from the medium and remains attached to the medium throughout these events. A guest sitter once asked Walter if the phenomena were independent once the ectoplasm had been taken from Stewart. Walter's reply was:

"If the link from Stewart was cut, then death would follow. The energy is a part of him. Ectoplasm is a dynamic living force; it is in all life, whether human or animal, it is in all life."

In fact, when the spirit people attempt to walk out into the room, there is a strong pull back to Stewart as Freda explains in Section 25.

Some inexperienced spirit people often find it a struggle and a 'flump' can be heard after they have tried to materialise. This is because they could not hold this 'physical' form and the ectoplasm dropped to the floor instead of sinking down gradually. You will hear Tom and Walter discussing this in Section 24.

Section 23

Katie's mother materialises.

Home Circle – 13th May 2003. (2min. 20seconds).

Mum materialised for the first time. Although I could not see her in the dark, she did very well indeed, but found the ectoplasm too heavy to support. She could not carry on as long as she would have liked and was unable to reach out and touch me.

June. It's been wonderful.

Gaynor. Someone else's out. Someone else is there.

J. Yes there's someone at the end. You're very welcome friend.

Ray. Come on then friend, whoever you are, come and see Katie.

Ann. You are very welcome friend.

Everyone speaks at once to encourage the spirit person to come out into the room. Footsteps can be heard

Katie. Good, keep trying. You can hear the breathing.

J. Keep talking Katie.

K. Yes I'll keep talking. She's trying to say something.

Spirit. Katie, Ohh! Yes...Mum.

130

Tom. It's Mum.

Katie. Oh lovely, Mum, lovely to hear you. I wish I could see you in the dark.

T. & J. The day will come, Katie.

Spt. Mum. I ... wished... to ...come ...to...you...but it's oh...so ... strange.

K. You are doing wonderfully well. I'm proud of you. Thank you, Mum.

Spt. Mum. God bless you love. God bless you.

T. God bless you. / **J.** God bless you, bye.

K. Christine sends her love.

Spt. Mum *(makes a kissing sound)* – 'I do...you.'

K. I love you. Christine loves you.

(There are more kissing sounds.) **T.** Ah, Well done.

K. Thank you. That was lovely.

A. That was well out to the left of me. She was trying to get through.

T. It was right out in front of Katie.

(end of section 23)

Section 24

Ronald says Ena is with him,
    and Walter demonstrates his spirit lights.

Home circle – 13th May 2003. (8min. 58seconds).

You will remember from Section 15 how Ronald Hill communicated for the first time to pass a message to his wife Ena. Ena passed over a few months later and in 2003, he materialised to tell us she was with him.

Following Ron, Walter then materialised and walked around the séance room demonstrating his self-illuminated spirit light to us all. This light is often shown in various forms – I have seen it as a pinprick becoming larger as it moves around the séance room. The spirit light has also appeared as a mass of diffused light, and I have witnessed it to be about 6"-7" (15 - 18cms) in diameter.

Walter carried this around in his hand and placed his other hand above and around it so we could see his fingers moving about. He then intensified a light to a smaller size that was bright enough to shine on his arm and hand as he walked round the séance room.

The best way I can describe the spirit light shining on the arm is that it is rather like looking at your own hand in intensified moonlight shining through a small hole in a completely darkened room.

Ronald. I have her, I have her.

Katie. You have her, yes, yes, Ena? *(other voices talk over the top of the spirit voice and the words cannot be differentiated)*

Ron. Yes. I have her. I am so grateful to you, I am so grateful to him. We both send our love E ..E.. .E...

K. Ena ./ **Ray.** Ena ... sends her love.

Ron. Yes. God bless you.

Tom. Well done. / **Gaynor.** That's wonderful. Gosh!

T. That's splendid.

Ann. The curtains are really moving, wafting about.

T. Lovely. The energy must be tremendous tonight. Great!   **June.** It must be, Tom.

(shortly after we heard somone else coming)

T. Come on then, come on then...Here we are.

J. Ok, friend.   **Walter.** Ok.

T. Ok. Hello, Walter.   **J.** Well done.

Walter. Folks, you can hear my voice?

J. We certainly can Walter.

W. I have to tell you that speaking in this manner, in this way is something which is very different to the way that I normally speak. (**T.** Right, right.) – You can hear my words?

All. Yes. Very well. / **A.** Yes. It's way above my head.

W. I stand before you this evening.

J. It's wonderful Walter.

W. I will tell you that it is some time since I last worked in this manner. I wonder if I can in any way try to show myself.

T. If you can, we would be delighted, of course.

R. We certainly would Walter.

T. We leave it with you Walter.

R. You'll do your best for us and....

T. We'll give you all the energy you want.

A. There's the light! / **T.** There's the light!

W. Ann ma'am. Look upon the light.

A. Yes...... Oh! there's a hand going across the front of the light ...The fingers are passing over it.

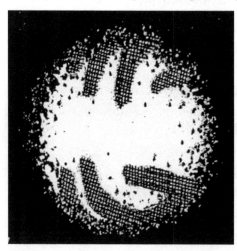

Walter carries a spirit light in his left hand and passes his right hand over the light.

J. That's wonderful.

W. Of course it may appear to be such a small thing to do. (**T.** But it is a big thing.) – Watch the light, Tom.

T. Yes I'm watching the light.

W. Can you see my hand?

T. Oh I can, passing over it, oh tremendous!

W. Katie ma'am, can you see the light?   **K.** I can yes.

W. Can you see my hand?

K. I can, yes. /   **T.** Passing across it.

W. Raymondo, see the light. Can you see my hand?

R. Yes, moving over it, yes.

W. What a darn shame that Michael will miss out on this *(laughter)* ... June can you see the light?

J. I certainly can. It's wonderful, Walter, thank you.

W. Ok, Ok.. Wait but a moment folks. Perhaps you may speak amongst yourselves.

J. Ok... Are you enjoying it Tom.

T. *(joking)* Oh no! What do you think about it, 'Rubbish'! *(a recent catchphrase, and much laughter from others.)* – Wonderful 'rubbish'! *(jokingly)*

J. It wonderful isn't it?

T. It's wonderful 'rubbish' isn't it? It's really great.

R. I think it shows you what they can do when the harmony's there, when the circle's right, Tom.

A. And the extra energy from Michael as well.

T. The potential in this room, it's wonderful. We don't need the trumpets flying around and those things.

J. No we don't.   **T.** This is what we are looking for.

W. Ma'am can you see the light?   **A.** I can Walter.

W. Then watch, ma'am.

A. I can see it reflecting off the hand below it. The hand is below it and the light is shining on to it like a torch.   **R.** Yes.

W. Can you see my arm, ma'am?

A. I can. I have just realised it wasn't as wide as the hand. Yes, and the fingers there. (**T.** Oh, Great!) It isn't .. oh I can't say....when you shine a light on to flesh colour..... it is slightly greeny ... but its... Yes. (*speech fades away*)

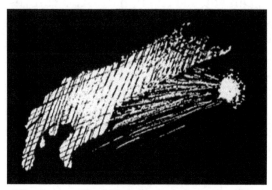

The intensified light is bright enough to show Walter's hand and arm.

T. Great stuff... Real progress.

A. Here's the light again.

T. Yes here's the light again you can see it.

W. June ma'am, watch the light.

J. I am watching the light Walter, Yes.

W. Can you see my arm?   **J.** I certainly can.

W. Now is that not something, folks?

T. It certainly is.

W. Katie ma'am, watch the light.

K. Yes, I'm watching the light.

W. Tom, can you see also at the same time?

T. At the same time. I can.

W. Can you see my arm?

K. Oh yes I can! / **T.** Oh yes! **J.** It's wonderful isn't it?

W. Now is that not something, folks?

T. That's something! / **K.** That's wonderful!

W. I can tell you this evening we have tremendous energy.

All. Good. /Wonderful.

(Footsteps are heard in the room)

All. There you are, there's footsteps./ Good./ Excellent, Walter.

W. Folks speak amongst yourselves. **All.** Ok.

T. Oh, that was tremendous. There are so many questions we want to ask. **J.** I know.

T. The first man – he walked back behind the curtain into the cabinet but I'm not sure that the second and third did. There seemed to be a thump as though they had gone.

J. On the floor. As though they had gone, yes.

A. Katie's Mum couldn't hold it.

J. I heard that with Katie's Mum.

T. Whereas Walter walked back.

A. Ron was so close to the cabinet, anyway.

T. He hadn't come out anyway. **A.** No, not very far.

T. Just sufficient to speak. Tremendous!

K. She did extremely well. **T.** Oh, Yes!

W. You are most observant. **T.** We try to be.

W. But it is important, folks. **T.** Right.

W. Can you hear my voice?

All. Very loud and clear./ lovely.

W. I tell you we are not always able to know with certainty whether our words are reaching you folks. (**T.** We understand.) – That is why we depend upon you speaking with us. Ok, Ok. Let me hear your voices. (*All reply*)

T. We were right were we, Walter, in saying that the first gentleman stepped back, you stepped back but the others seemed to just 'thump'?

W. Indeed, sir, the energy, they were unable to hold.

T. I've seen that happen. **A.** It is so hard anyway.

K. It would take a lot of practise to do this anyway. They need to practise don't they?   **J.** Oh yes!

T. Exactly. It's all a question of experience.

W. Ma'am I cannot begin to explain to you the amount of work, practise as you say, that is involved in proceeding so far to develop what you are witnessing this evening. You can hear my voice. (**All.** Yes, Walter) – Yes, Ok.

T. It's out in the middle of the room!

W. I have to tell you Tom, that it is many years since I were able to retain my form in this manner – wait a moment Stewart is waking.

J. Ok, Walter. / **T.** We leave it to you.

W. It is difficult for me to speak while he is as he is.

J. Don't worry, just hit him and put him back to sleep. – They do!

W. Ok, Folks. I have to tell you when I speak to you about remaining perfectly still so that the energy is not disturbed. I have to tell you, that even Stewart returning in some manner from the depth of trance that we hold him in disturbs the vibrations and therefore makes it difficult for us to debate.

T. All right, All right.

(end of section 24)

Section 25

Freda materialises for the first time.

Home circle – 19th August 2003. (13min. 54seconds).

For the very first time, Freda materialised and walked around experimenting with a self-illuminated spirit light. She gave a brilliant commentary telling us that she appeared to be floating, she also explained what it felt like and how extraordinary it was to speak through her temporary form.

Walter. Folks, we would like to try to do something we have not previously done. (**Various voices.** Right, Ok.) – Freda would like to try to come amongst you. Since this will be the first time that she has ever attempted to do this it will take tremendous concentration on her part just to be able to materialise her form.

(**Various.** We understand./Ok)

W. We are therefore making arrangements. We appreciate that you will not understand this but we shall...create, ...if she is able to express her thoughts, this will come via Stewart. (**Various.** Ok / Oh,right) – Gaynor ma'am, June ma'am (**G&J.** Yes Walter.) – If you listen carefully, whilst Freda is within the circle, listen within the cabinet and you may hear a trace of the voice as it is created and transferred to the form. (**Various.** Wonderful/ Ok.....) – I hope you understand, folks.

Tom. We do very well.   **Gaynor.** Yes, we do.

W. Ok, Ok.I shall return a little later.

G. Ok, Walter. Thank you for coming. Excellent job.

Tom. Thank you for dropping in

June. Nice isn't it?

Tom. Isn't it wonderful.

G. I love it when they touch me, don't you. I love the feel of them.

(There is a lot of chat here between the sitters at this point which cannot be separated but this is not detrimental to the proceedings)

G. So warm, so warm. Excellent. Come on, Freda.

J. So natural, Tom

G. Come on, Freda, you can do it...I can hear her building down here. ...Come on, Freda, keep trying... Oh lovely.

T. Oh, you can do anything you want.

G. She's coming out....

J. We've just got to listen for the voices, Gaynor.

G. Yes I will....she's out, she's out.

T. Right. Oh lovely. You're out.

The tap of footsteps are heard.

G. They're smaller. / **Ann.** You can hear the smaller feet.

J. Yes you can. That's wonderful, Freda.

G. I bet it's strange, Freda.

T. You've got try to listen for the voice.

G. Yes we will.   **T.** Nice and steady, Freda.

J. I can hear the breathing.

A. She's almost in front of me.

G. I can hear Stewart moving down here, Stewart's moving.   **A.** Well done, well done.

T. All right, Freda. We know the problem.

J. Take our love. You are welcome.

A. The voice is right here. Come on, yes. You are doing so well.

G. Gosh, Freda, what's it feel like? I bet it's weird.

A. I bet it's strange.   **G.** Oh, I bet it is.

Freda. Oh, my dears. (**T.** Oh, Lovely!) – It is strange.

Michael. That is tremendous.

G. Aren't you doing well! Aren't you doing fantastic, Freda. Well done!

Freda. I have to tell you all, that I'm feeling very unstable. (*many replies from the sitters*) ...Can you hear my voice?

J. Yes we can hear you, Freda. This is wonderful, Freda. We really appreciate this, Thank you.

G. I can hear Stewart moving, but... what ...brilliant, Freda.

J. Steady as you go.

G. Go careful....have to get some energy. Blooming heck, Freda, that was an excellent job.

A. Tremendous. / **G.** First time.

A. She was right in front of you, Katie, I think.

K. Was she?

G. Yes, she was, right in front of Katie.

K. I could hear her.

G. Yes she was, right in front of you....Here she is again.

J&T. Ok, Freda /Come on then. Nice and steady.

G. Hello, Freda.

F. I hardly thought it was quite so tiring.. (**All.** Oh!) – and I have to tell you all, it was very tiring.

T. They told us that, for the first time.

J. Thank you for doing that for us, Freda.

G. Brilliant.

F. I am standing here in physical form. At the same time it is most extraordinary, dears. (**G.** I'm sure) – I am trying to speak through my temporary form but at the same time I feel that I am speaking through Stewart. It is most extraordinary dears. You can hear?

All. Yes, yes. Wonderful./ Very Clear/ Really clear.

T. You are using the physical voice box.

F. I have to tell you, I do not feel that I have felt quite so unstable as I feel on my legs this evening.

All. Oh dear.

F. In fact I'm not awfully certain whether I have been able to materialise my legs in which case I'm not certain what it is that is supporting me. (**T.** You are very brave, Freda.) – I seem, Tom dear, I seem as if I am floating around (**T.** That's right) – somewhere between the ceiling and the floor. You can hear, dears?

All. Yes, very clear.

T. That's what they used to tell us, Freda.

F. Now listen. I have the signal here. I've been informed that we are going to try, not me personally but Walter and the others, they are going to try to awaken Stewart whilst I am within the circle. (**G.** Oh, right) – All we have to ask, all that we expect of you all, is that you all remain perfectly still. (**G.** Yes we will). – We have so many lines of energy criss-crossed about the room. I am trying to manoeuvre myself between them. (**T.** Very clever.) – Can you hear me?

T. Very loud, they can hear you at the bottom of the street!

G. Very loud. Louder than Walter even.

J. It's wonderful Freda.

F. Well I have to tell you I have no particular sense of the volume of my voice but I know you can all hear me because I can hear you all.

K. You can hear your voice moving around the room.

G. Yes.

T. When they waken Stewart are you going to try to talk to him?

F. I'm going to try to speak, dear. I'm facing the cabinet now and I'm watching all the work that is taking place. He'll be coming back you see. (**All.** Yes.) – He'll be coming back. Can you hear my voice?

J. Yes. It's wonderful, Freda. You are working ever so hard. It's absolutely marvellous. / **T.** Very, very clear.

G. Stewart's coming to.

F. You see what is important is that we must always err on the side of caution..... Sit still dear... I'm speaking to Stewart.

J. Yes I thought you were.

T. Now he's going to be surprised.

F. Sit still, dear.

T. I like it. A Spirit person telling him to sit still. Good.

(There follows a bit of amazed chatter between everyone)

F. Well you see that Walter's way is not mine.

G. No of course not, you're a lady.

F. I like to think that I am.

G. You are. Very much so.

F. What was that, dear? Yes. Walter is leaving Stewart as he is. (**All.** Ok.) – Leave well alone. Now can you hear, dears?

T. Keep going.

F. This is extraordinary. I'm trying so hard and I feel that I'm meeting with some success.

All. You are, definitely, you are./ **G.** Very much so.

T. Meeting with great success.

F. Can you hear my footsteps?

G. Oh yes, you've got your legs now, Freda.

F. Well I have to tell you all that I never felt, I never thought that I would ever see the day when my feet would once again walk upon the Earth.

All. Well there you are./ There you go, then! That's wonderful.

F. I thought I had said goodbye to it a long time ago and yet here I am, within your midst, speaking at full volume....

G. You're very clever. / **T.** Solid.

K. I remember you once saying that you watched them doing it and it looked very painful.

F. Well now I am in a position where I can confirm that, through experience, dear. It is painful.

T. Yes, yes so we understand.

G. You've tried so hard.

F. I'm not too certain how much longer I should be able to remain amongst you.

G. We understand, Freda.

F. Before I return to the cabinet and therefore to my world I would like to thank this gentleman. (**T.** Which gentleman?) – You, dear. (**T.** Oh!) – For what you have done.

T. Her hand's on my head.

F. For what you have done and that the work will be completed. I know that you know what I mean by that. The work will be completed. (**T.** It will evolve. Thank you.) – It will evolve. I'm happy to do that, dear. I was under particular instruction but even I had not have been so I would have still wished to do that. We are aware as you know of the wonderful work that you have done for some time now. It will be a lasting testament, dear. It will be a lasting testament and like Katie, like Katie also, the work will continue and it will reach many people within your world,...... many people.

T. Thank you very much. (*many quiet exchanges among the sitters*)

G. There's a hand on my head.

F. Now if there is nothing else that you would like to say then I shall return to my world.

J. Just to thank you.

T. Thank you for making that effort.

F. Perhaps, dears, I can do one further thing before I return.

J. Yes that would be nice.

(there are a number of quiet exchanges).

G. Oh I can see the light. Look there's the light!

All. Oh yes / Oh wonderful.

J. Brilliant, Freda. Well done.

G. It's flashing around again somewhere, or there's some spirit light flashing around.

F. I doubt I shall be able to return again.

J. Ok. Freda, thank you.

G. But you'll come another night?

T. In the future?

F. Well, thank you all for the love. You know, dears, these are wonderful conditions within this room. I know that we have said this so many, many times in the past but we can only continue to repeat ourselves. *(the voice is fading away)* It is wonderful here. (**G.** Thank you, Freda.) – Goodnight, dears.

G. Goodnight Freda, God bless you.

(end of section 25)

Chapter Twelve

LIVING MATTER THROUGH MATTER

At a home circle on 17th August 2004, I was witness to the passage of living matter-through-matter. During this experiment, Walter explained that everything is made up of molecules and nothing is solid; for example, what feels solid to the touch is simply on a different level of denser vibration. For Stewart's wrist to pass through a plastic cable tie was indeed something extraordinary. Below are the highlights of a recording, with accompanying illustrations, taking you through the experience step by step.

Stewart was secured to both chair arms by strong plastic cable ties which can only be removed by cutting them with pliers, and whilst the illustrations show what happened to Stewart's right arm, I can assure you that his left arm remained securely fastened throughout the demonstration.

Stewart's wrist is fastened to the arm of the chair.

Walter invited me to sit next to Stewart on his right.
Walter. Katie ma'am.

Katie. Yes, Walter?

W. You can hear my voice.   **K.** I can – yes, Walter.

W. I understand that you would like us to do something for you, so that you may have an extra experience that you may write about.

K. Thank you very much Walter.

W. Ok – It is my pleasure, ma'am.   Folks, may I ask you all to kindly place your hands upon your knees with your palms uppermost. Ok, Ok. (**All.** Yes.)

W. Katie, you have sat many times within the circle and you have observed and you have listened, whilst other ladies sitting where you now sit have experienced the passage of living matter through matter. We would now like you to have that experience so that this will add to the sum total of your personal knowledge.

K. Thank you Walter.

W. Would you very kindly place your left hand on the right hand of the medium – hold it tightly. (**K.** Ok.)

Katie holds the medium's hand.

W. May we ask you now to appreciate that the lady with her left hand is holding Stewart's right hand tightly. I know that you will accept that.

All. Yes, Ok, Fine etc.

W. Katie ma'am, would you kindly place your right hand on top of your left. (**K.** Yes.) – Understand if you will, that the medium is in an acute state of sensitivity so I ask you to be gentle ma'am. Very gently move your right hand up the arm of the medium. Can you feel the strap?

K. I can feel the strap.

W. Move your right hand away – you are holding Stewart's hand tightly with your left hand?

K. Certainly. Yes.

W. And you felt the strap, feel again ma'am – is it there? (**K.** The strap is there yes.) – Move your right hand away, ma'am. Hold Stewart's hand tight. (*A snap and swipe sound was heard and our hands, locked together, shot up into the air*).

K. Er? it feels as if the strap is broken.

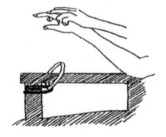

Both hands are up in the air with the locked strap still on the chair arm.

W. Ma'am, with your right hand would you kindly feel the arm of the chair and assure yourself that the strap is still there.

K. It is still there – yes – Stewart's hand is up in the air.

W. And you have not let go of his hand for a moment.

K. Not for a moment – no.

W. You have witnessed the passing of living matter through matter. Raymondo would you kindly introduce the light so that everybody can see the strap which is still on the arm of the chair.

(Ray shines a dim red light onto the arm of the chair)

Ray. The strap is there.

W. We have taken Stewart's arm through the strap leaving the strap still in place on the chair arm.

K. That's wonderful Walter.

W. So many people in your world would consider what has taken place to be some kind of a miracle – it is nothing of the sort. It is merely a small demonstration of what we can achieve when our two worlds blend together as a united whole, and when we have a medium who has suitable energy that we can extract and utilise. That is all, it is no miracle folks.

K. Thank you.

R. Thanks, Walter – Thank you.

(The spirit people then brought Stewart's arm back down and through the same looped strap that had been left hanging on the chair arm and the medium's wrist was secured once again. Walter proceeded with a further experiment while I continued to hold the medium's hand.)

W. Ma'am, place your right hand on top of your left hand. (**K.** Yes.) – Very gently ma'am, move your hand up the arm of the medium – stop – is it covering the strap? (**K.** It is.) – Is your hand holding the strap?

K. It is now – yes.

W. Keep it still, press down on the strap.   **K.** Yes.

Katie's right hand presses down on the strap while her left hand is still holding Stewart's hand.

W. Press down on the strap ma'am, you are holding Stewart's hand tightly? (**K.** Yes.) – Would you like the strap ma'am? (**K.** Yes please.) – Tell the folks here, you have your hand over the strap.

K. Yes, I have my hand over the strap.

W. And the strap is holding Stewart's arm to the arm of the chair?

K. Yes, it is indeed.

W. Would you like the strap ma'am?

K. Yes please Walter. (*A snap and swipe sound is heard*). Oh! Thank you.

The hands rise up in the air with Katie still holding the strap.

R. What happened Katie?

K. Stewart's hand is up in the air, the strap came off into my hand – I've got the strap now.

Katie removes the strap from Stewart's arm.

R. It came off, or did you take it off his hand?

K. I took it off his hand. It came off the arm of the chair.

W. Raymondo, is there a spare strap upon the table?

R. Yes – there certainly is.

W. I ask you folks to be perfectly still.

(We could hear Walter putting the spare strap around Stewart's arm).

R. You cannot do that with one hand can you? And Katie has the original strap.   **K.** I have it here.

W. Katie has the strap which a moment ago was around the arm of the chair. Ma'am you may keep that.

K. Thank you very much, Walter.

W. A small memento – a small gift from me to you ma'am. **(K.** Thank you.) – Ok-Ok-Ok. You are all so quiet.

All. We are all listening intently.

W. Katie ma'am. Do something for me. **(K.** Yes Walter.) – Reach on to the table and you will find that we have been able to link the two straps together – one through the other.*

K. I can feel them – they are linked together.

W. Take them and pass them to Neil. Neil sir, we would like you to accept these as a small memento of the occasion that you sat in this circle.

Neil *(a guest at the circle).* Thank you Walter.

Tom. The straps were separate loops at the start of the séance.

K. Yes – they were laid upon the table separate and now they are linked.

Neil. Thank you very much, Walter.

W. It is my great pleasure.

* *Two cable ties had been individually locked before the séance commenced, and placed on the table-top, a distance from each other.*

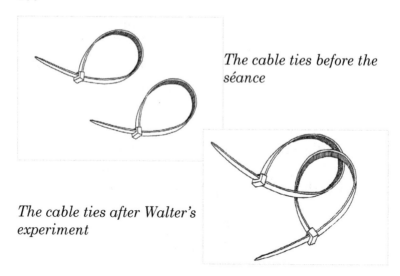

The cable ties before the séance

The cable ties after Walter's experiment

How the two became linked we cannot, of course, begin to understand the 'paranormal' *modus operandi* involved. But a wonderful example of spirit activity and a physical memento for the circle visitor.

At the beginning of another home circle in 2015 there were two separate already looped-up cable ties and a separate wooden ring resting upon the table-top. To our surprise when the light was switched on at the conclusion of the sitting, we found one of the looped cable ties had linked up with the wooden ring.

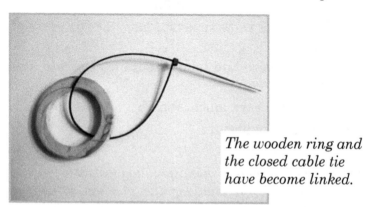

The wooden ring and the closed cable tie have become linked.

Alf and June Winchester from Cromer in Norfolk actually saw a similar experiment in the red light with ropes. Here is Alf's report:

> *"The demonstration of matter through matter is a regular occurrence at Stewart's séances but these experiments are held (certainly in public demonstrations) in total darkness. On one occasion in the nineties my wife and I sat at Stewart's home circle and were privileged to witness this phenomenon in red light. The practice at that time was to secure Stewart to his chair during séances by means of rope, (at least 6mm thick) which was firmly tied with secure knots. Walter instructed Ray that when he heard a knock he was to switch on the red light for 5 seconds. We were told to look towards Stewart's right arm and observe. When the red light came on, I clearly saw Stewart's arm shoot upwards and through the ropes that held it and at the same time there was a loud snap like the cracking of a whlp. The experiment was repeated with his left arm with identical results. The ropes were still firmly knotted and attached to the arms of the chair. My wife June's observations were identical to mine."*

These phenomena require a very different source of energy from those involving ectoplasm as is used in levitation, voice boxes, materialisations etc., and just how it is achieved was disclosed when Walter explained to Leslie Kean (a visiting journalist from New York) that he is no scientist, but is one of the souls who communicates, and this type of exclusive experiment is controlled and operated by the scientific experts in his world.

He told us that when the living matter through matter demonstration takes place, the spirit people extract from the medium a unique form of energy which is not to be confused with ectoplasmic energy. When the interlink takes place, Stewart's right arm and the arm of the lady who is holding the medium's hand exist not within the physical world nor within the spiritual, but between the two. As these limbs, existing now between the two worlds, are lifted up into the air that is the precise moment when the procedure is complete and that causes the snapping sound. When they lower the arms back to the chair, there is no resistance, for there is nothing physical and Stewart's arm returns through the looped strap left hanging on the chair arm.

Throughout all those years of sitting, we in the circle thought the snapping sound was caused by the strap, but it is not so, it is the coming together of the spiritual and physical energies. When the strap is being presented to the lady as a memento, the two energies gradually begin to move apart after the spirit people have re-secured Stewart and the arms become wholly 'physical' once more.

Chapter Thirteen

WALTER'S ECTOPLASMIC EXPERIMENTS

Over the years, Walter Stinson has given us a deeper understanding of physical phenomena and the scientists in the spirit world who 'generate' the ectoplasmic experiments. He has spoken to us of the scientific work that goes on in the background with the intention of showing us that life continues after death. It is through their work with ectoplasm that our spirit friends are able to walk among us in the séance room. In total darkness, they were solid enough to be able to approach me, remove my spectacles without any fidgeting or fumbling, fold them and hand them directly to my sister across the room.

During a sitting, before the spirit people start to walk around, we were asked to move our chairs back as far as we could go. Not only were they able then to walk around the room, but solid spirit hands touched and pressed against my back and those of other sitters even though our chair backs were tight up against the walls.

Like the living matter through solid matter experiment, this demonstrates how everything is made up of molecules and different vibrations, so nothing is solid.

At a home circle on 4th May 2004, seven spirit hands touched me at the same time. Gaynor was away that evening and I was sitting in her seat next to Stewart on his left. Here is an excerpt from my report:

*"Walter, (through Stewart in trance) then asked all
of us to move away from the cabinet and I did so as
far as I could and sat with the back of my chair right
up against the wall. Following the playing of music, I
felt a hand directly lift up my right arm and another
hand, with no fumbling, take hold of my right hand.
A third hand pushed what felt like a small booklet into
my right hand, this apparently was the writing pad
and at the same time a pair of hands touched my head
from the back and another pair of hands touched my
left shoulder also from the back – remember that
there was a wall directly behind me! Seven spirit
hands touched me at the same time – so there must
have been more than three materialised spirit people
in the room all at the same time."*

*Later, I found that written on the pad was – 'Mum
xx' and the spirit people said that this was for my sister
and me."*

(end of report)

Following that exciting experience of being touched
by so many spirit hands all at once, a spirit person
walked out of the cabinet and knocked on the door
which is situated at the furthest corner across the room.
Whoever it was then walked back to the cabinet and in
passing touched June on the head. Then Dr Barnett
told us that he had built himself into a full form and
he had also been able to create a speaking mechanism.
As we heard him walk out of the cabinet towards the
door, he said, "I do hope you will be able to hear my
voice." To which we all replied, "Yes."

When he returned, we talked about the hands that
were all around me, and he explained that they had
only materialised their hands and that it had been
unnecessary to fully materialise. He continued by

saying that they wanted me to have that experience, so that I could tell people, especially those who are so critical of séances. I replied, saying how solid the hands were.

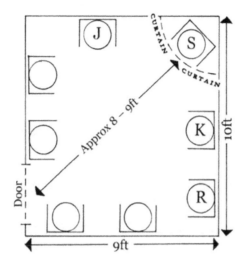

Diagram showing the distance a spirit person walked from the cabinet to the door.
S =Stewart. K = Katie. R = Ray. J = June.

Ectoplasmic Rods

Ectoplasmic rods, (also known as pseudopods), can stretch out from the medium as far as the other side of the séance room, sometimes tapping each sitter. They are very strong and solid to the touch.

At one time there were only four of us (including Stewart) sitting. As June, Ray and I were sitting very close to each other around the small table in front of Stewart, we knew nobody had moved. Walter asked us to switch on the red light above the table and to our surprise, lying flat on the table was a Plaster of Paris plaque of a North American Indian.

156

Approximately 9" long x 4" wide (22 x 10cm) and weighing 1½ lbs (685gms), it had been removed from a hook on the far wall and placed on the table by spirit people using an ectoplasmic rod. The distance between Stewart and the hook on the wall was 8 feet (2.4m).

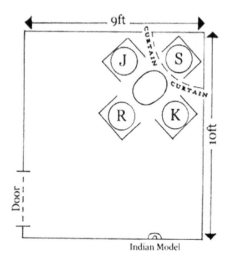

*Sketch of séance room showing the position
of the plaque before it was moved.*

Trumpet Phenomena

The ectoplasmic rods are also used to move trumpets around the room. Although the demonstration is always held in total darkness, we are able to see the luminous tabs on the broader ends of the trumpets. We also know that Stewart is still sitting in his chair because we can see the luminous tabs on his knees and he often converses with us whilst the phenomena are taking place.

With help and advice from Dr Barnett, the illustration opposite has been created to show what we would probably see if light was introduced during trumpet phenomena.

*The trumpets glide through the air with such ease
and tranquillity.*

It is a delight for the sitters to watch the trumpets slowly rise and soar up to the ceiling before descending (often rapidly) to a position directly in front of people's faces. They frequently communicate with the sitters using specific manoeuvres, for example; up and down for yes, sideways for no. In the presence of Tom and Ann Harrison, a family spirit guide called Sunrise often makes himself known with a circular movement of the trumpet in a clockwise, then anti-clockwise direction, as he did over seventy years ago in Tom's mother's home circle. The trumpet may tap a sitter on the shoulder, stroke an arm, or rest on a lap with the broader end facing the solar plexus. When this happens we know that energy is being withdrawn from the sitter. The sitters in the home circle are always willing to give energy and any energy taken is always replaced at the end of the séance.

My own experience is a feeling of revitalisation after a séance, as the spirit people seem to give so much more than they take – such is the love of spirit.

Double trumpets

One of the highlights of the trumpet phenomena is when one trumpet settles on top of the other and both levitate into the air locked together as one. As they sail around the room the double luminous tabs at their broad ends can clearly be seen. Although this type of phenomena is produced in total darkness, I have once again illustrated below what we might have seen had it been possible for light to be introduced.

A) First the energy / ectoplasmic rod forms pincers at the end to be able to grasp the trumpet.

B) The first trumpet is placed over the second trumpet.

C) With both trumpets held together by the ectoplasmic energy, they glide through the air with such grace and have never been known to separate or slide apart during flight or landing.

Stewart is often conscious during this procedure and can watch the double trumpet phenomena, and whilst this is happening he has remarked about a stronger pull on the solar plexus when the two are together. Our spirit friends wake Stewart up mainly to prove to sitters that he is not near the trumpets to wave them about, as some sceptics maintain.

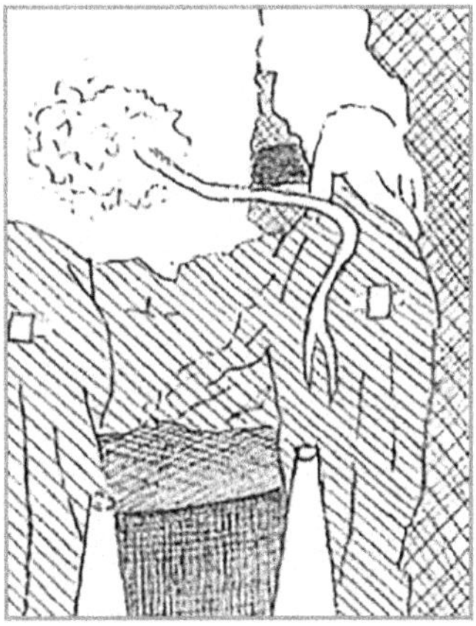

This is an enlargement of Stage A to show the grippers

Direct voice through the trumpet

When the trumpet is used for direct voice, an ectoplasmic voice box is formed below and around the chin area of the medium. A hollow ectoplasmic tube is

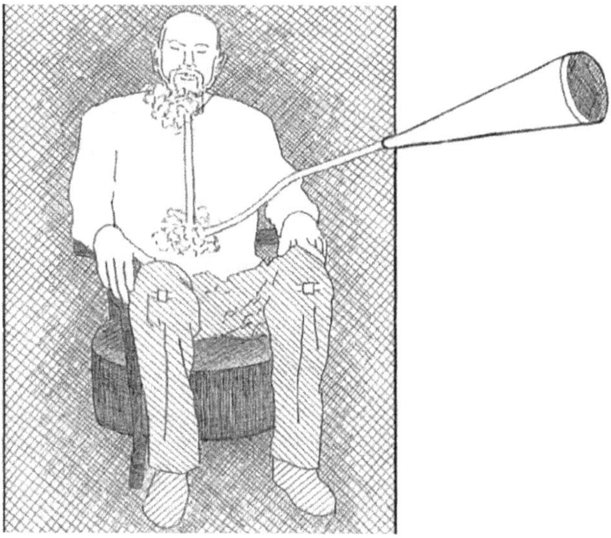

How the voice box is used during the trumpet phenomena.

then extended to the ectoplasm developed from the solar plexus which then attaches to the smaller end of the trumpet. Because this ectoplasmic rod is hollow, the direct voice is then able to travel through to the cone-shaped trumpet, automatically amplifying the spirit voice for the appropriate sitter. Stewart is usually in trance when this type of phenomenon takes place.

Once again all this is done in total darkness and we can only see the luminous tabs. The illustration on the previous page shows what we might see in the presence of light.

At the home circle on 18th November 2008, I asked Dr Barnett if he could help me with my illustrations regarding the trumpet phenomena. I needed to know how to draw the rod, how thick it was and if it was always straight and solid.

This is what Dr Barnett had to say:

> "No it is not always a straight rod. Take the small end of the trumpet and assume that the energy is within it and through it. You may then take this as roughly the size – the diameter of this rod.....There is no reason whatsoever why it needs to be straight, it does not follow the physics of your world."

Dr Barnett discusses the physics of our world.

Continuing his reply to my query he said:

> "If you were to present the energy line, the rod, in a completely straight line from the medium's solar plexus through to the trumpet, if you were to do that then of course that is precisely what people would expect. Miss Halliwell, you are applying your logic, the physics of your world, it is applicable to your world and not necessarily to ours. For example, I believe

that I am correct in saying that the existence of the energy you refer to commonly as ectoplasm – is not recognised by science in your world. Your science knows not where it resides nor could it detect such energy within the human body. That does not mean to say that it is not there, for it is. But never make the mistake of assuming that the science of your world is also applicable to mine, for it is not. There are certain similarities, but there are also a great many dissimilarities. I cannot be plainer than that...I wish that I could explain with far more clarity, but it would not be necessary – I think that is adequate."

Ectoplasmic rods are not always visible.

He went on to explain more about the rods:

"You do realise that there are many occasions when the energy would be invisible to your sight? Realise, that if it was possible – if we knew that it posed no danger to the medium by calling for the introduction of light at a time when the trumpet was in levitation, it may be that you would see nothing of the rod. No connection whatsoever between the medium and the trumpet itself. The energy is there connecting the two together, it is there but not necessarily visible to your sight. We would only make it so to satisfy your curiosity. People imagine that there should be a connection, a visible line of energy, but at present it would not endure any form of light. In a general sense, since the experiment is conducted within the darkness, there is no necessity for the energy to be anything other than invisible....It can be tangible, but invisible simply because we are conserving the energy – what would be the point in

wasting time making the energy visible when all that you are interested in is that the trumpets are in levitation and these are controlled by the intelligence of my world."

This phenomenon of the invisibility of ectoplasmic rods, was ably demonstrated in red light on 7th July 2011 and I have illustrated what everybody in the room saw.

Walter asked Ray to switch on the light for three seconds only. We all looked at the table top and saw a bell, a pair of drum sticks, two looped cable ties and a bunch of straight cable ties. Nothing moved.

Walter then asked Ray to switch on the light again, this time for 5 seconds, then off. We all watched the bell slowly move a good 3 inches (7.5cm) to the left towards Stewart, before Ray switched off the light.

Walter asked for the light to be switched on again for 5 seconds and this time we watched the bell move further to the edge of the table and topple over.

Because the glass surfaced table-top is covered with a red cloth, the bell would not have had the ability to slide freely; perhaps, therefore, it must have been lifted up very slightly by an invisible ectoplasmic rod for it to glide smoothly across the surface.

Table Levitation

This demonstration took place at a home circle and as we kept our hands palms down on the table-top, it started to vibrate and sway to-and-fro, before very

1. Four people (including Stewart) placed their hands on the table top touching each other.

gently rising into the air to a height of at least 12 inches (30.5 cm) where, for a few seconds, it hovered. Then, gently and slowly, it descended to the floor. Stewart's hands, also on the table, remained visible throughout the experiment.

2. The table levitates at least 12 inches (30.5 cm) into the air.

The same experiment has also been demonstrated at various public circles and on one occasion I saw the table levitate on its own – without physical contact! – as four people, including Stewart, sat round it holding hands, as illustrated below.

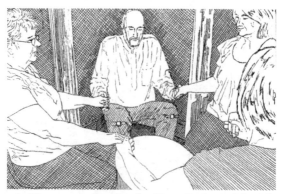

1. Four people, (including Stewart) hold hands round the table.

2. The table moves and levitates.

During a home circle on 29th July 2008, I took the opportunity to ask Walter how the table levitates. He explained that this was done by means of the dynamic living energy 'ectoplasma' (as Walter calls it) extracted from Stewart, and to an extent from the members of the circle. He then said that out of this ectoplasm, a lever is created to the very centre of the underside of the table and the energy is then utilised in such a way that it expands in an upward direction and the table begins to move and finally to levitate.

Another instance of table movement, – this time the table turns upside down. With no one touching it the table turns over without any visible support.

1. The table is upright with no-one touching it.

*2. The table turns
without any visible
support.*

Chair Levitation

Using a similar ectoplasmic technique as that used
to achieve table levitation, the energy can also be
powerful enough to levitate the chair with Stewart
sitting in it. During this procedure Stewart is conscious
throughout, and I show opposite what we might see if
we were able to use a red light. On this occasion, in the
darkness of the séance room, our eyes focused on the
luminous tabs on Stewart's knees as we watched them
rise to eye level and above.

Chair lifts and then moves forward

At a public séance which took place near Banbury on
20th October 2005, we witnessed Stewart's chair
levitate while he was tied to the chair arms with strong
plastic cable ties. We saw the luminous tabs on
Stewart's knees rise approximately 4ft (1.22 metres)
into the air. Soon after the levitation the same chair,
with Stewart still sitting in it and fastened to it, moved
approximately 5ft (1.52 metres) out, away from the
cabinet.

The chair plus Stewart levitates into the air.

After the séance ended, I asked Stewart what it felt like – as he had come out of trance at the start of the proceedings – and he explained that the chair seemed to come alive. It vibrated, and then started to rock to-and-fro as it began to levitate, and all he could do was to cling on tightly to the chair when his feet left the ground. Such is the power of spirit.

It happened again at a seminar on November 12th 2005 at a North Yorkshire retreat. I saw the luminous tabs on Stewart's knees rise up to a height level with the tabs on top of the cabinet curtains, which were approximately 6 feet (1.83 metres) from the ground.

A Hand Materialises

At a home circle on 17th April 2007, I and two other circle members were invited by Walter to sit with Stewart at the low table lit by a red light from beneath as described earlier. Stewart's hands were already on the table and we were instructed to place our hands, palms down, making sure we were all touching each others' finger tips. In the dim red light, a mass of ectoplasm was then seen rolling out from the direction of Stewart's solar plexus and moulding itself into a hook like shape, gradually developing into web-like fingers and a thumb before finally forming into Walter's solid hand. We then watched this hand tap the table-top and the sound we heard proved its solidity. Throughout this whole experiment, Stewart's hands were visible on the table for all to see.

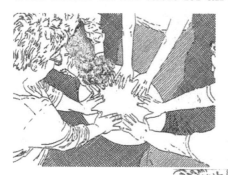

1. Ectoplasm rolls on to the table from Stewart's solar plexus.

2. It twists and forms into a hook-like shape.

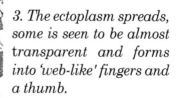

3. The ectoplasm spreads, some is seen to be almost transparent and forms into 'web-like' fingers and a thumb.

4. Walter's hand is now solid as we see and hear it tapping the table-top.

Different hands materialise

At another sitting, Walter's hand developed and then stayed on the table while a smaller hand developed alongside his.

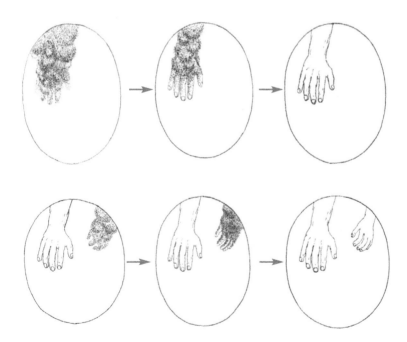

Transfiguration

Transfiguration is a delicate process in which a thin ectoplasmic mask is formed in front of the medium's face. It is best seen when the sitter is located close to the medium. This particular experiment can sometimes be fleeting, and stands in contrast to the ectoplasmic hand which is solid to the touch and is clearly seen for a length of time.

Although I have had the privilege to see partial transfiguration, such as my friend Bob's beard which is much larger than Stewart's beard and Gaynor's long hair as mentioned in the next chapter (page 183), I have witnessed sitters instantly recognising their so-called deceased loved ones' faces without a shadow of doubt. I can also report seeing some astounding transfiguration phenomena myself.

(Left) Stewart as we normally see him in trance.

(Right) The transfiguration of Bob's beard is much larger than Stewart's beard.

At a sitting on 8th December 2011, Ray was asked to switch on the red light, and we were invited to watch Stewart's face. He was in trance and his eyes were closed. His face then began to change with misty fog-like shapes moving across the surface. I saw a very dark area on and around the top of Stewart's head, but as I was sitting at a fair distance from the medium, it was not easy to see this in detail. I wondered if it was hair.

As the foggy shapes moved around, changing and forming around his face, I could see an open eye in front of Stewart's closed left eyelid. It was apparently the spirit person's eye, and for a split second there was an air of luminosity about it which made it sparkle as the spirit visitor looked around the room. The other eye was visible, but was slightly fogged over.

The features kept changing – showing dark and light areas, some slightly hazy and fogged – then the transfigured face began to speak and introduced itself as Ron, explaining that he was trying to show himself.

This was Ronald Hill, a soul I never met on the earth plane, but got to know through his wife Ena. As mentioned in Chapter 6 (Section 15), Ronald was killed in action during World War II and I now think that the dark area on top of Stewart's head could have been the partial development of his naval cap.

On 16th February 2012, I experienced a different form of transfiguration and have illustrated, to the best of my ability, the changes I saw.

The light was switched on and we all focused on Stewart's face. Sitters commented on the changes and we could see his face disappearing in parts and in certain areas it was darkening. Lindsey noted that the shape of his nose was changing, and also that some hair was forming. Carol noted that the phenomena were on and off, ("Now you see it, now you don't.") From the other end of the room, I could see Stewart's face coming and going.

Normally, transfiguration has a very thin layer of ectoplasm, but in this case, there appeared to be some build up, as something moved about in front of Stewart's face. His nose and the lower part of his face changed from time to time and some of the sitters could see small flashing lights.

(Left) Stewart as we normally see him in trance.

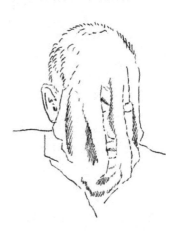

(Right) Stewart's features disappear/ reappear as the ectoplasm builds up and moves around his face.

Walter still continues with his experiments and because they are so unique, we never know what to expect. I must say that I am privileged to have been one of the few lucky people to have witnessed such wonderful phenomena at its best. The least I can do on behalf of the spirit team's fantastic work is to keep a record of new developments to share with others, as I have done up to press.

Part Three

Special experiences of spirit
'returns' and a
Christmas Tree Séance
with the
Stewart Alexander Circle

For Part 3 recordings listen to sections 26 to 38 on
www.alexanderproject.bandcamp.com

Stewart's sister, Gaynor is killed in a road accident in February 2009 and returns providing evidence of life after death.

*

Tom Harrison passes to spirit in October 2010 and returns to chat to the circle and later materialises to hold his wife's hand.

*

A Christmas tree séance provides outstanding physical phenomena.

*

A father returns to talk to his daughter one day after his funeral.

*

What a perfect stranger can do
– the roles we play during our lives on earth.

The Stewart Alexander Home Circle 2011

From the left: Jane, June, Christopher, Lindsey, Katie, (honorary member), Stewart (physical medium), Denise, Carol and Ray (circle leader).

Christopher and Jane had been full members of the circle for some time and travelled to the meetings from Easingwold (51 miles/ 82.11 km) until September 2015 when extra employment prevented them making the weekly journey.

Lindsey, Gaynor's daughter took her mother's place until she emigrated to Australia in February 2012.

Denise, (Ray and June's daughter) had by now returned to the circle after bringing up her family, and Carol is an additional new member.

Chapter Fourteen

GAYNOR SINGLETON

I received the awful news about Gaynor's fatal road accident on Saturday 7th February 2009. Shock, grief and total disbelief descended upon me and literally stopped me in my tracks. Understandably the home circle meetings and the guest sittings also came to a sudden halt. Over 300 people attended Gaynor's funeral, people from all walks of life who had been fortunate to experience Gaynor's warmth, love and friendship. As for the family that day, I was completely lost for words and all I could do was to give them a hug.

It is Friday 27th March 2009 and I find myself standing looking at a bench with the words,

'IN MEMORY OF GAYNOR SINGLETON 1952 - 2009
WHO SO LOVED COBER HILL – HER SPIRITUAL HOME'

carved into its back rest. This memorial bench is positioned between two beautiful cherry trees at the Cober Hill retreat on the North Yorkshire coast – the place where twice a year people from all over the world gather for the 'Stewart Alexander and Friends' weekend seminars. Gaynor was very much a part of those special gatherings and Cober Hill is a place that she loved. The vista from the bench is the same as that from the window of the bedroom she occupied whenever she visited.

Gaynor's seat is placed in the bank between two beautiful cherry trees in the Cober Hill gardens.

Sitting on the bench, my gaze fell upon the short narrow road that cuts through the splendid countryside and ends where the sea meets the sky and where, each day, the sun rises.

The view from Gaynor's bench.

Yes, I remember now, I had woken from a dream that Saturday morning on 7th February, the day we lost Gaynor I had dreamt of a large orangey/red sunset and little did I know then that the sun had already set on that day and a period of darkness was to follow. Even with our knowledge of survival, we grieve and suffer the physical and acute emotional loss of a dear one, but it is a comfort to know that they and we still live on after death, and like the sun always rises, we too rise into the spirit world. As I observed the scenery, I felt that this was the time to remember, the time to contemplate, to reflect, and recall some of the precious moments that I spent with Gaynor.

Stewart, Gaynor and their sister Joy at Cober Hill

As Stewart's sister, Gaynor was a keen and important member of the home circle, and, as long as I had known her, she had devoted herself to spirit. Unceasingly she supported her brother's mediumship and its development and over a period of many years

was one of the stalwarts of the circle. Always she sat at Stewart's left side, and with her happy effervescent personality she had the gift of quickly uplifting the atmosphere, which was needed when first time sitters at guest séances would, understandably, be very nervous. Invariably they would engage in serious conversation with fellow sitters – that is, until Gaynor arrived. She would breeze into the room, whip off her coat and ask: 'Hey! Did anyone see what happened in Coros'[1] last night?' Immediately, the whole atmosphere would change. With Gaynor around, there would be no more serious talk. She would laugh and joke thus enabling the first-time sitters to happily join in. This of course created the right and necessary conditions needed for a successful séance. She also gave encouraging support to our spirit friends who always needed to hear a cheerful voice.

Gaynor was irreplaceable. She had been a huge asset to the séances in many ways. She had the ability to distinguish the direct voices which generally commenced speaking so quietly other sitters could not hear them. She would encourage the spirit person speaking to keep trying until the volume and clarity of the words could be heard by other people in the séance room. She knew instinctively how to handle such situations. She also very often helped me, particularly during my early sittings with the circle, when I failed to hear what was being said.

Two days later, on Sunday 29th March, I found Stewart and his wife sitting on Gaynor's seat. After a few moments of general conversation, Stewart began to tell me an interesting story. Upon hearing it, I immediately realised that my work has not only been of service to the great truth of survival, but that it

---

1. Coros' is an abbreviation for the popular UK television programme 'Coronation Street'.

has touched people's lives. I felt both humbled and privileged. This is what Stewart told me that day.

A lady in America by the name of Annette Childs had purchased Part One of my trilogy in January 2009 via the Amazon website. Subsequently she emailed Ray Lister asking if he could send her the accompanying CD. She later obtained a copy of Part Two together with its two CDs. Ray informed Stewart that he had exchanged emails with the lady and Stewart felt strongly that he should make personal contact with her.

When he did so, he was to learn that she had a Ph.D. in Psychology, a private practice working with the dying to assist them in the attainment of spiritual peace, and that she was also a bereavement counsellor. Additionally, she had published important research findings on near death experiences, and since childhood she had possessed a mediumistic faculty although this apparently played a minor role in her professional life. She was also the author of two books[2] concerning matters of spiritual communication, and both had won literary awards.

Although Annette Childs had read many books and researched extensively in the field, she had known nothing of physical mediumship until she had come across my work, and knew nothing whatsoever about Stewart's personal life. However, feeling it was not by chance, that they had made contact, Stewart sent an email in which he mentioned Gaynor's passing and in return received wonderful words of comfort.

Later, because he understood the great value of communication through a third party, he asked Annette if she would try to link with Gaynor and to let him have any impressions that she might receive.

---

2. 'Halfway Across the River' (ISBN 9780971890220), and
   'Will You Dance' (ISBN 9780971890206).

Stewart, as Gaynor's brother, fully appreciated that anything that came through his mediumship would be of limited value for obvious reasons. But any relevant communication coming via a stranger – a stranger thousands of miles away in America – whom he did not personally know, and who knew virtually nothing of his personal life – would be important.

The result was that several days later the lady emailed information that she felt may have been communicated by Gaynor. One episode she mentioned from their childhood remarkably referred to a snake. Annette could not have known about a sickening incident that involved a pet snake and which, although at the time had been very repugnant, nevertheless, when recollected over the years, had caused the brother and sister great mirth. Stewart told me that as a young boy he had persuaded his parents to buy him a pet snake. Unfortunately, he was terrified of it and so had kept it in an empty biscuit (cookie) tin with holes in the top through which he fed it maggots. For many weeks he dared not remove the top, and when he finally did so he was to discover that the maggots had made a meal of the snake. Gaynor witnessed this and, they had in fact spoken of it only a few days prior to her untimely passing. Remarkable!

Dr Childs had also given the first letter of a town that she insisted was situated by the sea and which had a great significance to Gaynor. Stewart himself had no knowledge of it, but upon contacting Gaynor's youngest daughter Lindsey, it was confirmed that this piece of information was very relevant indeed to her mother. It was a town on the coast of Cornwall, where, apparently she would have purchased a house if ever she had been so fortunate as to win the national lottery.

The third piece of evidence involved a bouquet of flowers – a full description being given. The morning on which Dr Childs received the evidence was Mother's Day here in England and Lindsey had purchased flowers for her Mum that perfectly matched the description given by Annette Childs, proving that Gaynor had been very aware of her daughter's gift to her. All of this marvellous evidence showed that Gaynor had indeed communicated through a perfect stranger in America. The astounding aspect of all of this cannot be underestimated. Indeed, wonderful. Well done, Gaynor.

Gaynor has since spoken to the circle and to Lindsey several times.

On 17th November 2011, she tried to reach out to her daughter by materialising her hand in a way that I had never seen before. Below are my illustrations of this phenomenon.

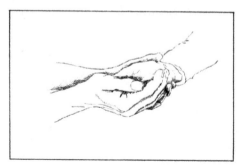

1) Stewart in trance cupped Lindsey's right hand in both of his hands.

2) He then moved his left hand over the top of Lindsey's hand and kept it there.

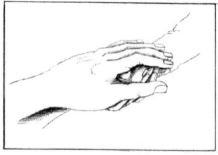

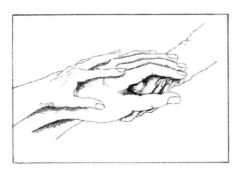

3) *Gaynor's hand materialised on the top of Stewart's left arm and hand and reached out to Lindsey.*

Three months later, on the 16th February 2012 we noticed a change in Stewart's face, and I observed what appeared to be long hair developing down the side of his head. For a good two minutes Gaynor made an effort to speak to Lindsey, while also attempting to show her hair and face in the red light.

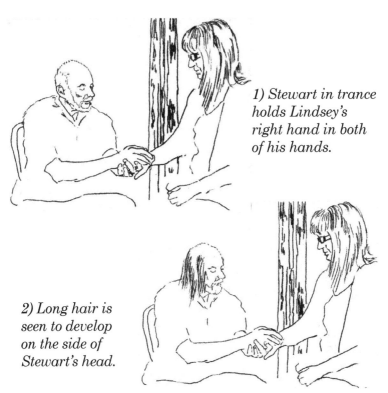

1) *Stewart in trance holds Lindsey's right hand in both of his hands.*

2) *Long hair is seen to develop on the side of Stewart's head.*

This was Lindsey's last sitting with us before she was to emigrate to Australia on 19th February, just three days later. Clearly Gaynor was trying her very best to get through at such a significant time.

Even though Lindsey is now living far away in Australia, time and space do not matter in the spirit world. Gaynor will always have the ability to blend into Lindsey's aura and be part of her life, as well as communicating with the Alexander home circle halfway across the world in Kingston-upon-Hull on the east coast of England.

Chapter Fifteen

TOM HARRISON

Friday 22nd October 2010 was to herald Tom's life coming to an end on this earth plane after ninety-two years. He was admitted to Hull Royal Infirmary in a coma and was not expected to come out of it.

That, indeed, was such a blow for me as I was so looking forward to seeing him at the annual Cober Hill Seminar the following weekend. I found it hard to contain my emotion as tears welled up in my eyes, for deep down I knew that his time had come. Yet, my inner self was happy for Tom's release from the physical body which had served his spirit well in this dimension. My thoughts and concerns were also directed to his wife, Ann.

Tom left his body the next evening and soon Ann was receiving numerous e-mails, cards and letters. Tom and Ann had travelled from their home in Spain to England to take part in the Stewart Alexander and Friends Seminar at the Cober Hill Conference Centre near Scarborough. With all the necessary business that a sudden death incurs and the rapidly approaching seminar, Ann prepared a letter that she could send by e-mail to many friends in the short space of time available.

She replied to my email message of support with this letter and I would like to convey to you some of Ann's words:

"Tom's sudden passing was a great shock but such a blessing too that he didn't have to go through the final dreadful stages of Parkinson's. He had dealt with that disease very well for six years but was now starting to show forgetfulness and unsteadiness when moving about – although at home before we left he had spent several days painting the newly raised garden wall – a tough job as it is heavily pebble-dashed but he was determined to keep active. I know that he meant so much to such a lot of people, including many, like some of you, he had never met. He loved to be in touch with people and it was a great joy that he could send emails all over the world, often spreading knowledge and healing but more often just being there for someone. His store of love was never in short supply."

His store of love was indeed never in short supply – this was so very true.

I cast my mind back to Tuesday 27th August 2002 when I was a guest at Ray and June Lister's home.

I was sitting in the living room watching a table being laid for a meal and to my astonishment, dishes piled high with food were being placed on the centre of the table, dish after dish until no more space was left. There was such a mountain of food on that table, I couldn't help thinking that surely we must be expecting some other guests. June must have picked up my thought because she looked at me and said, "Tom and Ann are coming tonight."

I counted five places and yet still wondered how on earth we would manage to eat all that food? And me being me, I was far too polite to say anything.

Sure enough Tom and Ann duly arrived and I can see it now so very clearly because I have never ever forgotten those precious moments, meeting them for the first time. I remember how Ann walked in through the kitchen into the living room and as she came towards me, June introduced us both. While this was happening, a tall and rather distinguished-looking gentleman appeared in the doorway; he didn't say anything, just simply stood behind the back of a chair surveying the mountain of food on the table with a concerned look on his face. His very first words were, "Er – June – we haven't got enough." Well, I just cracked and couldn't stop laughing at this gentleman to whom I had yet to be introduced. That was Tom – ever jovial, cheerful, caring and loving, and unlike me hiding the truth by being too polite and not saying anything about the food, he always knew how to make his own thoughts known in a very special and truthful way.

I had heard about Tom from Bob and Ena, when back in the 1990s they invited me to watch his video, *Visitors from the Other Side*[1], which included extracts from Tom's talks about the Saturday Night Club, (their home circle in Middlesbrough) and the remarkable physical mediumship of his mother, Minnie Harrison. I watched this video with fascination never realising in my wildest dreams that I was destined to meet and work with this wonderful man.

I often sat in the home circle with Tom and Ann and was privileged to witness the amazing communication with Sunrise, a North American Indian guide and guardian of Tom's mother, Minnie Harrison. Whenever Sunrise communicated with Tom through the trumpet phenomena, he would always make his special sound and Tom confirmed that this particular method of communication was just as it used to be in his mother's home circle more than fifty years earlier.

1. An interesting hour-long documentary, now available as a DVD from Saturday Night Press Publications. (www.snppbooks.com)

When the 2010 Stewart Alexander and Friends Autumn Seminar was drawing near, I asked what was happening about Tom's funeral or service. To my surprise, I was told that Tom did not want a funeral and his wish was to have a party instead.

It was arranged that the undertaker would take Tom's body to the crematorium and a party, a finger buffet, was to take place at Cober Hill on Sunday 31st October at the conclusion of the seminar, with music and singing afterwards. I know that many of my readers will perhaps find this rather strange, but I thought it a lovely idea. What is the point in putting family and friends through the trauma of a funeral, looking at a coffin containing an empty material shell, when the spirit of the deceased person is very much alive in the spirit world? Unlike Gaynor's life being cut short, Tom's passing, although sudden, was in many ways a blessing considering his ill-health, and although we shall miss Tom's presence on this earth, we do know that there will be a lot of rejoicing in another dimension – so why not join with them in celebration?

Tom's party was also to be in memory of two other friends who had recently 'earned promotion'– Ernie Crone and Prof David Fontana. Ernie was a regular visitor to Stewart's guest circles and always loved to be at the Cober Hill seminars. He had passed to spirit just two months earlier, on 31st August. Professor Fontana, a long-time supporter of Stewart's mediumship and a very close friend of Tom and Ann, passed to spirit on 18th October 2010, just five days before Tom. We raised our glasses to all three of them and a lovely and memorable time was had by all.

Earlier that day, Ann Harrison presented the talk that Tom was to have given at the seminar, and despite the grief she was suffering, she managed it with the utmost courage. I know Tom would have been so proud of her.

Ernie Crone (centre) with Tom and Ann Harrison
at the Cober Hill gathering 2008

The most astonishing event of the seminar that weekend was to be the wonderful communication at the séance held the night before. Ernie spoke to his wife Rose through Stewart's trance, until his emotion got the better of him, and shortly after Sunrise communicated through the trumpet. Many of the new guests in the séance room were not fully aware of who Sunrise was and therefore did not appreciated the value of his specific communication. To the accompaniment of communal singing, the trumpet soared around the room, finally stopping as close as it could get to Ann. Hearing breathing sounds through the trumpet Ann called to everyone to stop singing. After his special 'clearing' sound known so well to Tom and Ann and a limited number of other people, Sunrise spoke: "Sunrise greet little sister... All send greetings to you with love... All is well."

A very reassuring message.

Tom's presence was felt by many sensitive people that weekend but none more so than Gilly Woolfson, one of the participants in the mental mediumship workshop that Saturday afternoon. Gilly not only picked up the heavy and hot physical conditions Tom had experienced close to his passing, but he was able to convey to her special memories for Ann – from strawberries (the last thing he ate) to creamy marble pillars (in the posh restaurant where they had had a special meal with his daughters, two weeks before) and many more, accurate, pieces of evidence besides.

Showing himself to her as a vigorous young man, Gilly recognised her clairvoyant (mental) image of him in a photograph from 1948, on the following day when Ann gave the talk about Tom's mother's mediumship. Incidentally, Ann was not present in the room at the time Gilly received the communication – she was not even in the building.

Then only two weeks after the seminar, Tom came through Stewart's trance to speak, with a little difficulty at first, to the home circle. A little thing like death was not going to stop him communicating. So I invite you to listen to Tom's first communication with the circle in Section 26.

This was the first home circle sitting following the seminar. Having introduced himself, Tom had something special to say to Chris Eldon Lee, a regular visitor to the circle. Then Walter addressed the circle.

This is what Chris Eldon Lee wrote to Ann after the sitting:

> "As you will almost certainly know by now, Tom made a remarkable entrance at Hull on Tuesday. He chose a select audience, with just the five of us there – Ray, June, Lindsey, Stewart and a very privileged me. Funnily enough my eyes had been drawn to study the wedding photo on Ray's wall in which Tom stands so strong and statuesque. So it didn't come as a

complete surprise. His was the first voice to be heard and he came through almost at once, indistinctly at first calling 'June, June' and then more clearly. He told us off for trying to guess who he was before he'd had chance to introduce himself. But his voice gave him away. It sounded just like Tom*. It could not possibly have been anyone else. ...

I must say that for the very first time in circle, the hairs on the back of my neck stood up and tingled and tingled whilst he was present. It was a very powerful and moving feeling and I was so very glad to be present."

*And Chris should know the sound of Tom's voice as he spent many hours listening to it when producing the BBC Radio 4 Broadcast *'Christmas Spirits'* in 2003.

Section 26

Tom's first return.

Home circle 16th November 2010. (5min. 02seconds.)

A very breathy voice is heard trying to come and speak.

Chris E Lee (*abbrev to* **CEL**). Good Evening.

Ray. Hello, my friend. (breathy sound) Nice to have you with us. Come on, you can do it. (breathing again) You're most welcome here, you know. You're most welcome.

Spirit Voice. First.. tryv...tryv... Ohh! (*exasperated*).

June. Clive, no?

Spt V. No.   **J.** No-no-no-no.

Spt V. Don'...guess ... Don't ... guess. Ohh (*sighing, but it sounds like 'June guess'*)

J. No. It's difficult, come on.

CEL. Come on, come on, you can do it.

Lindsey. It sounds like don't forget.

Spt V. No, don't guess.   **J.** I've got to guess.

Spt V. No, no, ...don't guess.

J. Don't guess. We haven't to guess. *(laughter)*.

L. All right, sorry. We won't guess.

J. We've not to guess.   **R.** We'll leave it with you.

J. We'll leave it with you, darling, we've not to guess.

R. Come on. You're welcome anyway.

CEL. We understand.

Spt V. I...don't..know..if..I..can..say..just.. a ..few... words *(then a long breath)*

L. *(repeating)* You don't know if you can say...?

Spt V. A few ... words.

June & CEL. .. a few words.

L. You're doing well though.

CEL. We'd love to hear your words.

J. We'd like to hear you.

Spt V. Me...me *(a heavy breath then)* Tom.

J. Tom?   **L.** *(excitedly)* Yes, Tom. Is it you?

J. Tom, Tom.

Spt V. *(now recognised as Tom)*. Yes.

L. Tom, you are doing fantastic!

J. Love you to bits, Tom. Come on, Tom.

Tom. Really ... trying... hard.

L. Oh, you are doing great./ **J.** Oh, Tom, it is wonderful.

L. Thank you for coming. / **J.** This is wonderful.

T. Just thought it's time. **L.** You thought it was time.

T. For me to come. Yes, yes.

R. It's been too long.   **J.** That's wonderful.

L. Oh, Wonderful. Oh, thank you for coming and you've done ever so well.   **R.** You have.

CEL. We had a great celebration for you.

T. Aye, I know. **J.** He knows. *(laughter from the circle)*

T. Wonderful, ... wonderful.

L. Are you enjoying yourself over there?

T. Wonderful ... wonderful.

J. Ahh, that's wonderful, Tom

T. Tell... Ann... just had to come...I just had to come.

J. You just had to come.   **CEL.** You did indeed ...

L. Thank you so much   **CEL.** What kept you?

J. We love you, Tom.

T. If I could have come sooner...

J. ...you would.   **T.** Yes.

J. Yes. If he could have come sooner he would have.

T. ... Ann my love.

J. We will give Ann your love.   **T.** Thank you.

J. You're welcome, Tom. We love you to bits, Tom.

T. Thank you for being here, Chris ... Chris.

L. Chris.

CEL. Tom, it's wonderful to hear your voice, and don't forget that if it hadn't been for you I wouldn't be here at all.   **L.** Ohh.

T. Yes, *(speaking much more rapidly now)* but what... what is important now, is that you are here and everything I said about it, it is all that and more.

J. All that and more.

L. Brilliant. *(with comments on top of each other from the others too)*   **CEL.** Absolutely.

T. God bless.

All. God bless, Tom. / Love you to bits, Tom. / Thank you.

J. He grabbed my hand as he..   **L.** He tried ...

Cel. Is that the first time that Tom...?

J. That he's been through here, Yes.

Cel. ...spoken?   **J.** In here, yes.

There is a creaking sound and Walter takes over control.

J. Hello, Walter.

Walter. Now, folks, that was a surprise.

L. That was a really nice surprise.

J. It was a wonderful surprise.

L. He did fantastically well.

W. Well, let me say that he was most insistent.

J. Ohh, was he?   **Cel.** Funny you should say that.

L. Give him our love.

W. Of course; he has such a will.

J. He has and always will have.

W. You would expect nothing less.

J. No, no, definitely not.

W. Ok, so we thought that the time was opportune, particularly since our friend Chris...

Cel. Hello, Walter.   **J.** ... was here, yes.

Cel. That's very kind, Thank you.

W. You were able to hear him?

 J. Yes, yes we were.

Cel. I was looking at his photograph on the wall downstairs just a few moments ago. *(The photo is of Tom giving a Spiritualist blessing at Chris and Hannah's wedding in 2009.)*

W. Yes. He is insistent that his wife, Ann, is informed.

J. Ray will tell her, won't you Ray?   **R.** Yes I will.

J. Ray will let her know.   **W.** Ok-Ok.

(End of section 26)

Like Ray and June and the food set out on the table in 2002, Tom had prepared a huge mountain of food, but this time, not food to eat, but food for thought. The legacy Tom has left behind will encourage us all to spread the word far and wide. No matter how much of Tom's knowledge we take out to the world, people will always ask for more; they will never ever get enough of Tom.

And as for me, I shall always treasure his lovely greetings; he would place his hands on my arms just below the shoulders, hold me tight and take one good look at me, then give me a kiss followed by a huge hug.

After his transition, Tom made an appearance at various sittings. He often spoke very well indeed, but at times he sounded a little hoarse. His wife, Ann, once asked Walter if the hoarseness was due to Tom's picking up his own earthly physical condition. The answer was, "No, It's merely the difficulties he encounters when he endeavours to speak."

A point worth mentioning:

When loved ones in spirit try to speak, but for some reason do not sound quite right, we must remember that it is the message that matters, and quite often, the phraseology. For example, I was bowled over when Tom spoke a few simple words to Lindsey on 30th June 2011. "The day will come when she (Gaynor) will try to speak with you," was all he said. Those first four words hit me like a ton of bricks because it was Tom's style. I have another recording dated 13th May 2003 (Section 23) when Tom sat in the home circle and used the very same phrase, "The day will come, Katie."

'The day' did come for Ann eleven months after Tom had passed, on September 15th 2011. On an impulse, she had flown from Spain to sit in the circle and it was one occasion when I was sitting too.

We were only halfway through the introductory music, used to help Stewart go into trance, when Carol and June became aware of someone trying to speak through Stewart.

June. Come on friend. Can you turn the music down a bit, Ray?

Carol. We can hear you, friend, but it is very, very faint at the moment. ... Ray, can you turn the music down. He is talking but it's very faint. He's getting stronger if you can turn the music off.

J. Just turn it down ... Take my hand, darling? Come on, sweetheart, come on.

C. I think it's Tom. Yes. (**J.** I am sure it's Tom.) – If he can hear your voice Ann, he might be able to ...

Ann. Yes. Come on, love.

C. I'm certain it's Tom.   **J.** I am.

A. I've got an icy cold draught on my right arm.

C. He's probably holding it. *(Ray turns the music off)* – Come on you're nearly there.

A. Can you feel it Katie? (**Katie.** Hello?) **A.** No it's alright. (realising Katie hadn't heard her)

J/C – Come on, you're nearly there. You can do it.

K. Keep trying.

Spirit voice. Ohh...

J/C That's it you're there now, love.

J. It's you isn't it Tom?

C. It feels like his energy, so I'm certain it's Tom.

J. Yes it is Tom.   **C.** Come on, love, well done.

A. Come on, my love.   *(someone coughs)*

Tom ... I can hear!

Various voices. Yes./ You can hear?/ Well done/ That's good,/ excellent.

T. Oh..Oh ...   **A.** Come on, come on you can do it.

J. (*to Carol* – You got his hand?) Come on darling, nice and steady.

A. Take your time, nice and steady.

C. You're doing really well. ... Come on. Do you want me to hold your hand Tom?

J. Yes I've got it.

T. I... Oh! (**A.** Come on then.) – Can ... you ... hear?

A. Yes very clearly now – well done.

T. Oh! ... quite ... a ... quite ... a ... journey.

A. Yes . (**T.** Yes) – quite a journey.

T. (*breathily*) I am trying so hard to reach you. (**A.** Yes) – Sorry if this is ... ohh...

A. Take your time. (**T.** Yes) – You're doing well.

T. Oh I feel ... if I can speak better now.

A. Yes, you are much better.

T. Can you hear?   **A.** Clearly, clearly, well done.

K. Even I can hear him.   **A.** Even Katie can hear you.

T. Well good old Katie.

K. Hello Tom. Lovely to hear you again.

T. I ... this is like old times. I know that I ... Ohh, I know what I want to say but it's so hard – it's so very difficult to say a single word.

A. Well you are saying plenty of them. You are doing very well, Love.

T. Oh am I?   **J.** Yes   **C.** Very clear, Tom

Others all speak at once –

A. Very clear, Tom.

T. Ann darling, I am so happy that ... you ... are ... here ... yes. (**A.** Yes, so am I, so am I.) – You know people will not understand...the difficulty... the difficulties in saying what ... making myself understood. ... So hard.

but I want you to know ... I want you all to know that all is fine here ... (**A.** Good) – All is fine. I've met so many people ... yes ... wonderful. I'm often with Gaynor (**A.** Yes) – Gaynor, very often. (**A.** Good) – I know that Cober is not far off

A. That's right / **K.** No it's not far off

T. Be sure to give everyone my love.

A. I thought you would be doing that.

T. I'm trying ... trying, can't guarantee, no guarantee. (**A.** I'm sure you'll do it.) If I can't manage, tell them all... that I'll be with them. I'll be with you all. Yes, yes, yes. I was speaking to Sydney (**A.** Were you?) – and Gladys ... Oh ... Oh ... Oh ... Oh.

A. Have you seen Pat and Tony?

T. *(breathes heavily)* I ... was ... here. ... I ... was ... waiting ... *(a long breathy sound as he leaves)*

A. Yes. You were waiting...

Everybody speaks at once thanking Tom.

K. He'll be giving a talk at Cober.

Freda. Well, it may be a while yet, dears but I think he did wonderfully well,

A. So much stronger.   *(All welcome Freda and comment yes he did etc.)*

F. Well I think so, Ann dear, I think he did very well indeed.   And when one considers the difficulties involved, in just vocalising an occasional word, that I think that he is indeed doing exceptionally well. *(All comment agreeing with Freda.)*– Oh I do indeed, I do indeed. But don't think, Ann, that he is gone, he has not gone, (**A.** Good) – he will try again later. (**A.** Right, good.) – For now he finds it so exhausting. (**A.** Yes) So he has relinquished control and he is taking a rest. But he will try again a little later.

Freda stayed chatting for some minutes before handing over to Christopher so that he could use the opportunity to keep his hand – or rather his voice – in fluent control of Stewart.

However, it wasn't Freda who came later but Walter. He asked us to: "break for a period of maybe 5 minutes or perhaps even 10 minutes. Then we will begin again if you will ensure that you are sitting with your backs to the wall, draw a little further away from the cabinet – Ok. Then... we shall see what we can do."

After this short break, during which Stewart came out of trance, we moved our chairs back, to give the spirit people room to move about within the circle and Walter then asked us to sing to raise the energies. After singing parts of four songs we heard Stewart coughing and the curtains of the cabinet were wafted about vigorously with the rings clattering on the rail. Carol now became aware of Dr Barnett coming out of the cabinet, materialised.

Section 27

Dr Barnett and Tom materialise to touch Katie and Ann

Home circle – 15th September 2011. (9 mins 17secs).

Carol. I think Dr Barnett is about to talk. He's got his hands on my head now. Well done, Dr Barnett.

June./ Ray. Hello Dr Barnett. Nice to have you with us.

Ann. I can hear the breathing   **C.** Yes.

A. He's trying to speak

J. / R. He is / You're very welcome. Pleased you could come.

C. It's freezing around my feet.

J. Mine are. *(huge yawn heard)* Ok, friends, nice and steady. You're very welcome.

Dr Barnett. May I ask if you are able to hear my words.

All. Yes / Very clear/ Clearly etc.

Dr B. My friends, as always at this juncture I am very unstable in form.(**All.** Yes) – I have not been able to fully materialise in the way that I would wish to do, but I do hope that I shall be able, shortly, to come amongst you. (**All comment** Ok, Dr Barnett etc / **C.** We know you do your best.) – Yes, my friend, I most certainly do. As you know well, indeed, you will probably have grown tired of hearing these words come from my lips (**All.** Never) – but it is regrettable that always I am. ...we are singularly unable to guarantee that what we have alluded to, that is to say to come amongst you, we can never be certain that we shall achieve success.

There are so many, Christopher (*a circle member*), so many factors involved. It is not as you might think a matter of simply running through some kind of a process which will eventually lead to the successful formulation of my form. It is not that, I only wish that it were. It is rather always each occasion that I seek to materialise my form, it is literally...an experiment. It is literally a matter of trying so hard to follow a particular process, but that process varies such a great deal and itself maybe influenced in a variety of ways not least the atmosphere, the energy, the love within the room, all of these factors are so vitally important, and I know, we are aware of course, that we are extremely fortunate in that whenever the home circle meets then we enjoy the very best of conditions. But those conditions themselves can vary such a great deal. There are so many factors involved, my friends – so many factors.

Everybody talks at once.

J. Hands on my head, thank you.

Dr B. I hope that my voice is now clear to you.

J & others. It is / Very clear now

Dr B. I am so pleased to hear this. As I speak to you now, I have advanced a little way into the room. *(Everybody acknowledges that).* But always there is an uncontrollable urge to be, to rejoin the seat of energy, which is of course our medium and it is like literally being on one end of a very large elastic band. *(quiet acknowledging laughter/ comments from the sitters.)* You know what I mean.

C. I know what you mean Dr Barnett. Thank you, darling. He's got his hands on my head. God bless you.

Dr B. God bless you, my dear.

C. We love you so much, Dr Barnett.

J. We certainly do.

Dr B. That is precisely why we meet so often with a degree success here, because of the amount of love within the room. Raymond you can hear? **(R.** *(v.quietly)* I can) – We are taking vast amounts of energy from you, my friend.

Everybody speaks saying take what you need.

J. He doesn't mind at all. does he, Ann.

A. No not at all. He's got such a fund of energy and such a well known energy it makes it easier doesn't it.

J. Course it does. Yes.

Katie. He's walking in front of me.

Dr B. Of course

A. Thank you, Dr Barnett. Lovely. Patting my head.

K. Thank you Dr Barnett. Tapping my head.

A. Tapping my head.

K. Tapping your head as well. Have we got two people....?

Dr B. Well, my dears, yes there are two souls here.

A. Yes two people, we've got two hands.

K. I have got two hands on my head.

J. Two souls out!

A. And on mine *(others join in)* – Still tapping, tapping, tapping.

Dr B. Ann, my dear, **(A.** Yes, my dear) – there is no purpose in me spelling out to you whose hands are upon your head. **(A.** No, no not at all.)– **(K.** There are two hands on my head now/ **A.** Two hands are tapping on my head) – For they are so familiar to you **(A.** They are indeed) – Wait a moment **(J.** Just a minute) – I must transfer. One moment ...

J. Ok, Ok,.

C. You're all right Dr Barnett, go steady, love.

J. He's there, Ann. **(A.** Yes. Come on my love) – In front of Ann, he is. **(C.** Excellent)

A. Come on sweetheart. ... yes, yes – beautiful, you can do it. **(J.** *whispers* Yes you can) – yes you can.

(We hear slow laboured breathing)

A. I've got a hand tapping my knee, touch – taking my hand. *

J. It's your Tom / **C.** It's Tom

Tom. Ohh... **(A.** Oh, my love.) – Ohh, **(A.** Sweetheart) ohh, **(A.** Well done, my love.) ohh ....**(J.** We love you to bits Tom. / **A.** You are doing so well. It's brilliant) ..I....

A. Yes **(J.** Steady) – Steady, steady.

Chris. Take your time.

A. Too much – the emotion was too much.*

C. The emotion's intense.

W. *(very quietly)* Oh ...it is...   **J.** Is that you Walter?

W. It is folks as you might imagine.

J. Hello. Walter

W. Ok,... Ann, I want you to know this ma'am, (**A.** Yes, Walter) – that it would have been expecting rather too much for Tom to speak in addition to forming into a materialised soul. (**A.** Yes. yes) – Ok.

J. He did well Ann. He did very well, Walter.

W. My, Folks but I tell you this, that I would much rather speak through Stewart.

J. That's what Freda says Walter. *(and everybody comments)*

W. This is darned difficult, folks.

Quite a lot of chat from the sitters follows.

J. You did really well Walter, thank you.

W. Folks, but not for long.

(end of section 27)

* Ann told me later that it all happened so quickly she was unable to tell everyone at the time what Tom had done.

After playing with her hair Tom slid his hand gently down her arm, touching her hand and tapping her knee. He then picked up her left hand and cradling it between his two slim hands with their long fingers, she heard his familiar, emotional, "Oh, oh, oh," as he tried to speak to her. But he could not control the energy needed to hold the form together and, dematerialising, the ectoplasm returned to Stewart in the cabinet.

As Tom's hand left hers, she instantly found a larger hand was holding her outstretched hand. A hand she recognised – Walter's hand – and as he took control, she heard, very quietly, his so familiar accent.

The fact that Walter was also out in the room amazed us all. Was that what Dr Barnett meant when he said "Wait a moment – I must transfer." ? ... Was it so Walter could materialise?

Section 28

Tom materialises again to chat to Ann

Home circle – 15th September 2011. (7 mins 08secs).

Within a few moments of Walter speaking at the end of the previous section, Dr Barnett returned briefly to tell us he needed to begin again and a couple of minutes later we heard a materialised form building by the cabinet.

June. Ok, friends, nice and steady, please.

Ann. He's out again. (**J.** Ok, nice and steady.) – Yes, he's out with us again, isn't he? Well done.

J. Ok, nice and steady, you're very welcome.

Tom. *(quietly)* Oh... (**A.** Yes) – Oh ...Ann!

A. Come on then. Come on, love.

Carol. I know it's exhausting, Tom, but you're doing very well, love.

A. You are doing so well. It's brilliant. Absolutely brilliant.

C. What he's done tonight is amazing.

J. Just talk Tom. You don't have to move.

T. Ann... oh.

J. Ann knows you're here. Don't you?

A. Yes, I do. Come on, my love. It's wonderful.

T. Yes ...*(laboured breathing from beside the cabinet)* – wonderful, Oh.... My love! (**A.** Yes my darling) – if I say nothing else, I ... I want you to know this... that I am ... so settled, so settled. (**A.** Good) – Miss you, miss you.

A. I miss you too.   *(a kiss is heard from Tom)*

C. We do miss you, Tom.

T. It's Wonderful, Wonderful! (**A.** Good. That's lovely.) – Ann, you know I am often with you.

A. I know you are. I think you did something special, didn't you.   **T.** Yes, yes.

A. That was a lovely surprise.   **T.** Yes, yes.

A. Well done, well done, my love. Take care.

(We then heard a thump on the floor)

C. By, he did well tonight.

(Everybody remarked how well he did.)

Katie. Tom talked about that thump. That's the ectoplasm dropping down because they couldn't hold the weight (**A.** That's right, yes) – I remember him saying that. That was excellent Ann, wasn't it?

A. It was really good.   **C.** Hello

K. Hello, someone's running around. I got hands on my head, two hands on my head really, he's really shaking my head and slapping it.

A. And hands on my head too tap, tap, tap.

(Various chatter and comments of 'Well done.')

K. He's got my right hand.

(Dr Barnett was walking round, far from the cabinet, touching people for over 2 minutes. The curtains began to waft again and Stewart came out of trance.)

Stewart *(coughs)*, Oh can you feel the energy?

All – Yes, very powerful.

Jane. *(a circle member).* He's just reached me. He's really touching my head now. It's fantastic, thank you. (**June.** Yea, haven't you had that before, Jane?) – Yes but not so far from the cabinet. Fantastic thank you.

(There is a lot of excited chatter and then heard the curtains moving vigorously.)

Stewart. *(coughs)* Oh! Can anybody feel the energy?

(*June and Carol comment as Stewart goes back into trance and Walter returns.*)

W. Folks let me hear your voices.

C. Ok, Walter. Thank you for that.

R. Working very well tonight, Walter, Yes.

J. Fantastic that, Walter.

K. Absolutely.

J. It was absolutely brilliant, Walter, thank you.

W. Ok, folks we did our best. (*many replies overlap.*) (**J.** Well done.) – You know that for us, the process can be most frustrating. ...Those in ignorance concerning such matters may feel that the process should be simple. it is far from that, Hmm. (**A.** Yes) – The fact that Tom was able to come to you (**A.** Yes) – that in itself is a virtual miracle (**A.** Yes, I understand) – and I think that demonstrates quite clearly the love that he has for you. (**A.** And mine for him) – He made great efforts.

J. He certainly did.

A. It was fantastic, yes.   **W.** Ok.

(end of section 28)

It was a very special evening to have Tom attempt what he had seen and described so many times as happening in his mother's mediumship while he was here on earth.

And the special surprise Ann had had just a week before – a small crystal swan had been moved several inches across the shelf without disturbing the dust. She describes it in full in her book *Harrison Connections: Tom Harrison's Desire to Communicate*[1].

1. *Harrison Connections: Tom Harrison's Desire to Communicate*, ISBN 9781908421111 (Saturday Night Press Publications 2015)

Chapter Sixteen

THE CHRISTMAS TREE SÉANCE

Why a Christmas tree séance?

Because Christmas continues to be a wonderful delight to the children in the spirit world, and they like to play with the toys on the tree.

Christmas tree séances have been enjoyed for many years. I begin this chapter with an excerpt from Tom Harrison's book *Life after Death: Living Proof* describing the special Christmas party sittings their circle (known as the Saturday Night Club) used to hold for the spirit children in the late 1940s and early 1950s.

> *"As a family with five young children we naturally had a Christmas tree each year which we re-decorated especially for these sittings with small inexpensive toys like rattles, cars, aeroplanes, dolls, ships, strings of beads, baubles etc. and always told the spirit children they could remove them from the tree, play with them in the room and take away as many as they wanted — if they could manage it.*
>
> *Needless to say that every year they took us at our word and when the light went on at the end of each sitting, we saw that some of the toys had been removed from the tree and were not in the room. Aunt Agg, (our spirit communicator) told us that the children used to remove them from the tree, play with them on the floor and then dematerialise them to*

take them out of the house. We never knew the exact destination of each toy but were told the spirit children took them to the areas where very poor, deprived children lived and simply rematerialised them alongside such a child, who was overjoyed to find a new plaything – thus sharing joy and happiness in both worlds."

It would be so nice to share such joy and happiness in both worlds and I believe it is something we should do more often.

The Alexander Home Circle has conducted a variety of Christmas tree séances and I have selected one for you here, held at York Spiritualist Centre on Friday 8th December 2006.

Approximately thirty-five sitters sat in two circles and below is a plan showing the position of the cabinet with a wall immediately behind it.

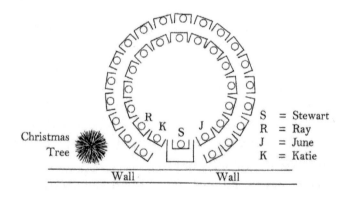

Christmas Tree

Wall   Wall

S = Stewart
R = Ray
J = June
K = Katie

As shown, a decorated Christmas tree was positioned outside the two con-centric circles of chairs. I sat to Stewart's left with June to his right and our circle leader Ray next to me in the inner circle.

All the chairs were touching one another, so nobody would be able to leave their chairs or even make a slight movement without it being noticed. As usual, at a guest séance, a first-time sitter was invited to check the cable ties binding Stewart's wrists to the chair arms and was satisfied that the medium was tightly secured.

The séance took place in an inky black hall and to take any items off the tree without bumping into anybody or knocking anything over would have been impossible. I estimate that the tree was approximately five feet (1.52 metres) away from the cabinet.

Stewart's principle guide White Feather opened the séance before Christopher, through Stewart's trance, sang 'We wish you a Merry Christmas.'

Section 29

White Feather opens the Christmas Tree Séance.

Christmas Tree Séance   8th December 2006. (7min. 16seconds).

White Feather. Once again White Feather is delighted that we have this wonderful opportunity to come amongst you all in this place of great love, where week by week and year by year the work of the Great White Spirit may be experienced and witnessed. Hmm. *(murmurs of agreement)* In this place the barrier between our two worlds so often is removed so that we may be as one together in love and in brotherhood.

June. Thank you, White Feather.

WF. White Feather know that you will all be delighted to hear that the conditions within this place, once again, are truly excellent. *(general sounds of thanks to WF.)* – White Feather and all on this side of life know that tonight we shall truly enjoy and share in a wonderful coming together.

Ray. That's nice, yes.

W.F. Always there is so much to be done. White Feather will pop out now.

June and all. Thank you, White Feather.

(creaking of Stewart's chair is heard)

J. Steady, friends steady. Steady! Steady, come on.

Katie. Take care. /**J.** Come on, take our love, that's it.

Christopher *(in spirit).* Yeah, just keep talking.

All. Oh, we will.

J. We'll do anything for you, Christopher.

Ray. You come in quick, Christopher, there, didn't you, old Wriggle-bottom.   **J.** Come on, sweetheart.

Ch. I'll be with you in a minute

R. Aye, you're wriggling about there. *(continued encouragement from June)* Are you in yet? Are you in, Christopher?

Ch. Well I'm not quite in but I'm not quite out either. *(laughter from the sitters)* (**J.** Oh, right.) I'm kinda in between states. Hahahaha. Yah,yah,yah.

J. Ok. You're getting there.

R. You sound all right to me.

Ch. I'll be with you in a minute.   **J.** Ok.

Ch. I'm just kinda – I'm settling in. I'm getting me feet under the table *(mixture of responses from the sitters)* yah,yah,yah... and I'm composing myself. *(laughter)* It's great, isn't it? (**J.** Lovely.) – I love my job.

R. You do.

Ch. There's a lot of people here tonight.

J. There is. A lot you know too.

Ch. Yah. Everyone will perfectly understand and make wonderful allowances for the fact I'm ... very, very nervous.

Everyone. Awww.   *(Ray laughs.)*

Ch. Ha Ha. Yah. I was laughing myself.

R. You was, wasn't you.

Ch. All right. I want to ask a very personal question. (**R.** Ok.) It's not that kind of personal but I'm being rather nosey tonight. I want to stick my nose in so that I know who's who and what's what and what's going on. (**J.** Ok.) All right. Is there anybody here tonight who hasn't sat with ol .. with Stewart – don't tell him I called him that (**J.** No, don't.) – before? Anybody who hasn't sat with Stewart before?

Many Voices. Yes.

Ch. Bloody 'ell, there's a few *(much laughter)* Yah. Well, I've got to be on my very best behaviour this evening. (**J.** Have you?) – Yea, it's very important so I'm going to speak very good. I'm going to speak very proper. Yea, I'm going to be very elevated.

J. All right, *(and laughter from all)* that sounds good.

Ch. Hahaha! HeHe! You got to laugh, ain't you. (**J.** You have, yes. I can't see it coming off.) – I don't even know what it means. *(laughter)* Hahaha! Well, whatever it is I'm going to be it. (**J.** Right.) – All right, because I've come from the seventh spheeff ... you've got to laugh! Yea, I've come from the seventh sphere.

Many. You haven't?

Ch. Yea. So you can tell how elevated I am. (**J.** Very) – Yea, there's only one problem I haven't a clue where the bloody seventh sphere is. Hahaha. *(laughter)* Yah,yah. I'm moving about a bit. (**J.** You are, aren't you?) – Listen everybody; if I don't keep moving about I'll fall out.

J. You'll be sitting with me then cos I've got hold of your hand.

Ch. Yeah, yeah. Keep a tight grip. (**J.** I am.) – You never

know what is going to happen. (**J.** You don't.) –
Yah,yah, yah. I've been I've been told... Yah, yah, I've
been told that I've got to start this evening, yah yah, in
a manner that is befitting for the occasion. (**J.** Ok. / **All.**
Ohhh!) – I'm bloody good, ain't I? (*much laughter,
including Christopher*) (**J.** Aren't you just.) – I think
so myself. (**J.** Ooo, you are.) – So listen, everybody ...
Yah,yah... all right, so I'm going to sing to everyone.

J. Oh, go on then. That'll be a change.

R. Going to sing! Now this is a first, isn't it?

Many. Yes.

J. No, he used to sing years ago to us.

Ch. A long time ago...

J&R. You did, didn't you. / It is a long time ago.

Ch. On behalf of my world, (**R.** Yes.) – We wish you a
merry Christmas. (**Many.** Awww.) We wish you a
merry merry, merry Christmas. We mess you a merry
very Christmas and a happy new one.. year.

J. (*and many voices with an appreciative sound*) Thank
you. Thank you, darling.

Ch. That was good, wasn't it? I've been practising. (**J.**
Have you... been practising?) – Yeah. Listen, people
who are nervous this evening... Yeah, I know there's
one or two, people who are here for the first time, people
who haven't sat with Stewart, just let me tell you
there's nothing to be nervous about. Nothing to concern
yourself about (**R.** Ok.) – I'm the most frightening
thing that's going to happen tonight, (*laughter*) so after
I've gone it's plain sailing.(*laughter*) Hahaha. Yeah. All
right. Listen everybody, people sometimes don't realise
when they sit with Stewart for the first time but I like
to tell everybody, (**J.** You do.) – I'm the star of the
show ...(**Several voices.** Oh!) when I've gone it's
downhill (*lots of laughter*) so make the most of it.
(*laughter*) – Yah, yah, No, listen everybody, it is

important as everybody knows that you have got to be very relaxed. (**J.** *(quietly)* Yes, it is.) Yah yah yah yah yah.

(end of section 29)

Our next spirit visitor was Walter, who spoke in his usual charming manner through the entranced medium, firstly to the sitters and then to a particular lady whom he invited to sit next to Stewart so that she could participate in the experiment involving the passing of matter-through-matter. Following Walter's successful demonstration, the two trumpets were then used to give a super display of levitation. As the séance was held in a large hall, with a very high ceiling, they travelled further afield than they normally do. One trumpet even reached a sitter who was sitting far away from the cabinet in the outer circle. After they moved gracefully around for about fifteen minutes, Freda controlled Stewart in trance to give astounding evidence of survival to various sitters.

Section 30

Christopher goes to the Christmas Tree.

Christmas Tree Séance – 8th December 2006. (4min. 50seconds).

Listen to Freda as she is interrupted by an excited young Christopher in the spirit world. A lot of joyous laughter was heard from the sitters as they listened to him playing with the toys on the Christmas tree. At one point, you will hear a piercing whistle which made everybody jump, including Freda herself. She amusingly remarked how this was the first occasion in her many years of communicating that she had lost control of Stewart. This section is a wonderful piece of recording, so uplifting with a lot of laughter... Enjoy!

Freda. I'm being pressed by Walter that the energy is such that we must move on. You understand?

Gerald *(a guest sitter).* Perfectly understandable.

Freda. Christopher, just a moment, dear.

June. Is he pushing as well? *(and various indiscernible comments from the sitters)*

F. Christopher if you wish to, then you must do so. I must tell you, dears, that Christopher is anxious to go to the Christmas tree.

J. That's all right, Freda. *(a general 'Awww' from the sitters)* If he wants to. Do you want me to come and sit back there, Freda?

F. No you may stay where you are.

J. All right, Freda. *(quiet murmuring from the sitters)* There's some chocolate on it, Christopher.

F. Who's responsible for the Christmas tree?

Ladies' voices. Jane.

F. Jane dear, (**Jane** *(circle member).* Yes?) – Christopher ... wants to know if he can take something from the tree. *(chuckles, ooos and aaas from the sitters)*

June. Anything. He can take anything.

Jane. He can take anything he likes.

June. He can take anything tell her... him.

Jane. It'll be brilliant.

F. Well, he's smiling ... I have to tell you he's smiling all over his face.

June. Tell him to help himself.

Jane. I'd be very pleased if he did take something.

June. You would wouldn't you, Jane.

(There is the faint tinkling of a bell)

Jane. ... I can hear something.

(A bell is rung louder and louder and there is then the banging of a drumstick, with the bell, lasting almost 10 seconds.)

June. That must be the bell.

F. I have to tell you, dears, I hope you are not finding this in the least boring. *(loud laughter)* – I'm always concerned, dears. I'm always concerned.

Lady's voice. It's quite exciting.

F. He's standing here with such a smile (**June.** Is he?) – You people who are clairvoyant you will be able to see him. Christopher, if you must, then you must. Go ahead, dear.

June. Tell him to take a teddy bear. **Jane.** Chocolates.

June and Jane mixed together. There's all sorts there for him. Just enjoy.

Lady's voice. Bring me a bar of chocolate, Christopher.

*(Out of the quiet there is a shrill, piercing, sound of a whistle blown **very loudly** and after the initial startled sounds of the audience someone shouts 'Oh, lovely,' and erupts into laughter. Everyone is laughing and chatting.)*

June. Well done! That's one of the whistles.

(gales of laughter continue)

Ray. I guess he found a whistle.

June. He found the whistle.

F. Well, I have to tell you, dears, this is the first occasion in many years that I have lost control of Stewart. *(more and more laughter)*

June. *(laughing)* Oh, Christopher, I thought you would have took a chocolate.

F. I think that is enough of that, dears.

(another burst of laughter)

Lady's Voice. That was impressive.

216

Jane. Very impressive.

F. I would not have described it as impressive. *(more laughter)*

June. Poor Freda.   **Katie.** Loud.

F. Yes, loud is the correct words to use. (**Katie.** Yes.) – Loud is the correct word to use ... Yes... Now listen, dears. Now listen,   (**June.** Ok, Freda.) – I'm unable to stay longer...

June. Ok, Freda. / **Sitters.** Awww.

Ray. Well, thank you, Freda.

Many voices. Yes, thank you. *(and many more comments).*

F. It has been a great privilege, dear, it has been a privilege. We understand how ... we... I'm listening, just a moment, dears. (**June.** Ok, Freda.) ... Yes, we understand the nature of our meeting here this evening and allow me to say I'm uncertain whether I shall be able to return again (**Many.** Awww.) – but allow me to say that I wish each and every one of you, as individuals and also in a collective sense, I wish you all the compliments of the season. (**LV.** Thank you and to you. Freda./ Same to you, Freda.) – That is on behalf of my world, dears. (**June and many voices.** Thank you, Bless you.) And when you are enjoying your festivities send a thought to my world.

June and many. Certainly will, Freda.

F. Send a thought to my world. We will ...Yes, I must go, dears. Goodnight to you all.

June. Goodnight. God bless you, Freda. *(and many more comments indecipherable individually.)*

(end of section 30)

Walter now speaks through Stewart in trance and I invite you to then sit back and enjoy 20 minutes of our two-hour long séance, as firstly, the spirit children play with the toys on the Christmas tree, then Dr Barnett materialises, walks round the circle, physically touching and talking to the sitters before walking around again to display his own spirit light.

The final section ends with the medium and his chair being levitated, and you hear Stewart speaking. This is an opportunity for readers to note how different his voice, and character, is from those of the spirit team.

To make it easier to listen to any part of this long sitting, I have divided it into four consecutive shorter sections.

Section 31

The spirit children play with the toys on the tree.

Christmas Tree Séance – 8th December 2006. (6mins)

Walter. Let me tell you what we hope to be able to do now, Hmm.

Ray. Ok, Walter, yes. *(other voices make comments also)*

Walter. In a moment we shall move Stewart back into the cabinet. (**June.** Ok, Walter.) and then Dr Barnett believes that he has...that we have sufficient energy for him to materialise. *(a general buzz of excitement, anticipation – wow!)* But as always we can only promise to do our best. *(there is a sound of a bell being moved by Ray.)* That is all....hmm.

Lady's Voice. That's marvellous.

J. Do you want the other trumpet moving, Walter?

W. Ma'am if you would kindly remove the trumpet.

Ray. Thank you very much, June. Ok, just put it behind, out the way?

W. Ok. (**R.** I'm just going to..) Katie, (**Katie.** Yes, Walter?) I want you if you will to continue to relax. (**K.** Ok, Walter.) You may close both eyes, but leave one open.   *(much laughter from the sitters)*

K. That's funny. Thank you, Walter.

W. June, (**J.** Yes, Walter.) – would you kindly do the same.

J. Yes, I will Walter, no problem.

W. Folks, we shall move Stewart back into the cabinet. (**R.** Ok.) – Raymondo, if we may ask if you would all kindly join together in song so that again we may lift the vibrations.

R. That sounds good, yes. (**A Voice.** A Christmas song.) Something bright, something nice. *(we hear the creaking of Stewart's chair)*

Distant voice. Rudolph, the red nose...

R. Go on then.

(All start to sing 'Rudolph the red-nosed reindeer.' During the singing there are chinking noises like ceramic cups being knocked together, which are the cabinet rings moving close to a microphone. Katie comments that there is wafting of the curtains and the sounds continue intermittently to the end of the song.)

R. Give us another one.   **Sitters.** Jingle Bells, Jingle Bells ...

(The chinking is heard again briefly. Many don't know the words and have to lahlah it.)

J. Eh, it just shows how many know a Christmas carol and it's Christmas! *(general laughter).*

R. Someone is tapping me on the head. (**Sitters.** Ohh!) (**J.** They are?) Yeah, two hands on my head. Thank you, friends. From behind me as well. Yes, I know it's a bit spiky but you'll be all right *(laughter)*. Thank you very much, my friend, yes. Thank you. Still touching my head...thank you very nice, just tapping it gently. Thank you, my friend, lovely, yes, wonderful, thank you, my friend. Lovely, right. Left me alone now. *(ripple of chuckles from the sitters)* Thank you so much.

(Out of the quietness comes the shrill sound of the whistle causing a great deal of laughter and a comment from Ray which cannot be fully heard.)

R. Oh dear me! I hope he hasn't put no coloured dye on my head. *(laughter again)* You never know what he is up to.

Brigitte. Ooo, he's got my hand as well.

R. Is it touching your hand as well?   **Br.** Oh yes.

R. Oh, that's good.

Br. Is it Christopher doing that?   **R.** Possibly, I don't know.

(The whistle is heard again but not so clearly blown or piercing this time, followed by some laughter.)

Man's voice. Losing your strength, I think.

R. I think they are round the Christmas tree, I think.

(A comment is made and Ray answers.)

R. Well it is children playing and there is one over near Brigitte, there.

J. They are children, aren't they Ray.   **Br.** Ohh.

R. Children, yes.   **K.** That's interesting.

(Someone starts to speak but the words are drowned by the whistle sounding again quite gently.)

J. That's nice. *(There is a clunk as something is dropped/ thrown.)*

A lady's voice. It touched my leg. *(and the whistle is blown with 7 short blasts followed by a sustained one increasing in volume. Laughter from the sitters 'Wow!*

Great!' are just two of the comments that can be heard in the general hubbub.)

J. Brilliant, that?

R. I guess you found a toy. *(laughter in response)* Off side!

(Brigitte makes some comment about chocolate.)

R. Well done, friends, keep going.

Dolores. Can you hear that, Ray?   **R.** Yes, I can.

Dolores. Tinkling at tree.

R. They're round the Christmas tree, yes.

J. Can you hear them, Dolores?

D. Yes I can hear them.   **R.** Yes, we can hear them.

(end of section 31)

Section 32

Dr Barnett materialises and walks around touching the sitters.

Christmas Tree séance – 8th December 2006. (5min. 58seconds).

Katie. It's absolutely freezing here.

(A faint hissing noise can be heard.)

June. Oh, Dr Barnett's coming.

Jane. Dr Barnett's ...yes.

June. Hello, Dr Barnett. It's nice to have you with us. You're very welcome.

Ray. Is he out in the circle?

J. He's just here next to me.

R. Good, good. Dr Barnett, yes.

J. Take the energy, Dr Barnett, take the energy. You're very welcome. *(there is the sound of someone trying to speak)* He's at the curtains, Ray.

R. We can hear you, Dr Barnett, yes. Thank you.

J. Just take the energy you need, Dr Barnett.

R. Yes. Anything you'd like to say to us, Dr Barnett?

J. You're very welcome.   **R.** You are.

Dr Barnett. My friends, you can hear my voice?

All. Oh yes. /Beautiful, thank you. *(and many more comments).*

Dr B. Asssss I ssssspeak with you I do so standing at the opening of the curtain. *(many comments including 'Great' from the sitters)* ... I regret that I am unable to say whether I shall be able to ... travel far from the medium.

R. Ok. *(and general comments from the sitters)*

June. We understand.

R. It's Ok.

Dr B. *(appears to draw a long slow breath.)* It is, as always, the weight of the energy which I find so difficult to sustain. *(Understanding comments from the sitters including 'yes it's heavy'.)* May I hear your ... voices. *(there is a sudden burst of sound as everyone answers.)*

R. You're doing very well, Dr Barnett. Wonderful.

J. If he comes out will you keep still and keep your feet under your chair.

R. That's right. If he comes out keep your feet under the chair.   **J.** I think he has, Ray.

Jane. Well done.

R. And he just likes to hear your voices. *(above the general hubbub Ray continues)* Well, if he hears your voices he knows in which direction to come.

(In the general conversation it is difficult to discern much but one lady does say 'It is a pleasure to speak with you. It's lovely to have you here.')

222

Lady's voice. Ray, I'm being touched.

J. You're being touched. So he's come out to you over there. Just keep still.

LV. You've done so well. Well done.

R. Who's he touching?   **J.** Leanne, I think.

R. Leanne.   **J.** Or is he touching Sue...

Sue. It's fantastic.   **J.** Sue.

LV2. Ooo! I'm being touched by Dr Barnett. That's absolutely brilliant. Thank you.

J. Just keep nice and still everybody.

LV2. Thank you so much. He's grasping my hands. Thank you very much indeed. Bless you.

LV3. Dr Barnett, Ooo, you're touching my head. Lovely. *(and she giggles)*

LV. It's beautiful isn't it.

Man's voice. He's touching my head. Thank you, thank you. He's touching my head.

LV4. He's doing so well. Ok,. Oh, lovely, Dr Barnett.

J. Keep talking, so he can hear you. *(and the chatter level, which had been growing quieter, increased and comments are hidden.)*

Brigitte *(guest sitter)***.** Do you want all of us to keep talking?

June. Just everybody keep talking.

Br. For energy, give you energy voices.

June. He needs your voices.

(For the next few seconds there is constant conversation as Dr Barnett continues to move around the circle.)

J. He's back here now.   **R.** My friends ... please.

J. He's back here now.   **Br.** Back in?

J. Back in the cabinet now.

R. Speaking with us again.

223

Dr B. My friends, it is always, regrettably, the weight of the energy which I find so difficult to sustain...

J. Yes. Very difficult, isn't it.

A Lady's Voice. Good of you to try.

(The chinking sounds that were heard earlier are heard again.)

J. Wonderful. Thank you for doing what you have done.

Man's voice. Done extremely well.

J. Extremely well. I do thank him.

(The deep breathy sounds are heard for some seconds, like someone breathing out very slowly.)

J. I don't know what he's doing but he's doing something.

Man's voice. Well done, Dr Barnett. *(and several others join in with thanks)*

Lady's voice. He tried so hard. / **Another.** Fantastic.

Man's voice. We're all very happy. *(The breathy sounds have continued all this time.)*

R. Ok, Dr Barnett. We're all here, Dr Barnett.

Br. Yes, we're still here.

R. I can hear him just at this side of the cabinet.

J. He's just in the cabinet, Ray.

R. He's what, love?   **J.** He's just near the entrance.

R. Near the entrance, yes. I could hear him.

Dr B. I am trying, my friends, to stabilise my form.

R. Oh, I see. *(many other voices reply also)*

Man's voice. His voice is much clearer. *(Several others agree with him but he is standing close to the cabinet microphone.)*

R. If you need the energy, Dr Barnett, please take it.

Ladies' voices. Please take it./ Take as much as you like.

R. Please take whatever energy you need.

Dr B. How I so wish it were quite so simple. *(burst of laughter from the sitters)*

R. Yes. The offer is there

Jane. You're very welcome here.

R. It is just nice to have you with us.

J. It certainly is. *(the breathing sound continues)*

R. I think he's done very well so far. *(replies of agreement from many voices)*

J. Yes 'cos he went quite a way out the cabinet to where Sue is.

R. Yes, he did; he extended it.

Sue. He went much further than me.

Man's voice. He came to me.

R. Well he likes to hear your voices while he's with Stewart.

Man's voice. We are here for you, sir.

(end of section 32)

Section 33

Dr Barnett walks round carrying his spirit light.

Christmas Tree Séance – 8th December 2006. (4min. 07seconds).

Katie. A light.

Ray. Oh, here's the light coming out of the cabinet.

June. He's got the light. *(There is a great buzz of comments from the sitters.)*

R. Can you see the light? (**Many voices.** Yes, yes) *(and much more with everyone speaking at once.)* It is a diffused light. (**Man's voice.** Yes. / **Lady's Voice.** Very good. *(and a lot more murmurs.)*

Dr Barnett. *(quietly)* My friends, ...

R. My friends ... *(said loudly to quieten the voices.)*

Dr B. Are you able to perceive my spiritual light?

All. Yes. *(and then a great sound of mixed comments.)* Aaah! / Well done! /Excellent! / Beautiful! / Thank you so much. / Isn't that lovely? *(this continues for around 16 seconds.)*

Man's voice. Are you holding it, Dr Barnett?

(We hear the breathy hiss again.)

K. He is right in front of me.

R. He's in front of you, yes.

K. He's moving away now.

Man's Voice. Excellent. Well done. ... Excellent.

R. I think he is moving it around so that we can all see it.

J. Yes, that's what he is doing. / **Br.** Well done.

J. Thank you very much, Dr Barnett.

Dr B. Please may I request that you should remain as still as you possibly can.

Many. Yes. / We'll keep still.

R. We'll keep perfectly still, Dr Barnett. Yes. Feet in, perfectly still please. *(The breathy hiss is heard again.)* Ok, Dr Barnett, would you like us to keep talking.

Dr B. Yes. *(Everyone replies and a buzz of chatter starts again.)*

R. It just gives him some sort of direction.

Br. It's out to here, it's on its way.

R. If you get touched, please let us know, yes.

Man's voice. Well done, Doctor.

Br. Well done. Well done. I know you are working hard.

R. Well done, Dr Barnett. Thank you.

LV. *(with a shout of surprise)* Oh! Touched my hair.

R. Touched your hair, that's good. Yes.

Another LV. Good. Come on, friends.

Another LV. He actually picked my hand up and spilled it in to my hand. Thank you.

And another LV. Thank you, Dr Barnett. I can hear you coming closer. Thank you so much. *(One after another can be heard saying 'thank you' amongst other comments.)*

R. Oh, is he coming round the circle, is he? Good. Well done, Dr Barnett. *(The talking continues as requested.)*

Br. Thank you very much indeed. Touching my head now. Thank you very much. Both hands on my head and holding both my hands. Thank you, Dr Barnett. Thank you for your healing. Thank you ever so much.

Man's voice. Thank you. Thank you, Dr Barnett.

R. Oh, That's good.

Voices. He's so strong. / Amazing. / He's got my hand, he has. / Marvellous. *(a chinking sound is heard again)*

J. He's back in the cabinet now.

K. They're wafting like mad.

J. Thank you, Dr Barnett. Thank you very much for that. **R.** Curtains are waffling? **K.** Yes.

LV. Fantastic. Thank you very much.

R. He must have come back into the cabinet.

J. He has, Ray, yes, he has, yes.

(People continue to talk and exclaim how wonderful it has been.)

R. Something else just dropped in the middle of the circle. **Br.** ... my chocolate?

R. Well done, Dr. Barnett. Thank you.

Brigitte. Well done, thank you very much. Fantastic.

(end of section 33)

Section 34

More physical phenomena before Stewart and his chair are levitated.

Christmas Tree séance – 8th December 2006. (3min. 49seconds).

Ray. I wonder what you are doing now, Dr Barnett.

Man's voice. We are still here for you.

Different man's voice. Having a drink, probably!

Katie. Here's the light coming out again.

Man's voice. There's the light again.

(a louder buzz of comments)

R. Is the light coming out again? Yes, there it is.

Many voices. Yes. There it is. / Look at that / Yes it's just faint, smaller than last time. / Quite High, Yes.

K. Light's coming down.

Man's voice. Can see that, Doctor, thank you.

K. It's gone back in the cabinet now.

June. Yes … It's amazing isn't it?

(Someone sings something about light.)

Man's voice. It was very bright at one point.

(There is a light clattering noise which then gets louder and louder as the drumsticks are banged on the table.)

Brigitte. What's that?

J. It's the drumsticks.

(Everyone starts talking and laughing more loudly and the drumsticks bang in rhythm.)

J. Om-tiddly-om-pom – *(and everyone joins in with 'pom-pom'; as the sticks bang out the rhythm on a different surface and the sound changes.)*

R. If we'd had a drum on the Christmas tree he could have played it.

(the chinking sound of the curtain rings is heard again)

Br. Next year.

R. I don't want a fairy on top, I want a drum. *(laughter)*

Br. It was enough with the whistle, I think.

R. Oh yes the whistle, yes.

There is a very light high-pitched tap somewhere.

Man's voice. That's a bang, Christopher.

Br. Yep.

J. He's just tapping Stewart's hand.

R. I don't know why they do that but they do it.

(The breathy sound is heard again.)

J. Ok, Walter. *(but the voice is Dr Barnett's)* Oh, its Dr Barnett. Ok, Dr Barnett.   **R.** Still Dr Barnett, is it?

J. Welcome back, Dr Barnett.

R. Nice to have you back with us, Dr Barnett.

J. Certainly is. *(As people start to make comments June hushes them.)*

Dr Barnett. We have such wonderful energy this evening... (**Voices.** Oh yes. / Brilliant etc.) watch if you will, what we from our world can achieve when souls gather together in love; when we have that vital energy then we can accomplish such a great deal. Watch carefully, my friends.

R. Watch carefully. (**Voices.** All right./ various other murmurs) I shall open my eyes.

(After 2 seconds of silence there is a loud thump which makes people jump and then there is a dragging sound.)

R. Sounds like they are moving the chair.

(There is another louder thump/crash.)

R. Yes, again.

(Stewart starts to cough, having come out of trance.)

R. & J. All right, Stewart?

Stewart. Was it Ok,?

R. Yes, Well it was...

Br. Yes, sort of... *(And there are many other comments and laughter in the midst of which is another heavy thump, presumably of the chair, followed by another.)*

R. We're still carrying on, Stewart.

S. Yes. I can feel my chair's rocking all over.

R. Is it?   *(The bangs increase in rapidity.)*

J. Is it? Yes is, isn't it.

(The banging continues as the chair is rocked backwards and forwards and people speak and laugh.)

S. *(resignedly)* Oh, my god! *(everyone laughs loudly.)*

J. Are you feeling seasick, Stewart?

Lady's Voice. Are they bouncing him then?

R. I don't know what they are doing with him.

S. I'm up in the air.

J. Ooo! He's up in the air! *(laughter and shrieks of amazement)* Can you see his knee tabs, look? Do you see them? *(more and more laughter)* Did you see his knee tabs? *(more indecipherable comments and there is one more loud thump as the chair is brought down to the floor)* Are you all right, Stewart?

S. I really.. hate ...that! *(more and more laughter.)*

(end of section 34)

After Stewart was safely lowered to the ground, it was time for the spirit people to make their farewells, wishing us all the best for Christmas and the New Year. White Feather and Ray, our circle leader, closed the séance and when the lights were switched on, everybody was surprised to find Stewart, (still tied to his chair) in the centre of the circle, (see Diagram A overleaf).

230

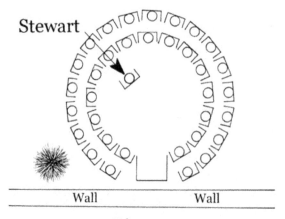

Diagram A

Diagram B shows the position of the toys and chocolates after they had been picked from the tree and left on the floor by the spirit children.

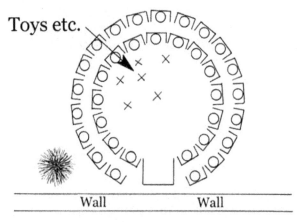

Diagram B

Chapter Seventeen

THE DAY AFTER THE FUNERAL

I would like to begin this chapter with an excerpt from a report by Lew Sutton, a lifelong Spiritualist, retired scientist, and researcher who attended the 'Stewart Alexander and Friends' seminar in October 2006.

His report was published in two spiritualist journals shortly after the event. When I told him of its inclusion in this book he wrote:

> *"Maureen's wonderful but poignant experiences are confirmation of how our loved ones in the Spirit World can be very aware of circumstances that affect us at a deep level. And reciprocally, how our loved ones in spirit can be affected by our own feelings – be they joy or sadness. A strong bond of love is not broken by physical death. Truly, a reminder of how important it is that we try to accept the loss of a loved one so as not to cause them sadness as they progress on their own journey in the Spirit World. Perhaps one of our great challenges that we may face during our soul's journey whilst on Earth."*

Maureen Abrol, who features in Lew's report, was a total stranger to me when I read it. Later, I had the opportunity to speak to her in person. It was then that I learned of the astounding evidence she had received at the séance, which she described to me in some detail.

This is Lew's report:

Séance Contact the Day After Funeral

"It was quite a rush for Mrs Maureen Abrol to travel straight from her father's funeral to attend a weekend physical phenomena seminar booked several months previously. Her determination not to miss the seminar was well rewarded when next day her father communicated during a séance held with physical medium Stewart Alexander. Maureen, who lives near Blackpool, travelled to the funeral and then on to the seminar which commenced late afternoon of the 20th October 2006. The bi-annual event, titled 'Stewart Alexander and Friends' was held as usual on the east coast at the Cober Hill Conference Centre near Scarborough.

Maureen and her friends who attended kept quiet about her father's passing and funeral so as not to prejudice any survival evidence given that weekend. Indeed even her friends didn't know of events at the funeral that were later to provide excellent survival evidence. Coincidentally, I had sat at the same table as Maureen and her three friends at meal times and they gave no clue whatsoever as to what the past few days had entailed.

The *Séance*

How well Maureen's silence paid off when she received outstanding evidence during the séance – verbal evidence complimented by physical phenomena. It was obvious from early on in the séance that our spirit friends had a particular need to communicate with Maureen. Three times she was called forward to sit near the medium. The first was for the now well established 'matter-through-matter' experiment which has been reported several times before.

A lady by the name of Wendy also participated in this experiment before it was Maureen's turn. The second time Maureen was called forward by Freda, one of Stewart's regular spirit communicators. She said 'John', who had been but a short while in her world, eagerly wanted to speak to her. This turned out to be Maureen's father whose funeral she had been to the previous day. Freda then relayed personal evidential messages to her from her father before letting him speak directly to his daughter. Perhaps the most evidential and moving part of the communication was the fact that her father repeatedly apologised to Maureen. He sounded heartbroken as it later transpired that Maureen had apparently been snubbed by family members at the funeral and not invited to the subsequent family gathering.

Facts that Maureen told me were unknown to anyone present as she had not even told her friends. An amazed Freda added at the end of the communication that she had never known anyone make contact so quickly after entering her world.

<u>Materialised Hand Seen</u>

Later Maureen was invited to hold what Stewart's main control Walter Stinson said was the materialised hand of her father, whose funeral she had attended the previous day. Those close by could see, under low red light conditions, a blob of ectoplasm form into a hand that then held and finally tapped Maureen's hand in the same manner as had been her father's habit. His hand then dissolved away. Maureen later told me that she was completely satisfied that it was her father who spoke to her.

Needless to say she was overjoyed with her father's return and very thankful she hadn't cancelled attending the seminar due to the funeral."

When I had the privilege to meet Maureen after the seance, her first words were, "Katie, I wish that I could have told everybody straight after the séance what really happened, but I was too emotional at the time to even think about it."

It was perfectly understandable to me how Maureen felt. Some of the things she told me I considered to be very private and confidential within the family, therefore I would not wish to be too open in respect of such sensitive issues. So, to put it briefly:

Going back some thirty years, it all began with an experience that occurred following her Auntie Alma's funeral. Clive Hudson, the husband of Auntie Alma, invited Maureen to attend Middlesbrough Spiritualist church to gain a better understanding of Spiritualism. During this time, Maureen's stepfather thought Spiritualism was rubbish and he made a firm statement by saying, 'Once you're dead, you're dead.' Maureen, being lovingly close enough to call her stepfather her 'Dad', promised she would not speak about the subject again in front of him or the family, which she subsequently never did.

Her mam, dad and the rest of the family were overjoyed when Maureen and her husband started their first business running a 'bed and breakfast' place in Blackpool. This opened the door for Maureen's parents and family to visit and stay with her for holidays and many a happy time was spent together gathering fond memories. Sadly, one member of the family never visited Blackpool or joined the rest of the family on holiday. Maureen never understood why. They never had any wrong words between them, but this particular member of the family decided to keep away. The gap between Maureen and the lady grew.

Maureen's mam and dad lived in a warden-controlled flat until her mam developed Alzheimer's over a period of eight years. Eventually she had to go into a nursing home. After Maureen's mam passed to spirit, her father stayed in the flat living an independent life. He was set in his ways and could not understand the estrangement between Maureen and the other family member.

The heart-breaking experience was felt after Maureen's father died, because the same family member refused to include her in the funeral speech, acknowledgements etc. The funeral was to be held on Friday 20th October (2006), and her first thought was to cancel her place at the seminar. Fortunately however, Maureen's husband persuaded her to go after the funeral despite the fact that she would be emotionally drained. He told her that it would do her good to get away for the weekend. On the day of the funeral, they drove from Blackpool to Middlesbrough to attend it and then afterwards down the east coast to the conference centre. Maureen met her three friends there and her husband drove back home to Blackpool. As mentioned in Lew Sutton's report; she said nothing about the funeral.

Here are Maureen's own words regarding how she felt when her father communicated at the séance:

"I walked into the séance room and took my seat, but after everyone was seated and the lights went out, I developed a strong sense of spirit around me. It was so strong I felt very hot, my heart was racing, and I had the flutters inside me. I knew then that something could happen. I sent out thoughts to spirit telling them, 'Please don't do anything here as I will not be able to cope.' (I am glad the spirit people took no notice). Later on, when Walter said there was a lady called Maureen sitting on his right-hand side, I knew it was me and I thought, 'Oh my God, what do I do?'

People then started to hold out their hands to help me over the chairs to get to the front. As I climbed over the chairs, I was pleading with the spirit people to keep me composed and not to let me break down and I felt privileged and humbled to be sitting at Walter's side. Walter demonstrated the matter-through-matter experiment. During the experiment Walter told me that Freda would like to talk to me later and his wonderful smooth voice made me feel so relaxed.

I returned to my seat and kept doing some deep breathing exercises to help control my emotional feelings and that also helped me to relax. Later Freda came through Stewart in trance and called out, 'Maureen, who is John, dear?' My heart suddenly started to race again as I told her John was my dad. Freda then asked me to come to the front once again and I clambered over the chairs to sit next to her. Feeling hot, flustered and in awe of what was happening to me, I was still asking spirit to keep me composed, (which I know they did).

As I held Freda's (Stewart's) hand she said, 'There is tremendous emotion here.' – I then knew I had to stay strong for dad to help him come through; I could feel the emotion, it was so strong. Dad managed to come through although he was heartbroken and sobbing. It must have been such an ordeal for him, but dad was strong minded and I said the right words to him to let him hear and see that I was all right. I have let everything go and have moved on and I wanted him to do the same.

I couldn't breakdown myself, as nothing would have been said with us both sobbing. I wanted it to work for dad so that he could be helped. I was getting my strength and support and felt all the love coming towards us both from the people around us in the séance room. I went back to my seat again and kept breathing deeply to control my emotions thinking what a wonderful experience it was to communicate with both my dad and my Gran."

Listen now to Maureen communicating with her father.

Section 35

Maureen's father speaks to her a day after his funeral.

Cober Hill Seminar October 2006. (10min. 24seconds).

This recording starts with Freda talking to both Maureen and Wendy *(another guest sitter)*. After Wendy had taken her leave, Maureen then communicated with her father.

(Some readers may find this recording quite emotional).

Freda. Who is John, dear?

Wendy. John? I can't think.

F. Just a moment then. Just a moment. The lady who came and sat with Walter.

Ray. Maureen. **Maureen.** Yes?

F. Maureen, who is John, dear?

M. I know ... Who? **F.** John.

M. Yes, John's my dad.

F. Just a moment, because he's here.

M. Yes, I know, thank you.

F. He's here, dear. He's here. **M.** Thank you.

F. I want to ask you, is there anyway whatsoever that Stewart would know that your father's name was John? **(M.** No.) No, of course not, dear. Well he's here and he's saying that this will be …Well I can't repeat what he is saying. *(laughter)* But I shall put this into my words, dear. That this is an enormous surprise for you. (**M.** It certainly is.) I know, I know. This is not long. He's been in my world but a short period. Just a moment, dear. Raymond, switch on your light. I wonder, Wendy, if you would kindly return to your place.

Wendy. Yes. Thank you very much, Freda.

F. It is my pleasure, dear. I'm so pleased. I only wish that we'd had the opportunity to speak more but I have this lady's father here and he so desperately wants to speak with her.

Wendy. That's fine. That's fine, thank you so much.

F. Thank you for sitting here, dear.

Wendy. And thank you for inviting me.

F. I shall not forget you. (**W.** I hope not.) I shan't, dear. (**W.** *(laughing)*, Thank you.) – You've done some washing very recently before you left home, dear. Can you hear? (**W.** Yes, it was like a Chinese laundry.) – Yes I know, dear. He's talking about this, he's talking about this and he was laughing like a drain. (**W.** I bet he was.) – He was, dear. (**W.** Thank you.) – Now you may go back to your seat. (**W.** Thank you.) – I wonder if the lady would come and sit here.

Maureen. Yes I will, Freda.

Ray. Careful, until this one gets past.

F. I wonder if I may have your hand, dear?

M. You may, Freda, thank you.

F. I have to tell you, dear, there is tremendous emotion here. (**M.** I know.) – There is tremendous emotion here... This is very... I have to say … He's … saying he was there at the funeral. (**M.** Yes.) – You understand?

M. That was yesterday.

F. It was only yesterday. *(a gasp from the other sitters)* He was there at the funeral (**M.** Yes.) – and he was saying, I have to tell ... I have to tell you, word for word, what he was saying. He's saying that he felt so desperately sorry for everyone. (**M.** Yes.) – You understand, dear? (**M.** I do.) – But he's saying the only way he could think that he can put things right and make this up to everyone; to try to... to try to make amends... you understand dear? (**M.** Yes.) – is to come this evening to you. (**M.** Yes.) – You understand, dear? (**M.** I do, I do.) – I wonder if? ... This is most unusual, he's only just arrived. (**M.** One week.) – I wonder if he will come and speak with you, dear? (**M.** *(hesitantly),* Well.) – Just ... I have to tell you... I'm feeling very emotional myself, (**M.** I am. I am.) – I'm feeling very emotional. I ask you if you will simply welcome your dad? (**M.** I will.) – That is all, dear, that is all. (**M.** I will, I will) – I'm not certain if he will be able to manage it, so ... Just a moment, dear. (**M.** Thank...) – He'll do his best.

M. Thank you.

(There is the sound of a heavy out-breath as the spirit communicator starts to try to speak.)

M. Come on, Dad. You can do it. I know you can, Dad. I know you can do it, Dad.

Dad. Ohhh....   **M.** Yes. Come on, Dad.

Dad. Mau... (**M.** Yes, Dad.) Maur... (**M.** Come on, Dad.) – I ..want .. to ... speak ... my daughter. (**M.** Come on, Dad.) – Is that ... (**M.** I can hear you.) – Is it you? (**M.** It is, Dad. It is.) – I don't know if you can hear. Had to come. (**M.** I know. I can hear you, Dad. I love you.) – Had to come. (**M.** I know.) – Felt ...so... *(sobbing is heard)* (**M.** Hmm ... it's all right Dad. It's OK.) *(Dad sobs.)*

M. It's all right, Dad. It's over now. *(more sobbing)*
You're all right. *(he sobs again)* Don't cry, Dad, please.
... It was all right. *(He continues to cry and Maureen
speaks between his sobbing.)* I know it wasn't nice was
it? .... I know it wasn't. ... Come on, Dad, it's not worth
it, is it?

Dad. If ... my... love ... so sorry.

M. Don't be sorry, Dad. We still love each other, that's
the main thing and me and you know, don't we?

Dad. Yes.

M. Yes. *(He continues to cry with heartbreaking sobs.)*
We do know, Dad, so don't get upset, please. Please
Dad. No worries.

*(There is a gurgling sound as he loses control of the
medium.)*

M. *(very quietly)* God bless you. .... God bless you.

*(Light breathing sounds are heard between Maureen
twice saying 'God bless you' as someone else comes to
speak and a lady's voice is heard calling 'Maureen'.)*

M. Yes.

Gran. Gran. (**M.** Yes.) – It's Gran. (**M.** Hello, Gran.)
Yes (**M.** Yes, hello, Gran.) – I just wanted you to know
I was here for him and met him.

All. Awww. *(in sympathy)*

M. Thank you.

Gran. I've got him. (**M.** Thank you, Gran.) *(now Gran
is crying also)* – I've got him. I've got him. I've got him.
(**M.** Thank you.) – I've got him. (**M.** Lovely.) – Look
after yourself. (**M.** I will and you look after yourselves.)

Gran. I do love you.　　**M.** I know. I love you all.

*(Gran loses her control of the medium and for a brief
second we hear the deeper sound of what must be
Stewart's voice. There is a few seconds pause during*

*which someone says quietly 'Take care, take care' then
Freda speaks again.)*

F. Well! *(breathing sounds are heard again before she
continues)* Well, I have to tell you, dear, (**M.** I know.)
– I think that I'm correct in saying that this is the first
occasion in all these long years that we have had a soul
return in such a short space of time from their passing.

M. That's right, yes, amazing. *(There are many
murmured comments from the other sitters.)*

F. It was so important for him to be here this evening.

M. I know that, I know.

F. He wants you to pass his love to everyone, and his
apologies. (**M.** I will.) – You understand, dear? (**M.**
Yes.) – He's so desperate that you do this (**M.** I will.) –
on his behalf... pass his apologies (**M.** I will.) ... and I
have to tell you something else, dear, (**M.** Yes.) – you
needn't to have sent out the message. He was going to
come regardless. *(general laughter from everyone)*

M. Thank you

F. He heard loud and clear. *(Maureen joins in saying
that with Freda)* (**M.** Thank you.) – But he was going
to come. He was determined.

M. I know. I thank you so much for this.

F. His mind is now at peace and he can now enjoy his
life ... his new life within this new world and I want to
tell you something else, dear. (**M.** Yes?) – I promise you
that I shall ensure that until he settles here I will be at
his side. (**Many voices.** Awww.) – I will do that for
you, dear. (**M.** Thank you, Freda.) ... I will do that for
you.

M. Thank you, so much. Thank you. Bless you. Thank
you.

F. You have a brother, dear?   **M.** I do yes.

F. He's speaking ... He's speak ... Who is Jeff, dear?

M. Jeff? …. Er.

F. Just a moment, I've moved on then. (**M.** You have. I can't think of.. Jeff.) – I've moved on. I've moved on. I have someone's brother here. He's shouting the name of Jeff. I wonder…? Raymond, would you kindly switch on your light. I wonder if you would kindly return to your place, dear (**M.** I will.) – but your father wants me to do this for him (**M.** It is for him.) – in the event that he is unable to return again. He's saying he's doing this not only for you but for them all.

M. It is, thank you very much. Thank you, thank you so much.

(As Maureen is speaking a kissing sound is heard.)

F. That is from him, dear.

A Lady's voice. Awww.

M. Thank you so much. God bless you.

F. Oh, it is my pleasure.

M. Thank you. My privilege. Thank you.

F. Now listen, dears, can you hear.

Ray and everyone. We can / Yes.

F. Now listen, dear, (**M.** Yes) – would you tell the people again and this is so important and I shall explain all in a moment (**M.** Yes.) – Would you tell all of the people here that the medium did not know (**M.** No.) – did not know that your father's name … (**M.** No.) – He did not know. That is all that I wish.

M. Nobody knows in this room that I …

F. That is all that I wish to hear.

M. Nobody knows that I was at my dad's funeral yesterday.

F. You see what is important, dears, what is important is this… You may return to your seat, dear. (**M.** Thank you.) – What is important to us in our world is this, as

Walter said a while ago we want no one to leave here with any doubts in their minds, you understand. Walter, I shall not be a moment, dear.

(end of section 35)

Maureen then told me that she never called her mam and dad by their names. No-one, not even her closest friends knew that her father's name was John, and that in itself is most evidential. She continued:

"I thought that was the end – how wrong I was. Later on, Freda called for me to sit at the front again, I remember my first words were, 'I have just composed myself,' and Freda said, 'Then you will need to compose yourself again in a moment.' I was asked to place my hand on top of the table which was lit up by a low red light. Walter then said, 'I want you, if you will, to welcome your father.' I replied, quietly, 'Yes.'

Then I could see a black blob slowly moving onto the table-top. It moved closer to my hand and stopped. It then started to form into a hand, the little finger came first, (like a bud), then slowly formed into a full finger, then the thumb and in turn each finger was formed until a full hand was in sight. The hand then slowly moved to the top of my hand and dad's hand felt as solid as my own and it was warm. His hand clasped mine, and I knew it was dad's hand, from the feel of it. Then I saw dad's thumb stuck out and his fingernail – it was definitely dad.

I felt so dumb-struck by what I was seeing, I couldn't speak. Everything around me was surreal, I felt so much love coming towards me, and I just wanted to stay there with dad sharing that precious moment."

244

Section 36

Maureen holds her father's materialised spirit hand.

Cober Hill Seminar October 2006. (12min. 47seconds.)

Listen to Walter's calming voice, after Freda leaves, as he materialises his hand, then asks Maureen to welcome her father who then proceeds to show his own hand to his daughter.

Freda. Oh, I have something here which is such a treat. The energy is flowing. Katie, you come and sit back here, dear. (**Katie.** Ok.) – The energy is flowing.

Ray. Oh that's good, *(and lots more jumbled comments from the sitters)* – take some more of mine if you want. *(Katie laughs)*

F. Raymond, Walter is asking for the table to be moved in front of Stewart and would you take everything off the table top ... and would you move the seat in towards the table and we are going to do something in a moment which we believe *(A bell is heard as Ray moves it from the table.)* – will make history in so far as Stewart's mediumship is concerned.

(more noise as things are moved and June says 'Oh, very good.')

F. Keep the light on, Raymond, keep the light on. I want you, if you will ... I want to invite back to sit, facing Stewart at ... the table the lady who sat here whose father has communicated ... Mau ... Maur...

Ray. Maureen.   **Maureen.** Yes.

F. Maureen you never expected to be coming back again quite so soon? (**M.** No.) – Walter would like you at the table, dear. (**M.** Right. I've just composed myself.) – Slowly and very carefully. *(As there are sounds of Maureen's making her way back to the centre* *of the circle Freda speaks very quietly to Katie.)* You are a dear soul, you are a dear soul. (**K.** Thank you. Freda, may I move slightly?) – Of course, dear, move in towards Stewart if you will. We want you to be comfortable. We want you to be comfortable. (**K.** Thank you.) – Yes, Raymond, shine the light, dear, so that the lady can see.

M. Oh I've got it, I've got it, thank you.

F. Move the chair in towards the table.

R. So your knees nearly touching it, in fact. All right?

M. Yes, touching now.

F. Lovely. There we are then.

M. Oh. I've just composed myself.

R. Can I turned the light out now?

F. If you will. ...Then you'll need to compose yourself again in a moment. (**M.** All right.) – Merely place your hand on your knee and we will tell you ... We want to discuss with you all because this is so important (**R.** Ok.) – that you understand, dears. From time to time we have worked now for many, many years in creating, we like to think successfully, various methods of communication and various methods of physical contact. We are, from time to time, able to manipulate the trumpet whilst, as you well know, Raymond, (**R.** Yes.) – Stewart is under total control? (**R.** That's correct, yes.) – This creates extreme difficulties because then we find that we have the greatest problems, the greatest problems in directing the energy. You understand? It begins to dissipate (**R.** Yes.) – and that is why, Maureen, at the present point in time we are unable to have contact with the medium when we proceed with this particular experiment. (**M.** I understand.) – I ask you to accept that. That is all that I can say, that is all that I can say. Now, Raymond, try the light upon the table, try the light upon the table.

Now if the people … outside of the centre circle … if you would like to stand so that you can see the table, you may do so, dears. I'm not guaranteeing that you will be able to see but at least there is a possibility that you will. *(There are sounds of people moving and someone says 'Thank you'.)* Can you see, dears? (**Voices.** Yes, yes.) – Oh, I'm pleased, I'm pleased. Now listen, dears, I am unable …   I am unable to say whether I shall be able to return again this evening because there is still so much to do and Dr Barnett is waiting patiently. (**R.** Oh, lovely.) – So in the event that I am unable to return may I say to you all what a great pleasure and what a great privilege it has been that I … that I've been given this opportunity to come and spend time with you. *(a burst of sound as everyone thanks Freda)* – Goodnight to you all, dears. (**All.** Goodnight Freda – God bless.)

(A few seconds pass and a breathy sound is heard before Walter speaks.)

Walter. Ok.

Ray and many others. Ok, Walter.

Ray. Welcome back, Walter.

Walter. Folks, you can hear my voice? (**All.**   Yes Walter.) Ok–Ok– The lady who sits facing Stewart (**R.**   Maureen.) (**M.**   Yes.) Your name ma'am – Maureen, (**M.** Yes.) – Maureen. Maureen we would like to display to you…the energy you know of as ectoplasm. (**M.** Yes.) – I want you if you will to watch carefully … and then I shall try to create my own etheric hand. Hmm? (**M.** Yes.) – What you are about to witness is the culmination of over forty years of development. (**M.** Wonderful.) – Folks, I hope that at the very least some of you will be able to see. Would you, Raymondo, (**R.** Yes?) – would you kindly keep us informed (**R.** informed, Ok, yes.) – as to what you are able to see …we need to know we are not always certain of our own success.

R. Ok, Walter. Ok, no problem.

(After a few seconds there is a strangled, gurgling sound from Stewart.)

R. Oh. Steady with the medium, steady with the medium. (**June.** Gently!) – I'm watching the table. I can't see anything yet. *(gurgling, masticating sounds continue as the ectoplasm is extracted from Stewart)* – It looks like patches all over it, you know, doesn't it? (**M.** Yes.) – I can see something now coming on to the table *(As other sitters see it they comment.)* – There's like a moving mass (**J. & M.** Yes.) – transparent in places. It's a live energy just moving on top of the table at the moment. (**M.** Yes.) *(The mouth sounds continue.)* – Still there, it is. Yes. I think is that a finger there, yes, (**M.** Yes, there's the.. Ooo.) – they're starting to form the hand now. (**M.** Yes.) (**Man's voice.** Oh, there we go.) – That's it now I can see (*various exclamations as the hand is seen – Oh Yes – two fingers – four.*) (**M.** Yes, Ooo, yes, it's a hand!) – That is Walter's hand. (**M.** Oh, marvellous!) – It's not an 'it', it is Walter's hand. (**M.** Marvellous, bless him).

Walter. Ohh.

R. That was wonderful, that, Walter.

M. Wonderful, that was. Marvellous!

W. Ok.

R. You did very well there.

W. Ma'am, (**M.** Yes.) – I want you if you will to place your right hand upon the table. (**M.** Yes.) – Ma'am, we have a visitor for you. (**M.** Oh right. Is that right, Walter?)

J. It's moving about.   **M.** Open up.

R. Ok. Keep as still as you can, please. (**M.** Hm-hm.)

W. May I ask (**J.** Keep still!) – if you would all – I know that this is difficult… if you would try to remain as still as you possibly can. Hmm? (**M. and other voices** Ok, Ok, Walter.) – There is considerable energy throughout the room. (**R. & M.** Ok.) – Ma'am? (**M.** Yes, Walter.) – I want you if you will to welcome your father. (**M.** Yes, Walter.) (**Many.** Awww.)

M. Yes. Come on, Dad. ...Come on, Dad. Come on, I love you, Dad. ...You know the love's there. *(slow breathing sounds are heard)* – Come on, Dad.

R. There you are you can see it coming on to the table, now.

M. Come on, Dad. (**J.** It's coming forward.) – Come on, we all love you.

R. There's a hand forming (**M.** Yes.) – from it. (**M.** Yes. – We all love you, Dad.) – Is it touching you yet? (**M.** It is. Yes, yes, I can feel you.) – She's got her dad's hand.

M. Yes. God bless you, Dad. (**Many voices.** *(sympathetically)*, Aww!) – He's holding my hand. God bless you, Dad. Thank you. Thank you, Dad.

R. Is he shaking your hand?

M. Yes. He's tapping it now.

R. Oh, he's tapping it.

M. Yes. He would do that. Thank you, Dad.

R. Oh good, good.

M. Thank you. God bless you. God bless you, Dad.

R. It's going back now, that's it.

Walter. I want to tell you ... (**M.** Yes?) – that you are only, I believe the sixth, perhaps the seventh person to make a personal contact in that manner. Hmm.

M. Thank you so much, thank you.

W. It has been my pleasure, but more importantly it has been your father's pleasure.

M. I know it has. I know Dad needed it. (**W.** Ok, Ok.)

R. How fantastic for him.

M. Thank you so much. Thank you so much, Walter.

R. Lovely, Walter, yes.   **M.** Thank you.

W. It is my pleasure, ma'am.

M. I shall never forget this. (**W.** Ok.) – Thank you.

R. Right those who are stood up now can sit down if you will, please. *(Some noise as they sit.)* Once you've sat down, could you keep still, please.

W. Raymondo, (**R.** Yes?) – your light. Ma'am, if you would kindly return to your place.

M. I will. Thank you so much. (**W.** It is my pleasure.) Thank you, thank you so much. God bless.

W. Proceed with caution, ma'am.

M. Yes. Thank you. *(She makes her way back to her seat in the circle.)*

R. I think that was wonderful, Walter. *(Others make comments like 'Beautiful', etc.)*

W. Leave the light on for a moment. (**R.** I will do, Walter.) – Folks, I want to address you all. (**R.** Ok.) – I speak to you all now in a collective sense, but at the same time I speak to you as individuals. Hmm?

R. Ok.   **Many.** Yes, yes, Walter.

R. We're listening, Walter.

W. Whenever we are able to gather together in conditions and in a manner which has been presented to us this evening, hmm, (**R.** Yes.) – then understand that we are always extremely careful to choose, what we hope you will all agree has been, wisely. That we have chosen a soul who desperately required to hear from her loved ones and I know that each of you, singularly, collectively, you will rejoice along with ourselves, with our world, for her.

Many. Yes /Absolutely. ... **W.** Ok.

(end of section 36)

Chapter Eighteen

THE PERFECT STRANGER

On February 2nd 2010, Freda spoke the about my series of books, the original trilogy, and asked that her words be recorded for the publication. As this recording was more than seventeen minutes long I have taken the step of dividing it into two parts.

Section 37

Freda talks about connections, the two teams, and working together.

Home circle – 2nd February 2010. (8min. 43secs).

One never knows what to expect in life. I marvelled at Freda's comments as she explained how Annette, (a perfect stranger) was a connecting link and how we all have a role to play in the scheme of things. Listen to what she has to say in this section.

Freda. (*shouting*). Now, Katie dear, can you hear?

Katie. I can hear you, Freda.

F. I'm shouting so loud – but you see there really is no necessity because Dr Barnett always arranges for Katie to be able to hear. Well, it is so important that she should do so, but you see I cannot rid myself of the habit, Katie, that whenever I speak to you, for some reason, I find myself shouting.

K. Everybody does that.

F. Of course. It's understandable. It's understandable. Now we understand, Katie dear, that you are well on with the final part of your trilogy. (**K.** I am indeed, yes.) – Yes I know. We are very grateful for all the hard work that you have invested into it, dear and we are very pleased with what you have done so far. As we have often said Katie it is a lasting legacy. It is something for you to leave behind, something that in the years ahead long after you have all left the earthly realm will be read by future generations of interested people. That's a wonderful thought isn't it? (**K.** It is a wonderful thought.) – We've done our best to inspire you at all times and we know that it has been extremely difficult for you on occasions but we have done our best to inspire you and we are very pleased with the results. And just remind yourself of this, and perhaps you do not, ... perhaps it does not really occur to you too often, but just remind yourself from time to time, that it was because of your work, Katie, that the connection was made between Gaynor, between Stewart, between the lady in America, Annette, and between the circle, for she was a directing force behind this. You supplied the means and the means were seized upon... (**K.** Thank you.) – by Raymond, by Stewart and then by Annette and that is a very nice thought indeed. (**K.** It is indeed.) – Had you not have written those books, Katie, then the connection, I daresay, would never have been met, it would never have been realised, so you have much ... we have much to be grateful to you for.

Lindsey. Well done. *(Agreement from the rest of the circle).*

F. Well done Katie. (**K.** Thank you.) But it is true, dear and you must remind yourself of that. If it achieves nothing else and it will, it will achieve a great deal but if those books achieve nothing else then you can ask for nothing more than what it has achieved so far for it has been the connecting link.

K. That's lovely. That's a wonderful thread of connection, isn't it...

F. Well it is. I think it is, dear. I know that I am not always eloquent in what I have to say but I think that you all understand.

All. We do./ Oh, yes./ It's lovely.

F. I think so, I think so I think it's a lovely thought and you see, dears, how you all have your individual roles to play. ... My team, my team, as you well know, is White Feather, as the doorkeeper, there is Christopher to enlighten the atmosphere... to lighten the atmosphere, to remove any tension, this is very ... this is vitally important. Of course, there is Walter, with all of his charm, but also with all of his experience and then myself, and I do my best to reunite people from both sides of the divide. Then there is Dr Barnett and we all know that he is responsible for developing the direct voice and the phenomena of materialisation. That is the team in my realm but just as we have our own individual responsibilities, so too do you, each of you, dears, each of you and although we do not always say as much, I can tell you that we are so very grateful to you all. June, you have sat there for so long now... (**June.** Yes, I have, haven't I?) – and we are so appreciative. You, indeed you are, a rock. Just indeed, as Raymond is also, a rock. It is upon you two that the circle revolves. The two of you, the circle revolves around you both and we are grateful. There is Lindsey who so gallantly took her mother's place and I cannot begin to tell you how important you are to this circle, dear, that is wonderful and then we have Jane and Christopher, who are not quite certain why they found themselves travelling week by week such a long distance to be here. Never quite certain – well I can tell you both, dears, that you supply so much energy, vital energy and you fit so well within the circle. And then we have Carol ... she provides a form of energy which indeed is compatible with the form of energy that we extract from Stewart in order to create the phenomena – the physical manifestations, so we are experimenting with her. You see how you all play a key role.

J. We have Denise but we haven't got her at the minute.

F. We have Denise ... but Denise will return when her life enables her to do so, she will return. We understand, dear. We understand. She is well loved in my world. (**J.** She is. We all love her.) – She is well loved. So we have a wonderful team, we have a wonderful team. United. Two teams always as one, always as one. Katie dear. (**K.** Yes, Freda.) –

As you know, and I have said this often before, Raymond has this thing that records our voices. I want you to listen to the words that I have spoken this evening, the words that have been spoken this evening. You see, this small circle ... is so vitally important not only to your world but to my world also, for from this small circle has sprung a channel of communication which has enabled people who visit from time to time to see for themselves, to experience, to witness the great reality of communication between my world and your world. ...

(end of section 37)

After a natural break in the flow of Freda's talk, she went on to say how death was feared by so many people because they lack the knowledge of the continuation of life. She also talked about her world and emphasised why it is so important to create wonderful conditions of tranquillity and harmony.

4

54

Section 38

Freda continues, speaking of the life to come in eternity.

Home Circle – 2nd February 2010. (8min. 42seconds).

Freda. From this circle has sprung the opportunity for
so many people in the past, and I have no doubt many
in the future, to derive solace, to derive great comfort
from the knowledge that their loved ones have survived
death which is so feared within your world. Feared
because of ignorance, ignorance of this great reality, as
Dr Barnett often says, this great reality concerning the
nature of life. This short span of time that you occupy,
your earthly plane, it is but a prelude to what comes
after – after death – that which awaits you all – that to
which you are all travelling from the moment that
you were born into your world. It is here waiting for
you all, but rather than being feared as so many in
your world...do...death is almost unspeakable, it is
unmentionable, it is dreaded by so many, but you see,
in reality...with knowledge comes reassurance,
certainty of what is to follow, that death is the opening
of the door into this wonderful world of eternity, this
wonderful world of ultimate reality.

As we have often said, your world, your world is this
world of illusion; our world is a world of ultimate
reality. That world which will continue on, to take you
forward, to cleanse the spiritual aspect of your nature,
and you will forever, with us all, move towards that
final stage of existence and the final stage of existence,
dears, may be likened to God himself for it is the 'all
pure' state but you will not lose your individual reality,
your own individual personality, your own individual
character, your memories. All that you are now you will
always be but as you travel through life so you will find
that there is more wisdom that will become yours and

what seems important now will be as nothing in the years to come. Once you have made the transition, once you have ... travelled into this world of beauty, of peace and of ultimate love, then you will know, truly, life in all its glory.

(Lindsey thanks Freda, and Katie comments that it was wonderful.)

F. That is what you are all travelling towards. Lindsey dear, death is not to be feared. It is to be welcomed for when it arrives so you will be born into this magnificent world, to once again be together with all those souls that you have loved and cherished upon the earthly plane but who have preceded you into the world of ultimate reality. We are all here waiting for you, dears, all waiting for you. What a wonderful thought.

Jane and others. Thank you, Freda.

F. What a wonderful thought. Now listen, dears. Jane dear, can you hear? **(Jane.** Yes, Freda.) – Now it had been promised to you that this evening we would allow you to feel the various aspects of this vital energy ectoplasm. You will forgive us, dear, you will understand, I think, that we must delay that until a further – a future – occasion.

Jane. Yes. No problem.

F. Well I think that I've spoken well this evening. *(all speak at once congratulating her)* – Well, I have done my best. You see we are all very aware that Katie's work is extremely important, and I know that she so hopes that we may say a few words that she may be able to relay to the readers of her final book and I hope that from what I have said, Katie, that you will be able to take at least something worthwhile.

K. Thank you, Freda. Yes, thank you.

Ray. Thank you, Freda. Wonderful.

F. Oh, it has been a great pleasure for me...

June. It's been wonderful, Freda.

F. – to be able to do this.

R. It's been a pleasure to listen to you.

F. I just wish, dears, I just wish that for a moment I could show you all, this world (**Lindsey.** Oh, that would be lovely.) in which I live. I wish that I could but I am unable to do so. But one day, yes June, one day we shall have the whole of eternity stretching before us.

J. Are we still sat in a field?

Lindsey. In a meadow?

F. Oh, of course. This is where we meet.

J. This is where we meet in the meadow yes, with the trees and the sunlight?

F. Yes indeed. We are all here together. (**J.** Lovely) It's wonderful and you can perhaps understand why it is that many in my world who communicate find such difficulty because in spite of the fact that you create these wonderful conditions in which we can work... you can imagine that for us to leave our 'all pure' state and to come to the earth, to your vibration, to come within these coarser vibrations, is far from simple, far from simple. It is only made possible because of what you yourselves create but nevertheless it is like an island upon your earth, an island of tranquillity and harmony amongst all else that is taking place outside of this room. We often despair, dears. We often despair. Indeed, we would rather not know. (**J.** I don't blame you, Freda.) – But we can together, we can make a difference and we can remove, in the eyes of many who are willing to see for themselves, to listen, ... to listen. For those who are willing to do that then maybe we can make a difference and touch them with this reality. (**J.** Let's hope so / **L.** Mmm.) – And now, dears, I think that I have spoken enough.

R. You've spoken very well. *(and everyone joins in)*

J. We do thank you for that, Freda.

L. Thank my mum again for making such a big effort. (**F.** Of course, of course.) – Fantastic.

F. Well I can tell you she's like the cat that's got the cream just now. (**J.** I bet she is.) – Oh, she is, she's so pleased, as we are all thrilled for her and you also. ... Katie dear. (**K.** Yes.) – Keep up with the good work.

K. I will. Thank you.

F. We are always there at your shoulder, dear.

K. Yes. Thank you. Thank you.

F. Goodnight to you all.

All. Goodnight. Thank you.

(end of section 38)

The circle members would always like to try to help as many people as possible to understand more about the truth as we know it. Although in certain ways we are separate entities, we are at our best when we become united as one harmonious whole, helping to weave the thread of knowledge into a wonderful pattern by thinking of others rather than ourselves. This attracts like-minded spirit people who strive always to help and inspire us to move forward. We are here for each other, – isn't that the (soul) purpose of life?

I think it is.

As you will have read in Chapter 14, Dr Annette Childs, was a perfect stranger to Stewart, but was able to tune into his sister Gaynor and provided outstanding evidence of her survival beyond physical death. It was interesting to hear Freda point out that had it not been for the trilogy, Dr Childs would not have emailed our circle leader Ray asking to purchase the CD. Ray would not have mentioned this to Stewart and Stewart would not have had the inner compulsion to get in touch with her.

Was Gaynor behind all this?

I am sure that she was.

Similarly, Anne-Marie Lewis was a perfect stranger to Maureen Abrol on the day that she walked into Maureen's cafe and sat at a table reading Tom Harrison's book. As Maureen served the food, she happened to glance at the cover photograph and commented: "That's Tom Harrison isn't it?" The link was made.

As mentioned in Chapter 17, Maureen's dad was opposed to Spiritualism, believing that 'Once you're dead, you're dead' and because of this, Maureen had not been able to talk about Spiritualism to him or her family for around thirty years. The Uncle Clive whom Maureen often accompanied when he visited the Middlesbrough Spiritualist church was Tom Harrison's brother-in-law and an occasional visitor to the Harrison home circle known as the 'Saturday Night Club'.

That chance meeting with Anne-Marie led Maureen to book a place at one of Stewart's Cober Hill physical mediumship seminars. Had it not been for 'the perfect stranger', Maureen would not have had that wonderful connection with her dad.

Knowingly or unknowingly, we all have a purpose in life and a role to play and I sincerely hope that this book, a revision and update of the old trilogy, may help to reveal the truth as we know it to be, bringing the comfort and reassurance that we live on after death. It is a lovely feeling to know that we, in both worlds, are here for each other. The spirit people are much closer to us than we think.

Perhaps one day, you may be the perfect stranger, linking that golden thread of knowledge to somebody's life.

If it is meant to be, it will be.

Go with the flow, don't rush and look too hard when seeking reality, because in your own good time, you will come across the truth on your level of understanding. Despite all the human errors, faults, misunderstandings and let-downs you may experience on this earth, learn to override all 'disturbulences', and be at one with yourself.

To find the truth that is right for you, listen to your heart.

Heaven is how you make it.

Part Four

Testimonies of healing and
some 'different' contacts by spirit
through the
Stewart Alexander Circle

For Part 4 recordings listen to Sections 39 to 41 on
www.alexanderproject.bandcamp.com

So far, this book has recorded my personal experiences with the Alexander Circle. Now, here are accounts of other people's experiences, healing and evidence of survival after physical death.

Freda gives evidence from husbands at a guest demonstration in the South of England.
*
Dr Hans Schaer has evidence from an old friend in a private sitting with facts unknown to him.
*
A sitter communicates with her family in the spirit world at a guest séance.
*
A 'Transatlantic Séance Experiment': the spirit team visits the USA and immediately reports back to the home circle in England.
*
The 'Book Test' another extraordinary manifestation by the spirit world.
*
Astounding evidence and spirit healing.
*
Personal testimonies of Dr Barnett bringing healing energies from the spirit world.
*
Freda makes a telephone call.

Chapter Nineteen

FREDA GIVES EVIDENCE

During Stewart's guest demonstration, in November 2000 at a spiritualist church in the South of England, Freda provided evidence from the spirit world. There were over eighty people present and Stewart was a complete stranger to everyone other than his immediate team. The séance lasted almost two hours and included physical phenomena as well as personal evidence. Here is an extract from the evidential communication.

Section 39

Freda provides evidence from spirit.

Guest séance November 2000. (14 min. 40seconds).

Freda. I have someone's husband here. Can you hear my voice?

Circle. Yes, we can hear.

Ray. We can hear you, Freda

F. I have someone hear who says that his name is Ted.

June. Ted? *(A Voice gasps)*

Ray. Anyone accept Ted?   **June.** Who is that?

(someone calls Ola – Ola)

F. Ola dear, You remember when you sat here and Walter was speaking with you and he said then that he knew far more about you than you might imagine but the time was not right then for him to say.... It is my responsibility, dear. It is not for Walter. It is for me and I have your darling husband here, dear. (**Ola.** Thank you) – you can hear my voice? (**Ola.** Yes, thank you) Well we would like to make your evening, this evening, dear. We would like to make your year! Ola dear, your husband is so thrilled. Raymond, I want your light. June, I want you to change places with Ola.

Ola. Thank you

J. Come on, sit in my chair, dear.

Ola. Ok.　　　　**Gaynor.** All right, friend.

F. Your husband would like to speak with you dear. You will understand that this will be far from simple but he will do his best. (**J.** (*aside to Ray*) Do you want this light on?) – Wait a moment. (**Ola.** Yes.)

J. Steady as you go friend, steady / **Ola.** Come on Ted (*Heavy breaths*)　　　**Ola.** Come on Ted

Ray. Come on Ted, come on. This is good.

(*Everyone encourages him with 'Come on Ted'*)

Ted. (*heavy sigh*) Yes. Oh, how wonderful!

Ola. I've been longing to hear you

Ted. Yes, yes, how wonderful, how wonderful. (*crying*). (**A voice.** You're doing well) – I'm always with you. Always ! (**Ola.** Thank you. I know you are.) – Ohh. Give my love to..(gurgle)

June. Oh, he's gone bless him. (**Ola.** Ohh!) – He did well.

Ray. It is so difficult for them

F. Oh, he tried so hard dear. He certainly thinks such a great deal about you. He's saying that he came here and in many ways it was quite a surprise. (**Ola.** Yes.) – He's saying – like many others have said before him – that he did not want to leave, dear, he did not want to leave. (**Ola.** No, I know.) – I want to ask if a chicken means something to you? (**Ola.** A chicken? I don't think so.) – Is there someone here who knows something about a chicken? What a strange thing? (**Ray.** It is isn't it, yes.) – There is dear, and it applies to you. There is something concerning a chicken. (**Ola.** I'm not chicken.) – What is it, dear? (**Ola.** I'm not a chicken I said. I'm not frightened.) – Oh no, I don't mean that. *(laughter from the group)* – No, oh no. I mean the actual animal, dear. There is some connection – there is something to do with a chicken. I'm not certain, I'm not certain... (**Ola.** Oh, I remember) – Well what is it?

Ola. I remember. When we were married – about four years .... my husband went out with some workmates and he got drunk and he lost the chicken. *(much laughter from everyone)* ... and I wasn't very pleased.

F. Then that explains, dear, why, when he said that, he was standing here with such a smile upon his face, saying, tell her about the chicken. Ask her about the chicken then she will know that it is me. (**Ola.** Yes it is. Definitely, definitely./ **Ray.** Good, good) – Well I want to tell you, dear, and I have to be serious for a moment, that your husband has forgotten nothing. His love for you today is as strong as ever it was when he was at your side. (**Ola.** Thank you.) – You must know that, dear. (**Ola.** I do know it.) – You must know that. (**Ola.** Yes. I do know it.) – And he's not in the photograph, dear. There is no point in kissing the photograph. *(laughter)* Do you understand what I'm saying? (**Ola.** Yes, I understand.) – There is no point. He's not there. He's with you whenever you send a thought out to him and he wants you to know how delighted and proud he is of you, dear. (**Ola.** Thank you very much. / **Ray.** Good.) – He's so proud. (**Ola.** He would be, I think.) – Oh, he is dear. It is not a question of he would be, he is dear. He is so delighted. From him to you, dear, I have to do this ... *(sounds of kisses being* *'blown')* (**J.** Ah, lovely) (**Ola.** Thank you.) – Just tell me – have you a small, this is quite a small glass container, this is very small. Two inches by inch and a half. (**Ola.** Yes, yes, yes.) – You know what I mean, dear. (**Ola.** Yes, yes) – It's a small glass receptacle of some kind.

Ola. He used to collect miniatures (**F.** I see) – I've still got it (**F.** I see) – a little bottle of beer. Two..

F. I see, I see, I see. He knows all about that, dear. I'm surprised you never threw it away. (**Ola.** No, no, no, no, no) – Oh I see, keep it as a keepsake. (**Ola.** I've got 150 of them.) – Oh I see, dear. I see, I see, I see (**R.** We could all get drunk.) – Raymond, I want your light, dear. (**Ola.** Thank you very much.) – If you will kindly return to your seat. (**Ola.** Thank you very, very much.) – It is my pleasure dear and when you return home this evening you will now know within your heart and mind that truly your darling husband is always at your side, dear. (**Ola.** Yes, Thank you very much, thank you.) – Thank you dear.

J. Ok, Ola, ... take you back, Take your time, no rush, alright?   **Ola.** Yes, thank you.

F. I want to tell you all something, dears. We have an evening of Teds. Is there someone else here, whose husband is called Ted in my world? No? (**J.** Ted, nobody called Ted?) – I see.

Sitter. An ex. Ex–husband.

F. An ex–husband ? Is he in my world, dear?

Sitter. He certainly is.

F. He's here this evening. Does that surprise you?

Sitter. No, not really.

F. Oh, I see. He's here this evening. He's sending his love. (**S.** Bless him. Thank you.) – He's sending his love, dear. (**S.** Thank you.) – You know what has taken place and what has gone, has truly gone? You know what I'm saying dear? (**Sitter.** I do exactly, yes.) – Have you a daughter,dear? (**S.** Er, Yes, I did have.) – Yes, in my world? (**S.** Yes) – because she is here also. (**S.** Thank you very much.) – is this his daughter? (**S.** Yes, it is.) – yes because they are here together.

S. Thank you. (*she becomes emotional*)

F. They are here together, dear. June, Raymond, I want your light. (**Ray.** Yeah, Ok, Lovely.) – What is your name, dear? (**Sitter.** It's that Sue again.) – It's Sue again. Oh, come and sit here.

J. Come on Sue. We'll put the light on for you.

F. Come and sit here. (**R.** Lovely, lovely) – Give me your hand, dear. Oh yes, oh yes, I remember well. (**Sue.** Do you?) – Oh yes I do. (**Sue.** Thank you.) – I do, I do. These people have come here together (**S.** Yes, I understand that.) – and your daughter has such great love for you, dear. (**S.** Bless her, thank you.) – She has such great love for you. (**S** Thank you.) – Did you realise, did you understand, did you accept and did you appreciate that in her short life there was no one upon the Earth quite like you. (**S.** No I didn't appreciate that.) – Oh you, well I'm here to tell you this evening, dear, because she's telling me. (**S.** Thank you.) – She's saying whatever, *whatever* the situation may have been. You understand what I'm saying? (**S.** Exactly. Yes I know what you mean.) – deep within her heart, dear, (**S.** I know.) – unspoken words, (**S.** Yes thank you.) – and what a great shame, and I speak to you all now, dears. What a great shame it is that very often because we are humans, we find such great difficulty in truly expressing our emotions for a whole variety of reasons and some times we find life can be extremely cruel. We suddenly awaken one day to realise that it is too late. (**S.** Yes. That's right. Exactly. I know what you're saying.) – but listen everything that you have sent to her has reached her. (**S.** Thank you.) – You understand? (**S.** I do, I do, yes.) – everything has reached her, dear. (**S.** Thank you very much.) – she's saying that in the past she has wanted so much to come to you, oh yes, but the time has never been right but this evening perhaps because of all the love and energy available within this room. There is not a mother within this room, dear, that does not feel for you at this moment in time (**S.** Thank you very much.) – and I can say that because I myself, I am a mother also (**S.** Really? Right, thank you.) – Oh yes, oh yes, oh yes. But he is saying that he has her. (**S.** Good.) – Do you understand? (**S.** And that is the way it should be. Yes) – Yes, he has her (**S.** Thank you) – but he is her father and you are her mother. (**S.** that's correct) –nothing will ever change that, dear. (**S.** Bless you, thank you.) – nothing will ever change that. (**S.** Thank you.) –You know that she is always with you, Sue? (**S.** Thank you) – She is always with you. (**S.** Lovely, thank you) Do you know something about a ribbon, dear?

Sue. Doesn't spring to mind at the moment.

F. There is something about a ribbon.

Sue. I used to wear ribbons when I was little and hated them.

F. Let me ask (**S.** Huh, hmm) Do you know someone by the name of Doug, – Douglas or Duggie? (**S.** Yes.) – Is this in my world or is he still in your world? (**S.** In the Earth plane, Earth plane.) – There is some connection here and I'm not certain what this is. Is this someone who you have spoken to? I'm speaking of in recent times. (**S.** er... No, not recently, no.) – No, in the last few months. No? (**S.** No, not really, no.) – Oh I see.

Sue. There may be a Duggie in the spirit world. I've lost contact with him 20 years ago. (**F.** Oh, I see.) – A friend of my father. (**F.** I see, I see) – He was Doug, Duggie.

F. I see, I see, I see. Because you were a pretty little thing, dear (**S.** I was, yes) (*others laugh*) – You still are. Forgive me, forgive me. You still are, dear. (**S.** Oh, you are sweet.) – Oh, well, I suddenly realised what I said. (**S.** Thank you.) – but as a little girl you were extremely pretty (**S.** Was I?) – and one of the recollections that this person has of you, was ribbons in your hair (**S.** Oh, yes.) – This is what it is, dear (**S.** Oh yes, I was young then, much younger, that was it.) – You're still a darling (**S.** *laughs* Thank you.) – So again, when you leave here, Sue, you will know your darling daughter has been for you this evening. (**S.** I certainly will. Thank you.) – Would you know who Helen is, dear? (**S.** I would have called her Helen) – You would? I see. Because that is the name that she has. (**S.** Thank you. I asked that question. Thank you.) – You have. People sometimes tend to forget that very often communication exists upon an emotional level, on a mental level sometimes the unsp.... People do not need to speak, sometimes we are able to receive directly from their minds what they wish to say and yes, Eric is here. (**S.** That's my Dad. Yes he is. (**S.** Thank you. Thank you./ **Ray.** Oh lovely.) – He's here for you this evening. (**S.** Thank you.) – He is here for you this evening. It is him that is speaking of the ribbons, dear. (**S.** Oh he would.) – Yes he's speaking of the ribbons. You were always his little girl, dear. (**S.** Yes I know that.) – You were always his little girl and you still are. (**S.** Oh, I love him. Thank you.) – One day..... One day in the future you will all be together again (**S.** Yes, I know, I know, thank you.) – I think we've had quite a reunion, dears, this evening.

Many voices. Oh yes. We have, we have, thank you. (*laughs of pleasure*)

F. It's been wonderful. Raymond I want your light. Sue dear, if you'd be so kind.....I want to say one further thing. I want to ask. I want to impress this upon people. I understand that people are people. I understand this so I want you Sue, if you will, to announce aloud that everything that you have just been given, by me, that Stewart knew absolutely nothing about it whatsoever.

Sue. No, no, nothing at all. We met briefly two months ago that's all. (**F.** Yes, yes.) – and just shook hands, that's all.

F. Because I would hate for anyone to leave here and think, but perhaps Stewart knew the lady? (**S.** Definitely not.) – He does not, dears. (**Many.** He does not./ No, no.) – He does not. And I'm only saying that because I want you all to realise, to accept and embrace this great truth.

Ray. Yes, yes.

Molly *(a sitter)*. Freda, we've had wonderful evidence from you. (Agreement from others)

F. Oh you are very kind, dear.   (**S.** Molly is kind.)

F. You're very kind. She's a sweet lady (**S.** She's lovely.) (**Molly.** Person!)   – Molly we do, we do appreciate all that you do. You must understand that, dears. (**M.** Ok,Ok) – We appreciate all that you do.

(end of section 39)

Chapter Twenty

DR HANS U. SCHAER IS GIVEN EVIDENCE

Dr Hans Schaer, an investigator from Switzerland, sent me details of a private sitting he had with Stewart on May 22nd 2002. He told me in his letter, "These messages were given far away from Stewart's home circle, on the Island of Ibiza – and since they are so very evidential, I thought you might wish to receive them."

Now with the kind permission of Ulla (George's wife – see below), I am able to include this wonderful piece of spirit contact.

Walter Stinson provided this communication, speaking through the medium in trance. But before you listen to, or read the details of the recording, allow me to give you Hans' description of the evidence in his letter to me of 1st June 2002.

"Walter's comments about the passing of 'George', a dear and close friend of mine, who had passed to the spiritual world only 5 weeks before this sitting took place are even more evidential. George had lived in Ibiza only about a kilometre from my house – and Stewart had briefly met him on his last visit before this, about 2½ years ago. Stewart knew that he had died, but he had no idea that he had a daughter in the spirit world called Sandra – and of course he did not know that she had run a bookstore in Santa Eulalia, (the second biggest town on the Island of Ibiza). George, for various reasons, had indeed been an extremely

*heavy burden on his wife, Ulla, during the last months
of his earthly life and had had a very restless mind.
He knew that his end was near and did not want to
die, because he was afraid that he might be reborn
as a low–level animal. I had many conversations
regarding this subject with George, and I know from
my own experience that Walter was right saying,
"that for the first time in many years his mind is at
peace," – realising now that life continues for him and
that he would not have to come back on the earth as
an insect or a rat as he was somehow afraid of."*

Section 40

Hans receives evidence from an old friend in spirit.

Private sitting – 22nd May 2002. (10min. 30seconds).

Walter. Let us speak as old friends, Hmm?

Hans. Yes, delighted.

W. If there is anything you would like to ask then you
must ask. (**H.** Ok.) – Ok. Incidentally, Hans I am
delighted to tell you also that George has met with his
daughter Sandra. (**H.** Oh, really?) – Oh yes. He has
been around, and he wants his wife to know that he is
well; that he has arrived safely within my world; that
he is now together with Sandra. Hmm? (**H.** She will be
delighted.) – I can also tell you, hmm, that for the first
time in many years he is truly at peace; that his mind,
his very being, is at peace. He is so revitalised within
my world... He is so revitalised within my world. (**H.** I
am delighted to hear that.) – He is well. All is well. He
has merely left behind his old, old body but now he is
living within this world of eternal joy.

H. Was he surprised when he woke up there?

W. Indeed he was. He was even more surprised when

he found himself looking into the face of his darling daughter. (**H.** How nice for him.) – Well he is delighted. The only regret that he has is that he has left behind his darling wife and also that he was towards the end such a burden upon her but he knows (**H.** Yes.)… he hopes that she will understand the frame of his own mind…why he was as he was, Hans. (**H.** Yes.) … Ok. Ok. but she knows that at one time and for many, many years they were as one. (**H.** Yes, yes.) – Ok, ok so he wants and he hopes that you will convey his undying love for his wife, to his wife. (**H.** I undoubtedly will.) – He would be pleased; we should all be most grateful. (**H.** I most certainly will.) – Tell me Hans, would you know if his daughter was involved in some manner with books? (**H.** That's correct.) – Because she is still involved with books. (**H.** Oh, really?) – He is trying to think of something that he can say which will be most evidential for his wife. Her love of books is the same as it was when she was upon the earth.

H. That is very evidential.

W. Yes, she is still involved with books.

H. She had a book store in Santa Eulalia.

W. Oh, I see. I see. Well I cannot think that she still has a book store within my world but she is so interested in books but in a slightly different way to that which she was when she was upon the earth because books are living things. They convey the thoughts of the person who has created them. They contain the thoughts and the feelings, the very essence of the person who has created the book; who has given birth to the book but that within your world is all that you can hope to realise, to feel but in my world it is somewhat different. But no matter. Tell me if she was … Did you know the lady, Hans? (**H.** No I never met her.) – Well I ask only if she was quite slim?

H. Well she suffered from cancer.

W. Yes I know. (**H.** I guess, but I can ask Ulla, George's wife.) – And towards the end before she left the earth it was as of pain to those who loved her, who looked upon her, you understand. (**H.** Yes, I'm sure it was.) – But the cancer is no longer there and has not been there since she left the earth. She is well and he is well and they are together. He has met so many old friends.

H. I am very pleased for him.

W. He has met so many old friends. He has met someone.... I am not able to understand this word but the name begins with W, hmm? Yes. I want his wife to know this also. he has met someone he refers to as W. and I want also to know if a wolf means something. (**H.** A wolf?) – Yes I want to know if wolf means something. (**H.** Yes.) Ok, Ok, but he is well.

H. That's important, that's also important for her.

W. He sends his regards to you Hans, of course.

H. Oh, thank you. Give him my regards please.

W. Oh yes, he knows that. He knows what is taking place today. He knows (**H.** He does know?) Oh, of course!

H. May I play the tape to his wife?

W. Of course, of course we hope that you will. We hope that is some way it will be of some help to her.

H. Well, I'm sure it will.

W. But if ... What is the lady's name? I have met her before. (**H.** Ulla.) – Ulla. Then Ulla, I want you to listen to my voice. I am speaking to her directly now Hans so that when you play this recording she can hear my voice, my words to her. (**H.** Yes.) – Then Ulla listen to what I have to say. I want to reassure you that your husband is well; that your husband today is in a world of eternal love and joy and peace, a world of eternity. He no longer suffers in the way that he did and he sends his apologies to you, if in any way he was, as he knows he was, something of a burden but you will understand he did not realise this at the time. But all that has now gone and he is .... your husband is as you knew him for so long and you have suffered the terrible consequences of bereavement and that is natural, but understand that your husband has merely progressed a little further on the road of life. It is something that all who walk up on the earth will one day do. For no one can live upon the earth for ever and everyone must sooner .... man must one day leave the earth and travel into their new lives, into my world, my world of eternity. You think she will understand these words? (**H.** Oh, she definitely will.) – I'm delighted, I'm delighted. So, Ulla, you must be assured by me, by Walter Stinson, that your husband is so well and he sends his love to you. You must dry your tears and know that all is well and one day in the future, but not for a long time yet, one day in the future he will be there to greet you when you yourself leave the earth and you will be together again, Ulla, there is no doubt. Ok, Ok, Hans I have said enough to Ulla.

H. Yes. That is very encouraging for her and very important for her. I hoped that we would get a sign from George.

W. But we do understand. Hans, we do understand. Even those who call themselves Spiritualists when death occurs and they lose from their side a loved one then it matters nothing as to whether you are a Spiritualist, if you are a Christian or Buddhist. It matters nothing as to what your religion may be, all suffer the pangs of bereavement and that includes Spiritualists. (**H.** Yes, it hits everybody.) – Yes of course it is only natural but then the day invariably comes when the Spiritualist will draw comfort from their knowledge that truly life is eternal.

(end of section 40)

Chapter Twenty–one

GUEST SÉANCE AT BANBURY

On 24th March 2005, a guest séance was held at Jenny's Sanctuary near Banbury in Oxfordshire. The thirty–five people sitting that night witnessed trance communication; living matter passing through solid matter; direct voice; full materialisation and spirit lights.

With Freda's help, one of our guest sitters, Gilly Woolfson, was able to communicate with her people in the spirit world. When Gilly gave me permission to use this recording, she confirmed that Stewart knew absolutely nothing about her family, her friends or her private life.

Section 41

A sitter's communication with her family in spirit.

Guest séance – 24th March 2005. (10min. 27seconds).

Freda. Yes just a moment, dear. I'm sorry. I'm listening to someone who is most insistent. There is someone here who has someone in my world by the name of John. Can I hear a voice. (**Gilly.** Yes) – What is your name, dear? (**Gilly.** Gilly.) – Gilly. Now I ... Just a moment.. Switch on your light, Ray. Are you the Gilly who came here and sat with Walter?

Gilly. I am. I feel I am getting a lot of attention...

F. I thought so, well I want you here, dear. Would you kindly allow Gilly sit in your place, June.

(There is some chatter as places are exchanged)

Ray. Well as I said outside. If they want you they shall get you.

Gilly. Well here we are. Good evening.

F. Gilly dear, I suppose you are starting to feel at home sitting there? (**G.** I am, yes.) – Then give me your hand, dear. Give me your hand. I want you here. Once you were sat with Walter there were numerous souls from my world who were gathering very close to you (**G.** Oh, right.) – and one or two would like to communicate with you this evening. I have a gentleman here by the name of John. He is very insistent of the great love in his heart for you. There is a great deal of emotion here (**G.** Yes.) – and he wants to be allowed to speak with you so I think I am going to stand to one side and allow him to come and talk (**G.** Oh that would be wonderful!) – Now may I say to you dear, may I say that this will be the first occasion that he has ever tried to speak through Stewart, you understand and I will say to you this, it is extremely difficult and we ask you all only to encourage him as much as you … Have you a dog, dear? (**G.** Yes I do.) – Yes, I know. He's talking about the dog, he's talking about the dog. You have a few over here (**G.** Yes) – Yes because he's saying he's got them; it's a menagerie, dear.

G. Yes *(laughing)* I've always had a menagerie.

F. Yes I know and he's taking c... Is your father in my world? (**G.** No, no he isn't.) – Well, just a moment, who is Peter? (**G.** That's my husband.) – It's your husband. because this gentleman here is talking about Peter. (**G.** Yes) – Just a moment, you come and do it yourself. Just a moment. I'm going to allow him to come... He's speaking of your father, dear. Has your father not been well?

(**G.** He is not at all well.) – No, this is what the concern is. The concern is for....and John is saying that everything that can be done is being done. (**G.** Oh, that's good.) – When will you see your father next? (**G.** I'm going down next week.) – Does he understand Spiritualism? (**G.** Yes) – Are you able to talk to him about this dear?

G. Yes, his mother was a spiritualist.

F. I see. She's in my world. (**G.** She is) – because she... was this a lady of about.....I'm not very good with heights 5 foot 5, 5 foot 6, 5 foot 4 – around that height (**G.** About my height.) She's coming forward now, dear. She loved you and she still loves you. Who is Martha, dear? (**G.** That's an aunt, a great aunt.) – She's in my world? (**G.** Yes) – Because she's here also. There's a whole crowd here.

Gilly. (*laughing*) There's so many of them there.

F. They are all coming forward now and there's someone who loves to play draughts. (**G.** Yes.) – There is someone who loved to play draughts and he's brought them tonight and he's shuffling, you understand. (**G.** Yes, I do.) – Yes. Just ... and there is a schoolteacher of yours over here.

G. Oh yes, another great aunt. She....

F. She's here. You know the name of Dobson, dear? (**G.** Yes.) You know the name of Janet. Just a moment this is not you. Who is it here who knows the name of Janet in my world? Is there someone here who knows the name of Janet in my world?

Voice among the sitters. Yes I do.

F. And what is your name, dear? (**Voice.** Anne.) – I want you in a moment. Just a moment.(*speaking to Gilly again*) I have someone who would like to speak with you, just a moment. (*There are gurgling sounds from Stewart as they prepare to speak.*)

June. Encourage him.

Gilly. You are doing really well.

Male Spirit– John. Can you hear? I'm not certain if I should be doing this. Is that you? It's me, John. (**G.** Hello, John.) – I don't know if you can hear my voice.

G. I can hear you very well, very clearly.

John. It is so hard to do this. Listen, I've never stopped. I've never stopped (**G.** You are doing well.) – I've never stopped. I knew you were there. I knew (**G.** Yes) – How are you?

G. I'm fine. I'm so much better for hearing you here.

John. I'm trying so hard. I don't know if you can hear.

G. I can and I love you so much.

John. I've never stopped loving you. (**G.** Oh, that is so lovely.) – I am always with you. (**G.** Yes, I know you are.) – I try to let you know. (**G.** Yes you do) – I expect…How's Peter, how's …..

G. Yes he's alright. Yes, yes he's not too bad at all.

John. Give him my love (**G.** I will) – Tell him I've been, tell him I've been.

Ray. Tell him I've been (**G.** Yes, I will) – by that was good for a first time. **June.** Brilliant.

F. I have to tell you dear. He is here. There is so much love bursting out of him. He is so delighted. Have you a ring of his, dear? (**G.** At home, yes) – Yes. He's talking about the ring. You've held on to it. You've kept it.

G. Yes I have, yes I have.

F. Well he is so proud of you, dear. (**G.** Well that is lovely.) – I can tell you that he is.. so.. proud… of… you. I was going to ask you something rather silly there. (**G.** That's all right) – I was going to say to you – 'Who on earth is Gilly' and it's you, dear. *(a lot of laughter)*

G. It's a fairly silly name. I'm Gillian really.

F. Oh no, it's wonderful. Who is it who had something to do with encyclopedias?

G. Oo! My goodness, that's my father. He used to bind them. (**F.** Yes) – in leather.

F. There is someone here who is saying that he used to work with your father (**G.** Yes.) – and he's mentioning the encyclopedias.

G. That's right I have a set at home.

F. Yes, I know you have. I know you have and this is to demonstrate how close our world is to yours. You understand dear. (**G.** Oh yes, it is.) – It's very, very close. You'll be surprised what we see, dear.

G. Quite worrying actually.

F. Oh no, not at all when the time comes for us to stand to one side.

G. I know and I talk to you all as much as I can.

F. I want to ask would you understand a reference to breaking a ship. (**G.** Yes I do.) – You would understand a reference to breaking a ship?

G. Yes, because my son is to do with all that.

F. I see, I see. Is that Tony, dear?

G. That's the older one. It is the younger one, this is.

F. Well there is someone here talking... Is this your mother's favourite? There's a connection here.... Something to do with Tony.... I'm not certain, I missed this, dear... If I explain, I'm between two worlds. I'm trying so hard to keep control and listen... There's something to do with Tony here and I'm not certain. Is it you that likes black coffee? Is it? (**G.** Yes, yes and he does too.) He does also. (**G.** And his girl friend.) – No, no! just a moment let me do this.

Ray. Don't feed him.

F. I would much prefer to be referred to as a 'she'.

Ray. Yes ... *(words are lost in everyone's laughter.)*

F. I just want to say a word to you, dear and this is meaningful What is this to do with a flap? I want to ask. Your Tony, dear, has he injured his leg (**G.** Yes.) – Has he injured his leg (**G.** Yes) – Well there is something to do with a flap. Is it a flap of steel. What is this? There is something to do with his leg.

G. He had to have a metal piece in it, yes.

F. This is it. There is something. They are talking about this being a flap. The flap had to be placed in there. (**G.** Yes, yes that's right.) – And you may be surprised to hear that when he underwent the operation my world drew very close to him (**G.** Yes) – Very close to him and your mother is... *(some one coughed and covered the words)* – No, I shall leave it there, dear, I shall leave it there.

G. That's wonderful.

F. It is my pleasure, dear.

G. Thank you very much.

F. It is my pleasure. Sometimes, dears, I feel so frustrated because trying to keep control of Stewart's mind to communicate in this way and also at the same time trying to listen to my world is very confusing.

G. Of course. You have done a wonderful job.

F. I've done my best.

June. Thank you, Freda.

G. You've done very well It was wonderful.

F. I've done my best. Raymond, switch on the light.

(end of section 41)

Chapter Twenty–two

THE TRANSATLANTIC SÉANCE EXPERIMENT

This fascinating experiment took place when direct contact was made by our spirit friends from the séance room in Kingston-upon-Hull in Northern England to Oswego in New York State, North America. These two places, so far apart in the material world, were joined together in one thought space – and this is not telepathy! The book test adequately illustrates this.

For over thirty years, Stewart made an exhaustive study of Spiritualism's history – particularly as it relates to physical mediumship. During the late 1980s he made contact with Riley Heagerty who was living in America and, like Stewart, had spent many years researching this subject.

This mutual interest was to result in some years of lively correspondence. However, with respect to what follows, it is important to understand that what passed between them was principally related to their research. Very little of a personal nature ever arose.

In the Autumn of 1994, Riley Heagerty proposed what later became known as the 'Transatlantic Experiment'. He wanted to ascertain whether Stewart's spirit controls could possibly lock into his own vibration, and in order to assist, he sent over to England a lock of his hair and also a small photograph of himself. Stewart's circle – although never having previously attempted such an ambitious experiment – agreed to try, and sent Mr Heagerty a copy of their séance music. Stewart's spirit controls were keen to take part in this and asked that he sit at exactly the same time as the circle in England and play the séance music throughout.

On 1st November 1994, the attempt was made with Mr Heagerty sitting at his home in Oswego, USA, and the circle in their regular séance room in England. Within minutes of the start of the séance, Stewart was controlled by his regular spirit guides and it quickly became clear that the entire proceedings would be concentrated upon this unique experiment. The séance was recorded on cassette tape and a copy of it was despatched to America the following day for Mr Heagerty's analysis.

Two weeks later Stewart and the circle received a detailed report from him. The following March an account of this highly successful experiment was published by two spiritualist journals. What follows is Riley's report in brief, which, in my opinion, illustrates unequivocally that distance is no object to the spirit people.

I feel that this experiment goes a long way towards establishing the independence of the manifesting personalities, Walter Stinson and young Christopher, from the [persona of the] medium. I am satisfied that both demonstrated their own individual intelligence. I take the view that, for posterity and for the great truth of 'Survival', the details of this experiment must be recorded and preserved.

The Noel Riley Heagerty Report

Introduction

Stewart's circle arranged the séance procedure. I sat at 3 o'clock (Eastern American Time) in the afternoon, in dim red light and played the exact musical tape which the circle played as they sat at 8 o'clock [evening](English Time). I then concentrated my thoughts and vibrations upon Walter Stinson, White Feather and young Christopher[1] . That is all I did. I had absolutely no idea, until I received the tape of their sitting that Walter and Christopher actually came to my house.

Stewart and I never once mentioned to each other that the spirit controls would be coming to America. I had more or less expected them to simply take a 'reading' from the lock of hair and the tiny picture. I was absolutely stunned, wondrously so, when I heard the tape; absolutely shocked. There has never been a spiritualist in my sitting room, ever, and I have never described my room to any person on this earth, nor my house, or any of its contents or structure. I have known Stewart for some years. Our interests are in research and physical mediumship. We have shared very little on a personal level outside of our obvious love of physical mediumship.

The Report

First, I must say what a tremendous, mature and powerful circle you have; one shining light in the firmament of reality. Now, let me tell you that, yes indeed, I was sitting right at the exact time as all of you were, right to the minute. I had the international operator give me the exact time and I set my clock accordingly. My thoughts were centred on your circle, your energy and your spirit controls especially. I visualised a white beam of light going from here to there. I had the exact music playing and soft, dim red light throughout.

---

1. Freda and Dr Barnett are not mentioned here, as they were not communicating through the Alexander Circle in 1994.

Core Specifics

Let us now consider Walter and some of the hard core specifics of the experiment. Although I was intending to wait until the end of this report before commenting upon the accuracy of the experiment, I have decided not to do so. Brace yourselves – I would score it almost a clear and complete 100% success. As I listen to the recording once again, I shall translate it and record my comments.

'A large house' – *correct. I live in a very large, pre-civil War house, built in 1847.*

'Five steps up the front door' – *correct.*

'A very large door' – *absolutely correct.*

'Up the stairs we go, a railing' – *correct.*

'Natural wood' – *explicitly correct; the rail and the stairs are pure mahogany.*

'Stairs turn' – *correct.*

'They then continue to go up' – *correct.*

'Home of peace' – *absolutely correct in all regards.*

'We now go along a long corridor, and there are rooms on each side' – *both of which are correct.*

'At the end of the corridor there is a room' – *correct.*

'Walking up to the top of the house' – *absolutely correct. I live in the attic of the house.*

'The richness of the room; several pictures on the wall; a room that is filled with the power of the spirit' – *nothing could be more correct than these statements about this room.*

'Opposite the door, to the right, a desk' – *perfectly correct.*

'Above it are bookshelves' – *correct.*

'To the right, as with the shelf above the desk, is a bookshelf – all being filled with books' – *correct again.*

'A burial ground not far from the house' – *correct.*

'Opposite the door to the left, a window which is covered over' – *this is astonishingly correct.*

'The gentleman sits without shoes' – *correct. (For the experiment absolutely no shoes were worn).*

'An irritation in the right arm' – *On the very day of the experiment I was in our back yard trying to get our snow-blower working. I replaced a spark plug and pulled the rope to start the machine up. With full force my right elbow hit a stack of firewood directly behind me. I thought that I had broken it. As I type this report, (15th November) it still hurts and when I sat for the experiment my elbow was extremely painful.*

'A strange smell in the room' – *correct – the room has a continuous cranberry candle aroma.*

Let me now move on to Christopher's input.

'A big bookcase, lots and lots of books' – *perfectly correct, of course.*

'Third shelf down, 14th book in from the left – a pamphlet and next to this is a book with a torn cover' – *The pamphlet is of all things – 'Visits by Our Friends from the Other Side' – written of course, by Tom Harrison and there is a book with a torn cover next to it.*

(Readers will be interested to hear that the author Tom Harrison should have been sitting with the circle on the night of the experiment but at the last moment was unable to attend.)

Most incredibly, Christopher refers to a drawing of a ship – (A sailing ship – he says) – *and there is a beautiful painting right above my old leather chair of a group of sailboats. If you were to stand back, or better still, stand back and refer to it as a child would, it looks like one ship.*

'**Dogs barking**' *– they are barking all the time over here. There is no doubt in my mind that during the experiment a dog was barking. The four houses that surround my house all have dogs!*

'**The slight step up into the room**' *– This has got to be the floor right in front of my door. Because of the chimney the floor goes up like a hill, and then down again. Amazing indeed.*

This completes my report. The sailboats; the cemetery; the covered window; the bookcases; the Harrison pamphlet; no shoes; the internal details of the house. There is absolutely no getting round the accuracy of this 'Transatlantic Experiment'.

Chapter Twenty–three

THE BOOK TEST

We know that the spirit people are able to communicate in many different ways, most commonly via clairvoyance and clairaudience. However, there is one unique method of communication that cannot be explained in terms of telepathy or mind reading between the medium and the sitter. It is known as a book test.

In 2006, Susan Farrow Topolovac experienced a series of such tests through Stewart's mediumship and in 2007 her report was published in the 'Psychic News'. As editor of the paper at the time these tests took place, she has kindly given me permission to republish her article here on this very interesting subject. Sue writes:

The book test first emerged as a form of evidence through the work of the re-nowned trance medium, Gladys Osborne Leonard (1882-1968). Since that time there have been, as far as I am able to discover, no known examples of this phenomenon occurring through other mediums, save for some tests given through Stewart Alexander in an earlier phase of his mediumship. However, in March 2006 a book test was given to me through Stewart's mediumship, and since then, further tests have been given to sitters in the UK, Switzerland and Spain. This is an exciting development and provides a fascinating insight into the apparent ability of the spirit world to demonstrate discarnate intelligence and, at the same time, disprove telepathy as a possible explanation for the successful tests. As a form of evidence the book test is distinctive in one further respect: it can be subjected to independent validation; it is a matter of factual accuracy (or inaccuracy) and not of individual emotional response to information given.

According to the eminent psychical researcher, Nandor Fodor, the book tests through Gladys Osborne Leonard first began in response to a question from one of her sitters. The trance control did not answer the question in the usual way. Instead, he told the sitter that if he would go home and locate a particular book on a particular shelf, he would find the answer to his question on a given page. The tests which have come through Stewart Alexander's mediumship have followed a similar pattern.

The first of the recent tests – in March 2006 – was given to me by Stewart's guide, Freda Johnson: 'Sue dear, you have a bookcase. Take the second or third shelf from the top. Take the third or fourth book from the left. It has a red cover. Turn to page 84 – a left hand page. Near the bottom of the page there is a full stop. Following it is a reference to either 'fish' or the 'sea'.'

This is what I found: '...walked along the jetty towards the shore. Some man was standing on the jetty, smoking and spitting into the sea.'

This test proved correct in all respects; shelf, book number, page number and text. The cover was multicoloured, predominantly red.

* * * * *

Since that first test, many more have been given to sitters in three different countries. On 24th June 2006, Stewart held a physical séance in Basle, Switzerland. The following account is reproduced by kind permission of a Swiss sitter present on that day:

'Freda conducted a very interesting experiment with me. She told me I should go to my bookshelves and take out the seventh or eighth book from the third shelf, open the book to page 89 or 102 and then read approximately the fifteenth line. I should then find something about a crocodile there or, at any rate, definitely something about an animal with fangs (snappers). She (Freda) wants to bring us the proof that our loved ones from the world of spirit are amongst us and also that they follow what is happening in our lives.

The following day I immediately went to my bookshelves with great expectation. And there are three big bookshelves which could have been the one to look in. In the first set of bookshelves, third shelf, eighth book, page 89, I found a picture of a sleeping tiger!

In the second set of bookshelves, third shelf, seventh book, a further picture of a sleeping tiger. Oddly enough, the first and second books are identical, and are the only books I have ever bought in duplicate.

In the third set of bookshelves, third shelf, eighth book, page 102, I found a picture of a crocodile with his mouth stretched wide open. Freda was correct on all accounts. We were deeply impressed and touched.'

A further test was given to a guest at Stewart's home circle on 17th August 2006. This test is of particular interest in that it relates to a book which the sitter herself has never read. This is her account:

'Freda asked me to go home and check that the third book from the left had gold writing on the binding. She said if I were to look on page 84 or 89, I would find, two-thirds of the way down the page a reference to a dog

or other animals. I checked this out and sure enough there was a book third from the left with gold lettering on the binding, and on page 89, two-thirds of the way down it mentions cattle, sheep and chickens. I have never opened this book before and I find it amazing that this happened. It is wonderful that I have been able to witness this for myself.'

It will be seen from the Swiss test report that the book chosen was of special significance to the sitter – the only book she had ever bought in duplicate.

In my own case, the first book chosen was a copy of Bulgakov's *The Master and Margarita*, the first gift ever given to me by my partner. This was in fact, an English translation of a Russian classic, but it seems that language is no barrier to the spirit world when giving these tests, since my third test, given in July 2006, turned out to relate to a book in an East European language. I have a rudimentary knowledge of this language but am by no means fluent in it and could not possibly have read the book myself. Freda told me that half-way down page 84 I would find a reference to 'wood'. I knew the word for wood but, wishing to be as diligent as possible in carrying out the test, I checked the dictionary before doing so. I discovered that there was an additional word for wood and so scanned the relevant page with both options in mind. It was, inevitably, the one I hadn't known!

Spirit communicators have always been at pains to point out that they can be fallible in such tests; when asked why this should be so, the reply has been that they themselves cannot understand the reason for inaccuracies. In the words of Freda Johnson, 'Sometimes we can be very accurate, dears, but at other times we are dreadful!' It is well documented that there were many wholly inaccurate tests through the mediumship of Mrs Leonard, alongside the plethora of successes. There have been a few unsuccessful book tests in Stewart's séance room too, but, most interestingly, a significant majority of the tests have proved to be successful, whether in whole or in part.

At the time of writing I myself have received a total of six such tests. Of these, three have been accurate in all respects, one accurate in all respects but one (correct book location, correct page, correct words but one missing) and two inaccurate.

In a recent variation on the book test theme, Freda has started to give photograph tests to sitters. The principle is essentially the same as that of the book test: a photograph is described in detail and the sitter must then go home and locate it from the information given. The description offered may include physical characteristics of the person or people in the photograph, the position of individuals in relation to the camera, the location in which it is set or perhaps a particular distinguishing feature such as a building or object.

My own first photograph test was given in these words: 'You have a photograph of his (my partner's) mother. She is facing the camera front on, not in profile. She has dark hair and wears it in a bun. She is a round lady, not slim.' Interestingly, I had never met my partner's mother because she had passed to spirit many years before I met him, and I had seen the photograph in question only once in my life several years earlier. I had to search hard to locate it and was delighted to find Freda's description of it to be accurate.

An even more precise test was given to a sitter in Scotland. The sitter writes:

'At a trance demonstration by Stewart Alexander on Saturday 15th April 2006, Freda, one of his controls, came through with my Grandmother. She asked me to go to a box of photographs and to go to the eighth or ninth one, saying that the photo showed three ladies with hats on.

So, next morning I lifted seven photos out of the box and there, side by side, were photos eight and nine. My Grandmother and two friends were there, complete with hats. They were on a day out.'

The most recent photograph test to date was given to me on 12th October 2006 at Stewart's home circle. Freda said: 'You have a photograph of your boy with no tie, with collar open. This is in a cafe. There is some romantic connection – a wonderful memory.'

This test was spot on in all respects. I took the photo myself in a Coffee Republic cafe and there was most certainly a romantic connection to it – a particularly wonderful memory.

It will be seen from the foregoing examples that a considerable degree of accuracy has been exhibited in the outcome of the tests. It is of course fair to say that no statistical analysis of the results has been undertaken and thus it is not possible to give a precise percentage success/failure rate. However, it can be stated with certainty that the majority of the tests, both book and photograph, have been successful.

At the time of Mrs Leonard's mediumship, there were those who cited telepathy as a possible explanation for the successful tests. In my own view this is a doubtful proposition for two reasons. First, it is hard to conceive of anyone who has every word, punctuation mark and page number of every book they possess, stored away in their short or long term memory, except, conceivably, those rare individuals who have a photographic memory. This would be particularly unlikely in the case of anyone who, like myself, owns many hundreds of books. Second, the tests have often related to a book which has not even been read by the sitter concerned (e.g. the East European language book referred to above), and in these cases the possibility of information being accessed telepathically seems well nigh impossible.

It seems appropriate to conclude this article with a most spectacular (and prophetic) book test, the first ever given through Stewart's mediumship. It occurred almost twenty years ago, well before the advent of Freda Johnson into the Alexander circle. At the time, Stewart and his circle leader Ray Lister were in the habit of travelling once a month to the home of the spiritualist pioneer, writer and medium, Alan Crossley.

He had a wealth of experience in physical mediumship and had formed a group of like-minded people to sit with Stewart in order to develop particular phenomena. This circle became known as 'The Project'.

Alan Crossley had a keen interest in book tests, and out of the blue, one day, Christopher (Stewart's child guide) gave several, many of which proved correct. In the very first of these tests a circle member was directed to a particular book and passage. A month later, at the next meeting, the circle heard the result: the test was completely accurate. And the final word of the passage? FREDA.

Thank you Sue.

Referring back to my introduction at the beginning of this chapter, who could have guessed, when the spirit communicators experimented through Stewart's mediumship with the first ever book test in the late 1980s, that Freda was destined to become a prominent member of our spirit team? Her first communication in the Alexander home circle took place in 1996 – almost ten years, after the name was given in that initial book test. Then it was a further ten years before Freda herself assumed sole responsibility for the book tests.

Until recently, however, no one in the circle had realised that her name had been the final word of the book test – the very first book test all those years earlier. One can only marvel!

This is why, in my opinion, it is so important to keep a record of any evidence given by a medium, even if it does not mean anything at the time. At a later date it may be highly evidential and in that event – just as with book tests – it certainly rules out telepathy or mind-reading as an explanation.

Chapter Twenty–four

ASTOUNDING EVIDENCE AND SPIRIT HEALING.

An unexpected change of events took place during the Stewart Alexander and Friends Seminar held at the Cober Hill Conference Centre in the north of England on the evening of the 31st October 2015.

In the corridor, Stewart's wife sat reading outside the already closed stage door. It was her job to make sure that no-one would inadvertently walk into the theatre, thus disturbing the trance demonstration taking place. Suddenly, the door opened and she was shocked to see Stewart (who appeared to be in a semi-trance state) leave the theatre earlier than expected. For some reason, the demonstration had been unusually cut short. He was accompanied by his two circle members June and Carol who ushered him into one of the nearest bedrooms.

June later told me that as Stewart sat down on the bed, he was thrown back into a deep trance and Freda came through announcing that there was unfinished work. She called for Christine Rae and her son (also called Stewart) to be brought into the room.

Their names were called out to a puzzled audience and everyone including me wondered why they had to quickly, and quietly, leave the theatre.

The next morning, I found myself interviewing Christine in private:

"I thought something had happened to my family"

exclaimed Christine as we commenced our interview, (and I have put the main part of her story in italics).

> *"It was quite a shock to be called out of the theatre. I was taken into one of the bedrooms and found Stewart still in trance, Freda spoke through him and asked me to sit beside her which I did, and she held my hand saying that she had unfinished work and that they had to close the trance demonstration in the theatre early because what she was about to tell me was too private."*

I discovered that it was indeed a very private message because only she and her son knew what happened in April 2015, and emotion welled up as Christine began to tell me her story.

"I want people to know about this," she said, as she started to sob a little.

I did my best to console her, asking her to relax, take it easy and to take her time. She paused to compose herself in order to continue her story:

> *"Dr Barnett then came through and told me that he had been with us at the operation.*
>
> *Last April I was taken into hospital for an operation on my spine and I had had the pre-med and was all dressed and prepared and my son and I had said our goodbyes before I was wheeled into the theatre.*
>
> *I saw the surgeon in his green robes walk up to me and he held my hand and said, 'I am so sorry, I can't do this operation, I have been up since 5am looking at your scan and I cannot say that you will walk again if I do this operation on your spine. The nerve is wrapped round your seventh vertebra, I have looked at it from different angles and I would have to take out the seventh, sixth and eighth vertebrae.I would have to free a nerve that must never be touched. I cannot*

warrant that I will not touch it, all I can say is this, that if the pain returns and it is so unbearable – then I will operate on it.'

I was reduced to tears as he kept on saying 'I am awfully sorry, but I cannot do this.' He was ever so nice. He finished off by saying, 'You walked into this hospital, but you cannot expect to walk out after the operation, you could be in a wheelchair for the rest of your life.'

I was then taken back into the small room and as I was given a piece of toast and a cup of tea, I felt a strong awareness of Dr Barnett and began to wonder if it was me or if it was real because I was in a right state of shock and as they had given me the pre-med I couldn't go home, the only way I could get back home was by taxi and that would have cost me £25.

Nobody knew what happened but my son and me.

Everything had been set up; my son had arranged to take time off work and you can imagine how I felt."

"So only you and your son knew about this and Stewart Alexander did not know?"

"Yes, – only me and my son knew. A few hours before the trance demonstration, I was in the conservatory when Stewart Alexander asked how I was and I said it was quite a long story. At that moment Stewart started to sway a little bit and he said they have never let this happen before – as the spirit people were about to take control, he was getting taken over and he commented that this doesn't normally happen, in fact, this has never ever happened – it is quite unusual. I came away crying and thinking, 'What is going on?'

I so wanted to get Stewart on his own because I hadn't yet told him about my operation.

Going back to the unfinished work on Saturday night, Dr Barnett talked about the operation and he was telling me things that I knew Stewart would not know. Dr Barnett then said, 'I've got somebody here who wants to talk to you'. He brought my father and in fairness I have to say that my father never bothered with me, I only saw him five times during my whole entire life. After I was born, he just went away, but I am still his daughter. Dr Barnett brought my dad so that he could say sorry. Nobody knew about that.

The other thing that dad brought up was an incident with a pan that happened in my house. I was making rhubarb jelly and when I lifted the pan, the handle came off and the hot rhubarb jelly was spilt all over the floor. I tried to walk and went full length onto the floor and in doing so I screamed out for my son, he rushed down and also slipped full length onto the floor. Nobody could have known that and dad said that he had been there and that he was looking after us. When my son heard this message, he started to cry because he realised that it was valid evidence of survival. No-body knew of that incident but the two of us.

Dr Barnett then took control and as Stewart (still in trance) stood up, his hands went right up and down my spine feeling each vertebra and then at the bottom of my neck concentrated on the seventh and (the sixth in particular) vertebra, − this is the one that is untouchable, I would not let anyone massage my neck now.

Dr Barnett said that he will do healing on the seventh and eighth vertebra every night and when he told me that the nerve has found a place, a small place where it is comfortable, I suddenly realised that what Dr Barnett said was almost exactly what the surgeon told me. The surgeon said, 'I don't know how you get away with all this, it must have found a comfortable twist.'

> *In the twist it is obviously comfortable enough, and if ever the pain was unbearable I have got to phone the hospital and they will operate on me straight away. I also have to tell you this, a medium at a spiritualist church told me that I was going to have an operation and that he sees a wheelchair. I asked him to stop and said that what he told me was irresponsible; his message affected me so much that it was on my mind as I walked through the doors of the hospital."*

Was there a purpose for this and a reason I wondered as Christine carried on talking?

Christine broke down as she continued:

> *"After being told about the cancellation at the hospital, I went to my bed.*
>
> *The sister of the ward saw me on the bed and said, 'What are you doing here?' I told her that the surgeon had decided at the last minute not to operate on me. The sister then said, 'I have never known that before, I have never ever known that before.' As all this was going on, I felt that Dr Barnett must have stopped the operation, because I do not believe to this minute that the surgeon would take me all that way to the point of cancelling."*

Christine was now very emotional, and as the interview finished, I realised now the reason – and the purpose – why Christine was brought out away from the audience at that large trance demonstration. With so much emotion, she simply would not have coped on the stage.

I take my hat off to her because at the end of the seminar, she bravely plucked up the courage to go on the stage and tell the delegates what had happened and why.

So it would appear that our spirit friends plan things in advance. Freda told us at the trance demonstration that there were so many souls there – it was like a football ground. It did make me wonder how Freda could manage with such a multitude in the spirit world. I guess any deceased loved one in spirit would naturally want to communicate at the very first opportunity.

There is a purpose and a reason for helping souls with a greater need than others and what better way than to end this chapter with a letter sent after the seminar to our circle leader Ray and June Lister from one of the delegates.

Hi Ray and June

I thought the séance was absolutely amazing and love it that we still hear from White Feather, Christopher and Walter. I have always had a soft spot for Freda and just love her voice. She is such a lady!

The evidence was spectacular on Saturday, but you know what made it even better was when I heard about Christine and her son having a one to one with Freda after the séance had ended. That brought home to me how spirit are mindful of our privacy and knew that Christine would have found it very difficult to have her personal private life opened up in public. I think that was truly wonderful. I can't stop thinking about it.

Chapter Twenty–five

FURTHER TESTIMONIES OF SPIRIT HEALING

In this chapter I give you a few testimonies written by more sitters who were privileged to receive spiritual healing direct from Dr Barnett after he materialised and walked out of the cabinet.

Tom Harrison

"My wife Ann and I were on a brief visit to the UK from our home in Spain to see my specialist[1]. On Tuesday 23rd November 2004, I was extremely privileged to receive a 'hands on' healing session from the spirit gentleman then known as 'Vanguard'. All the sitters clearly heard his voice at normal head height from in front of the cabinet curtain. We then heard his footsteps as he moved his materialised body away from the cabinet. I 'sensed' he was standing in front of me and within a few seconds was thrilled to feel his large warm hands being placed on mine which were resting on my knees. He then moved his hands up on to my shoulders. He removed his hands and in a quiet but clear voice asked me to stand up and turn round to receive some healing for my health problem.

The back of my chair was touching the wall behind me and Dr Barnett (Vanguard) asked me to move the chair so I could face the wall and press against it. He then asked Ann to steady me by holding my left arm.

---

1. Three months earlier Tom had been diagnosed as having Parkinson's disease

As I stood there, I felt his strong hands firmly pressed on to my shoulders for about half a minute. Slowly his hands moved down my back to waist level, before moving upwards slowly to my shoulders again for about another minute or so. During all this period of about three or four minutes, I could feel and hear his breathing behind me and felt a very calming influence. It was an extremely interesting and unique experience.

As he was finishing he asked me, that when I 'retired' on a Tuesday night, to send out my thoughts to him and he would continue the healing process. I am sure this has continued for the past four months and my condition is progressively improving. I now feel better than I have felt for at least two years. Tuesday nights continue to be very important and special for me.

My grateful thanks to Dr Barnett (Vanguard) and the band of spirit healers."

Ernie Crone

"On Thursday 9th September 2004 I was privileged to sit with a group of friends in Stewart Alexander's circle. In June of that year, I had been visiting my son in Milton Keynes with my wife Rose and had been taken into hospital. I spent thirteen days in hospital and was discharged, but still on medication. During the sitting Dr Barnett, (Vanguard) visited the circle and told me I was not in good health, and that he would help me if I wished, to which I agreed. I was sitting about five feet from the medium, (Stewart), who was secured in his chair.

I felt a presence and then felt two hands on my shoulder; they stayed there for about a minute and then moved to my stomach area and started to vibrate. This lasted for about 30-40 seconds after which they returned to my shoulders. These hands were warm and large. Another gentleman in the circle was also given healing before the Doctor returned to the cabinet.

I had an appointment to see a Consultant Gastroenterologist about a week later. I was able to cancel this appointment because my stomach and bowel symptoms had improved so much.

Thanks to Dr Barnett (Vanguard) and his spirit healers I am now back to some sort of normality. (whatever that is?)."

Alan Player

"I am a hairdresser operating a very busy salon in Wells-next-the-Sea in Norfolk and I have been privileged to have taken part in several of Stewart Alexander's séance circles at June and Alf Winchester's home in Norfolk.

For a week I had battled on at a salon-chair suffering from one of my attacks of sciatica in the lower part of my back and I was all for not attending a séance on the 14th October 2004. As an afterthought, I had a feeling that maybe sitting in the séance and in the power of spirit, I might receive some kind of help. I decided to go, and with the help of some pillows on my chair, I sat through the séance.

As is usual, we had all the amazing and wondrous phenomena and I felt so glad I had made the effort. Towards the end of the séance, I was subjected to an amazing healing act which I will never forget and which I can quite honestly say did exactly what was needed.

Don't ever think that the touch of a spirit person in a situation such as this is a cold icy touch as I will tell you here and now, it most certainly is not, because I always thought that, and up to the evening in question I thought and believed exactly that.

I was asked to stand and a spirit being came and

gave me healing; my thoughts and fears raced through my mind, but as Dr Barnett (Vanguard) shuffled towards me and got closer to where I was standing, I felt this wonderful feeling of love and warmth. As I embraced this wonderful spirit person's energy, my fears completely melted away.

When Dr Barnett (Vanguard) was standing close to me, the feeling was that of a huge spirit being, he felt so enormous. The other sensation I had was that of standing under a shower, a feeling of a white light showering down, over and through me.

Dr Barnett (Vanguard) spoke with a tremble in his voice. I was so in awe of his powerful energy and because of his complete warm calming influence, I could not quite hear what he said to me. As his warm hands rested on my shoulders and then moved up and down my spine, I knew and felt that I was in the wonderful presence of a powerful and yet gentle loving spirit being.

I felt quite re-assured and comforted and will never forget that wonderful and most valuable experience of the power and love of spirit materialisation. The healing touch was as real as the touch of a human being. Thank you, Vanguard for the privilege of that healing and also for the chance to pass this on to others.

On a final note, may I mention that I rested from the duties of the salon for one week, which is hard for me as I don't normally give in. The spirit people most certainly helped me to relax and my sciatica has not returned since."

Here is an excerpt from a further letter from Alan conveying details of another séance he attended on Saturday 23rd July 2005 at Cromer.

"As we reached the part involving spirit materialisation, Dr Barnett moved around and asked how my back had been since his healing. I was deeply touched by the wonderful presence of this Being, so gentle, so full of love and compassion. He said he was very pleased to be working with me and I returned the gesture by saying how much of a privilege it was to receive such a personal message and to know how very much aware Dr Barnett was regarding myself. Further to this, he came over and with his large powerful hands, shook my hands several times up and down, then placed his hands upon my head. I gave Dr Barnett my blessing, thinking how very special this soul is."

Stephanie Lees

"I have suffered from a damaged back (which caused me to have sciatica) for some years and in December 2003, I was told that I would be required to have a back operation in eighteen months.

Through meeting Cathy Hirst at Stanstead Hall when we were at a course for self-hypnosis, I had been introduced to York Spiritualist Centre and subsequently my partner, Graham and myself were invited to a séance with Stewart.

After various people had been introduced through Stewart's wonderful trance, Dr Barnett came from the cabinet and walked around the inner circle of guests. As he approached our seats, I was hoping that he would stop in front of us. Cathy was sitting on my left side and Graham to my right. I suddenly felt gentle hands on each side of my head and my hair being stroked. Then Cathy's right hand and Graham's left hand were picked up together with both of my hands and Dr Barnett said, 'God bless you.' We were thrilled to experience the firm warm touch, but also to hear so clearly his voice.

Following this wonderful confirmation of the Doctor's presence, I have found that the back pain which I have had for some years had disappeared. Whilst I had required frequent painkillers prior to the Doctor's visit, I now, some months later (and despite even six hours gardening at times!), very seldom need to have even mild painkillers. It is now eighteen months since I was told that I would need an operation and in my present condition I would not consider that to be necessary."

Ken Wood

"On Thursday 9th September 2004, my wife, Jacqui, and I were privileged to sit with a group of friends in Stewart Alexander's circle.

I had been ill for ten days prior to this date and my doctor's diagnosis was a virus which included symptoms of a very high temperature and severe diarrhoea. Within the previous seven days before attending Stewart's circle I had lost 7 pounds in weight and having taken the maximum medication from my GP, I was told that the next step would be hospital. I asked my GP to give me another three days as I was due to go to Stewart's circle. I felt I had to go, even though I wasn't sure I would get there.

We stayed overnight in Hull and I spent the afternoon in bed before attending the circle in the evening. When we arrived for the séance, I sat close to Stewart, who was secured to his chair in the cabinet. During the sitting, Dr Barnett, (also known as the Vanguard), materialised and gave myself and another gentleman healing. He took my hands into his hands for 40 to 60 seconds and a warm glow, full of peace and calm, flooded throughout my body. When Dr Barnett returned to the cabinet, the calm stayed with me and upon returning home I felt so much better. The symptoms subsided and my GP was pleased to see I was well again.

Thank you Dr Barnett, I have not had any illness since. Love to all our spirit friends."

Judith Cottle

"I have known and loved both Stewart and his wife, Sue, for many years and have the utmost confidence in his work and love for spirit. I have sat in his séances on many occasions, both in his home circle and at various other séances around the country. I now sit and hold his strapped-in hands each time he visits the Sanctuary at June and Alf Winchester's home in Norfolk, where I now also live.

About seven years ago, I was diagnosed with Osteoporosis, after my spine was fractured in six places.

Some years ago the voice of Dr Barnett which emanates from beside Stewart, became much stronger, and when asked what he was to be called, he said he was the 'Vanguard' for all who worked behind the scenes in spirit. We called him 'Vanguard' until he was confirmed as Dr Barnett.

He asked that my chair should be put in front of the cabinet so that he could work on my back. Each time we sat in these séances, he called me to have healing in this way until the last time, when he asked me to stand. His hands, much larger than Stewart's own, vibrated up and down my spine.

The heat and power were tremendous and my Consultant, after I had my last "Dexa" scan, said that the bone density was certainly improving. I still wear the morphine patches and take my weekly medication, but the pain I used to suffer has subsided a great deal, and this is due, in no small measure, from the help and healing received from this wonderful doctor and his friends in spirit.

I have now papered and painted one of the rooms in my house and have worked very strenuously in my garden. Without this healing on me by Dr Barnett, I know that my condition would have deteriorated, and I thank this beautiful soul for this continuing progress."

Chapter Twenty–six

FREDA USES THE TELEPHONE

Alf and June Winchester have been friends of Stewart's for more than 30 years and have organised the 'Stewart Alexander and Friends' bi-annual seminars at Cober Hill for eighteen years. Although they live in Norfolk (about 151 miles or 243 km from Hull), they remain in close contact with not only the Alexander Home Circle, but with the spirit team as well.

As Alf and June are too far away to attend the weekly home circle in Hull, the spirit team (especially Freda) would often ask Raymondo to record and pass on messages to them, and June has some interesting spirit connections to report.

Freda uses the Telephone

One day, in the circle, it was suggested that they try an experiment. The circle wondered if it would be possible for Freda to speak through Stewart in trance and talk directly to June via the telephone. A phone would be placed just outside the door of the séance room. When the time came for Freda to talk to June, Stewart would remain in trance while a member of the circle would bring the telephone inside and dial the Norfolk number. June would be on standby to pick up her receiver.

The experiment was successful. With the telephone on speaker mode, the circle was able to listen to June and

Freda talking to each other, as in a normal phone-call.

This is what June had to say about the experience:

"*Speaking directly with Freda over the telephone is no different from speaking with a close friend, and she seems excited to be able to chat. I always feel so happy to hear her voice. She phoned on one occasion to thank me for asking Stewart to give a special trance demonstration at one of our seminars because it would give her priority to reunite people with their loved ones. On that occasion, Walter spoke to me first and said I had made someone very happy, before Freda came and thanked me. She was so delighted to have a special slot in the programme to be able to have more time for her unique reunions.*"

The Power of Thought

Another connection June made with Freda was, this time, using the power of thought concerning her father:

"*In 2001 my father came to live with us and had a number of mini strokes until he was unable to speak or move. The only way I could make him comfortable or really care for him was to say, "If the answer is yes Dad, close your eyes." "Are you hungry?", "Are you tired?", and that is how we managed.*

When he became very frail, I needed to be with him constantly but had a part time job at Cromer Hospital (ward hostess). I felt I should resign, but we needed the money. I really didn't know what to do.

One Tuesday, as I took our dogs out for a walk, I asked Freda for advice. As I walked back home, I decided to write giving in my notice. But as I posted it I wondered if I had made the right decision.

That evening, the circle sat at Raymondo's house"

in Hull. At about 10.30 pm, Raymondo telephoned and told me that Freda had been at the circle and had asked if he was recording the sitting. She then asked him to send me a copy of the recording but to be sure to tell me that she was with me when I was walking the dogs and that I had made the right decision.

No one, not even Alf knew my thoughts and my questions to Freda."

June and Alf Winchester seen here discussing the programme for a Cober Hill seminar.

Father's return

When June's father passed to spirit at the beginning of April 2005 he made a very quick return to speak to June and three months later materialised at their home in Norfolk. Here is what June wrote:

"My father passed to spirit on 11th April 2005. The funeral took place on Friday 22nd and we took his ashes to Mum's grave in Kent the following Monday.

On Friday 29th April we were at a weekend seminar

and sat with Stewart in a trance sitting at the Edinburgh College of Psychic Studies.

Freda came through and told me that she met my father when he passed to the spirit world and he seemed to know her. I replied 'He did know you because I often spoke of you to him.' Freda then said, 'He wants to speak to you himself; he hasn't been able to do that for some time has he?'

Dad spoke and thanked Alf and me for making his last few weeks bearable and said that now it is the time for us to do all the things we hadn't been able to do because of looking after him. There wasn't a dry eye in the room.

On 29th July, when Stewart paid a visit and went into trance in our séance room in Cromer, Dad materialised and spoke at the end of the sitting.

Someone very tall stood at the side of the curtained recess next to me. The voice came from very high up. I heard deep breath and the person said 'It's John.' After that he struggled to speak and it was difficult to make out what was said. However, when we played the recording (the microphone had been attached to the ceiling above the curtains) he clearly said my special name and it is Dad – who happened to be 6ft 2ins tall.

How wonderful, consoling and exciting it was – just beyond words."

Author's note:

When you send out a thought, it is received. The spirit world is a world of thought and this is why we need to be aware of our motives. Thought is a very powerful form of energy, and as like attracts like, we are what we think.

Conditions of Thought

Sit in the silence of your thoughts, for that is your entry into the spirit world – A World of Thought.

Thought is creation whether it be negative or positive, and positive thought is extremely important when you sit in a circle.

Positive thought is open thought; it allows love, truth and goodness to flow through whenever you hold a séance.

You sit for the love of the spirit world.

You sit for the beauty of natural harmony.

You sit for meditation and peace.

You sit to be of service to others.

You sit for the goodness and healing of life everlasting.

Let the Light come in

and never allow negative thoughts to enter.

Negative thoughts close the door to truth and harmony.

So listen to your own thoughts –

Are they positive or are they negative?

Negative thoughts are fear of the unknown –

Suspicions of any fraudulent activity or –

Selfish and wanting thoughts

of perhaps expecting too much too soon.

Study your own thoughts carefully.

Always think of your departed loved ones being happy and free in the World of Spirit. Give them your love and your thoughts will be open to them – and do not expect – for this opposes the law of free will and the harmony is lost.

Time does not exist in the spirit world, so sit, – be patient, – be free in the World of Thought.

Be your own self, be at one, be unselfish and give, – give out loving feelings in harmony and bless your own consciousness.

Bless the beauty of your life and send out love, for love is light. Sincere unselfish love is an open door to those in the spirit world.

Think seriously about your own thoughts for they are the result of your sitting.

Be at peace with yourself.

(K.H. 2002)

Part Five

Reflections on my journey
and
tips for avoiding potholes on
the path of life

Researching the Meaning of Life

*

Touching the Next Horizon

*

The Stewart Alexander Home Circle 2019

Back Row from left: Ray (circle leader), Danny (Denise's fiancé), Stewart (physical medium), Denise.
Middle Row seated from left: Diane, June,
Katie (honorary member), and Carol.
Front Row from left: Emily, Shelby (Denise's daughter).

Chapter Twenty-seven

RESEARCHING THE MEANING OF LIFE

Have you ever asked yourself these questions:

Why am I here?

What am I looking for?

Why am I reading this book?

You are not alone, because people all over the world ask themselves the same questions as they ponder on the wonders of life itself. But what about life after death? Mediums can tap into the dimension known as the spirit world; some people have had a glimpse of it; others like to think it does exist and many genuine seekers hunt high and low for evidence of this everlasting sphere.

Our spirit friends in the home circle tell us that there is much more to life than the physical.

❖ As Freda puts it, "The mind is all that you are, all that you were and all that you will be—it is your personality—it is your complete memory—it is you in totality."

❖ As Walter demonstrates in his living matter through matter experiments, the fact is that nothing is solid and everything is made up of molecules vibrating at different rates and on different levels.

❖ And Dr. Barnett informs us that the logic and the physics of our world do not necessarily apply to the spirit world.

There is so much we don't know. Because we are limited – usually – to our five senses under the control of a finite brain, any strange or unusual happenings seen or heard are likely to be considered a trick of the mind by people without knowledge.

Those with a greater understanding of consciousness recognise that there is more to life than meets the physical eye. Such people can bring together a nucleus of energy, a condition of thought generating a sense of love and harmony, making that fantastic breakthrough into the spirit world possible.

For this reason, I am pleased that the Stewart Alexander and Friends Seminars have accommodated many a hopeful delegate who has gone back home with answers to some of the missing pieces they had been searching for, thus adding food for thought to their personal journeys. Professors, psychologists, scientists, doctors, spiritualists, psychic researchers, journalists, men and women from all walks of life have attended these special seminars which were held twice a year at the Cober Hill Conference Centre from 2000 to 2018. All had the same focus – to understand more about physical phenomena and the spirit world, a dimension beyond our finite knowledge, which we can only witness given the right conditions and opportunities.

The seminars, organised by June and Alf Winchester, played a big part in encouraging such people of like minds to get together. They were an opportunity for those who have witnessed spirit communication and genuine physical phenomena to express their knowledge and share their experiences without being ridiculed by individuals with conflicting beliefs. Delegates usually realised that it is much better to know about something directly than simply to believe in something. At these weekends, they could relax and enjoy a few days away from their daily concerns.

One of the key events in the programme, which included lectures, talks and workshops, was a large séance seating up to 100 people in the theatre.

Seated ready for the séance at a Stewart Alexander and Friends Seminar.

On these occasions, our spirit friends had the dynamic opportunity to demonstrate physical phenomena to an audience which was always amazed at the spirit team's ability to speak in direct voice, move the trumpets, materialise and walk among us, touching and talking to us all. Even with such a large audience, the trumpets could often reach out to those sitting at the back, and personal messages from so-called deceased loved ones added to the highlights of the weekend.

The seminars inspired many discussions relating to our temporary life on earth and the continuous life in spirit. Although it is a fact that human beings have a tendency to explore the vastness of the universe and the depths of the ocean with keen interest, how many have considered exploring the mind and the existence of the spirit world? This is why it is so important to have seminars like these, where people of like mind could strengthen the links between themselves and the two worlds.

Speaking of links, I for one have met many interesting people from different parts of the world at these seminars. One recently happened to be a respected investigative American journalist and a New York Times bestselling author by the name of Leslie Kean. She started visiting our seminars in 2015 when she was in the middle of writing a new book on research into the question of survival after death. Leslie was strongly impacted by the physical phenomena she witnessed at a seminar, and this resulted in further visits to the Alexander Home Circle where she experienced even more within a much smaller harmonious group. Her book, *Surviving Death: A Journalist Investigates Evidence for an Afterlife[1]* is a highly recommended read and is now the basis for a six-part documentary series.[2] The book includes her descriptions of the first few times she sat with Stewart's home circle, as well as a chapter written by Stewart himself.

Leslie and her fellow sitter, Mike Anthony (also from America), are now honorary members of the Alexander Home Circle. They sit every Monday at the same time the circle sits, and from New York City they participate in the séance via the iPad. Yes – this is another experiment that works. Facetime is connected to the New York séance room before the séance starts, and the iPad in Hull is then turned upside down on the table to block out any light. This enables Leslie and Mike to listen and join in with the conversation involving the

1. *Surviving Death: A Journalist Investigates Evidence for an Afterlife* (Crown Archetype, 2017)
2. For details see Leslie's website, www.survivingdeathkean.com.

circle and the spirit team. The only thing they can't do is see the phenomena. The spirit team has said many times that for them the distance means nothing, and that Leslie and Mike's voices sound no different to them than those of the people physically present in the room.

As far as we know, this is the first time in the history of Spiritualism that such a link has been made between sitters in distant locations on a regular basis.

In the meantime, both Leslie and Mike are continuing their research into the enigma of life beyond so-called death.

Mike Anthony and Leslie Kean

Having said all that, let us now return to our own personal research, which is the most important aspect of the journey for each and every one of us.

Reading this book will have created a connection between you and me, even though we have never actually met. Because this non-physical link has been made, now is the time to put our heads together and consider the power of our own thought processes.

Chapter Twenty-eight

TOUCHING THE NEXT HORIZON

This book has detailed some of my most meaningful experiences with spirit communication, an incredible journey of discovering trance and physical phenomena.

So having shared my venture along the path of trance and physical phenomena, we now approach a fork in the road where you and I will continue to walk our own separate ways— but before we part, I would like to offer you an invitation to sit with me a while, so we can ponder what has been learnt.

Our paths will have a number of different horizons on offer and we have freewill to choose our own way of life as we would like it to be.

As you know, mine has involved researching spirit communication and physical phenomena. It was a path of surprising discoveries leading to the ultimate experience of witnessing materialisation – being able to hear, see and touch the spirit people through a rare form of mediumship, supported by the Stewart Alexander Home Circle. I marvelled at Stewart's physical mediumship and I would consider him to be one of the finest in our era. I do hope that someday you will get the opportunity to experience similar physical manifestations at their best. For me, it was a life changing experience.

Even if you do not get the chance to encounter such phenomena, this need not stop you from conducting your own search for evidence of life after death. There are numerous spiritual paths to walk, some with very different views. Always remember that the patience and harmony of an open mind is the key to a successful connection, and even if you do not join a circle or a group, it is always beneficial to be at one with yourself.

What do I mean by that?

It is being kind to yourself as well as to others – because your unique version of heaven on earth is what you make it. It is a state of consciousness and unconditional love bringing about the freedom of the spirit.

> The freedom of the spirit
>>should be as a bird can fly
> With enlightenment in its heart
>>as it soars towards the sky.
> No bias or other personal beliefs
>>can block that feeling within
> Since open-minded thoughts
>>are as free as a lark can sing.
> So look up to that heavenly space
>>with unconditional love
> And send out thoughts of beauty
>>to the entity above.
> Truly like attracts like,
>>it is the natural law
> Be happy for your loved ones
>>who have only gone before.
> Be as free as a bird can fly
>>and allow your thoughts to sing.
> Happiness is the key to it all
>>and a connection it may bring.
> Remember always when you sit,
>>it's love that must be brought
> The energy of your very being
>>is the freedom of your thought.

(K.H. 2019)

Amid the hustle and bustle of everyday life I believe it is a good idea to stop and pause a while—to be mindful of a flower—to appreciate its beauty—to smell the scent and look deep into its incandescent colours—to be at one with its essence, and in return it will give you a moment of peace and tranquillity. It will give you your own space to find that still quiet voice within, to become at one with yourself so that you will begin to feel the relaxation of your whole being. It is then you may become inspired to sense something beyond the material world, a chance to discover the truth as you find it, and to maintain a unique balance of spiritual wellbeing.

Too many of us are locked into this modern technical world, so much so, that we tend to forget who we are. Despite saying this, I do appreciate that it is not easy to simply cast away our cares and worries, but a little time out, now and then, will certainly do no harm.

Sitting in meditation, listening to soft music, strolling through the woods or losing one's self in an interesting hobby may open the door to a spiritual connection. For me, insights sometimes gently flow through my thoughts when I am deeply involved with my artwork, and I often have to stop painting to write down the inspiration received.

I have learned that wherever you walk, there will always be another horizon, such is the continuation of life. When you have climbed a hill, you will then be able to look back and view your own vista of knowledge – according to your own personal development – with the opportunity to discover more about how and why you came to be as you are. You can assess what you have learned and how you came to discover new insights unfamiliar to you at the time.

Believe it or not, we are all actually our own teachers and only we can enlighten our own thoughts by seeking the level of truth we are able to accept. Another person's philosophy is fine, if we choose to become a follower for a while. We can learn from such a teacher, because they can show us and tell us what they know, but this may only skim the surface of true understanding. It is like someone telling you how to swim, but you won't really know how to swim unless you take the plunge yourself. This is why I believe that personal experience is our best and greatest mentor. We must always listen to our inner feelings.

At the beginning of my journey, when I started to seek out my own truth, I tried to understand the purpose of life and why I was here, but had no idea how I would find it. It was only when I chose the path leading into Spiritualism that I could recognise the hidden help within.

Because I chose to investigate and search further into the enigma of spirit communication, I slowly began to adopt a condition of acceptance, thus developing a new way of learning. I would ask myself questions and then somehow come up with my own answers; but were they only coming from me? A truly good teacher will place questions before you but won't give you any answers until you have made your own effort to investigate. Our individual inner teachings will also encourage us to seek and search, and will always accompany us along our tentative path of learning—growing stronger over time.

This is how my spirit friends were able to support me without any set rules and regulations that would have interfered with my own freewill. But the evidence was not presented to me on a plate; it was earned over a long period of time and the scenery was not always pleasant! There were potholes along the way.

I have come across fraudulent mediums. So let me assure you that I am aware (as is the spirit world) that there are conscious and unconscious mediumistic frauds just as there are frauds in most professions. Conscious frauds are those who purposely set out to deceive vulnerable sitters for monetary gain. Unconscious frauds are pseudo-mediums whose gifts, rather than being genuine, owe everything to an over-active imagination. They are, in fact, people who unknowingly deceive themselves into believing that they are what they are not.

For example, a so-called medium came into my house and said 'Thank you spirit' when she heard a click. I politely told her that the click she heard was the central heating timer switching on, but she wouldn't admit to being mistaken. Such people can be the betrayal of true and honest mediumship. Sadly, they are all around, so it is advisable not to accept everything at face value. When possible, try to record the message, store it, and monitor the outcome. If in doubt, simply file the reading and continue on your path of life. One important piece of advice is this – please be patient. When the time and conditions are right, a more meaningful form of experience will present itself, even if it does take some time to do so.

Emotion can cloud our senses to such a degree that we are unable to focus properly using our own judgment. The conditions of our thoughts need to be clear to be able to recognise the true nature of a medium and above all, we must always take care not to become a vulnerable or gullible recipient.

Please don't be upset if somebody receives excellent evidential communication and you don't. Each and every one of us has an aura which changes according to our moods, so if you are grieving, a brown or grey aura can upset the delicate connections of communication – in other words, your loved ones in spirit are around but are unable to reach out because of your intense grief. Grieving people are often disappointed with being unable to make that connection promised by a loved one because the sitting has perhaps taken place too soon after the transition.

Stewart once told me of an embarrassing situation he found himself in.

Two ladies came to a guest séance, travelling the 230 miles (368 kms) from Bristol to Hull. The first lady was hoping to make contact with her deceased husband and the second lady came with her only to give moral support. However, it was the second lady who received the evidential communications and not the friend she was supporting, who received nothing at all. One can understand why the first lady was upset. It would have been very difficult to tell her at the time that she herself had unknowingly created some kind of a blockage, most likely, due to her grief.

There are many reasons why a loved one in spirit is unable to make that breakthrough; one of them could be that the spirit person's energy may not blend with the medium's energy. Just like the fact that we on the earth plane do not always gel with some people, it could be that a loved one in spirit may have the same dilemma with a certain medium. If such a loved one does not feel comfortable at 'merging in' with a certain medium, then communication may not be possible. If this is the case, then a medium who could give one person an excellent reading may not deliver a reading of the same calibre to somebody else. A sitter can always visit a different medium if this happens, being very careful to select someone who comes via a personal recommendation and has a good reputation for accuracy.

We have been told that measured time does not exist in the spirit world and perhaps because loved ones in spirit might be experiencing such happy times in their 'heavenly' abodes, it is likely that they do not realise how much time has passed on the earth plane.

Some spirit people may not even realise that they have died, because they may be thinking, how can they be dead when they find themselves very much alive in another dimension? As Freda explained in Chapter 10, she thought she was in the middle of a dream when she saw people who had long since preceded her into the spirit world. This of course was a tremendous shock for her as she always thought of Spiritualism as absolute nonsense.

I have known people who have been disappointed because they have not received a message from a deceased loved one who promised that he/she would communicate soon after the passing. Some may have read books with accounts of spirit people making contact soon after their passing, and because of this, it is natural for people to expect this to happen for them. My consoling words would be that we on the earth plane do not know of the difficulties our friends and loved ones in spirit encounter when trying to make that important breakthrough. If it was easy, everybody would be doing it.

Wanting something to happen and it doesn't, can lead to disappointment. I made the mistake of expecting Mum to communicate quickly through a medium, but she didn't until after a few years. Other deceased friends and loved ones came through, but not Mum and I wondered if it was because I was trying to make things happen with too much expectation. I was to learn that the best communications came through when I least expected them. The spirit people will come through when the time is right for many reasons that we on the earth plane do not understand.

One example of a delayed 'agreed' message was delivered in a séance on 31st July 2008 when Gerald O'Hara received a secret code word via Freda, some thirteen years after the death of his friend, Michael Cunningham, in 1995.

Gerald's friend Michael had suffered a lengthy period of ill health before his passing. Whenever he had well-meaning visitors who would inadvertently make him feel drained and unhappy, his code word to Gerald was 'Jam'. If, on the other hand, his visitors enlivened him and made him happy, his code word to Gerald was 'Marmalade'.

It was then decided between them both that Michael would use one or other of those words after his death to verify his identity to Gerald.

Although Michael had come through various mediums after his passing, there was no code word provided for a long time. Then Freda provided the simple word 'Marmalade'. On hearing this word, Gerald recognised that Michael was not only saying 'It's me,' but he was also telling him, 'I am happy.' This special code word was personal evidence of his survival and happiness in the next world.

Love and happiness is the key to successful communication, and in my opinion, mixing with like-minded people will always help steer us in the right direction. You may perhaps suddenly realise that you thought you knew something when in fact you didn't. This happens to most of us and it is all part of understanding the different levels of knowledge and experience.

Occasionally, messages from the other side will not be understood at the time, but, once again, it is always advisable to record them on the chance that back-up evidence may be received at a later date, thus proving the message to be valid. These are usually the best messages because they dispel any form of telepathy.

A sceptic will forever demand irrefutable evidence,

and scientists will only accept definitive proof in order to recognise events from the séance room or other types of spirit communication. What they fail to comprehend is that the right conditions of thought that are developed within will help create a state of harmony. This loving atmosphere is essential for the development of physical phenomena and is a very important part of the equation. If sceptics and negativists were to sit with a circle like Stewart's, their conflicting energies would likely block the ability of the phenomena to occur.

Sitting with Stewart, I have done my best to illustrate the wonders of the occasion. But looking at my drawings alone will not necessarily affect a person's mindset. The images cannot capture the exceptional atmosphere of the séance room and the feeling of love that penetrates the core of your being. The sensation of being 'at one' with the spirit people has to be physically and personally encountered. Only then will you experience the two worlds blending together.

If you ever have the privilege to be invited to sit in a physical séance, please be aware that certain sitters who have not witnessed genuine ectoplasm can sometimes be misled by their own imagination. I have sat with people who were convinced that they were seeing ectoplasm when there was absolutely nothing there, and such individuals (unless they happen to be clairvoyant) can create an element of confusion for the other sitters.

As ectoplasm develops, it can be seen in its various stages, sometimes it looks like a thick paste, a blob of rubbery substance or candyfloss – but believe me, ectoplasm in its developed form is not some wispy energy or moving vapour, it is solid matter. The spirit scientists can make it into anything they wish – flesh, hair, clothes – solid to the touch and physically visible to every sitter in the room if it is possible for light to be introduced.

These drawings (as shown earlier) depict how every sitter in the room saw the ectoplasm on those occasions.

Here we must be careful not to engage in auto suggestion. This is a common problem, especially in transfiguration, when somebody claims to see a face and another person excitedly echoes the announcement driving others on. It is always advisable to be aware that desperate and overly eager sitters with 'wanting' thoughts can be deluded into seeing something that is not really there. Fraudulent mediums (often feigning trance) will use the opportunity to move and twist the features of their faces in a very dim red light making it hard to see exactly what is happening.

Before commencing to sit, it is essential to open the session by asking the spirit world for protection, especially for safety to be concentrated around the medium and each person in the room, and to be permitted to work with the highest level of good.

Bob and Ena always emphasised like attracts like, and if you sit with the genuine intention of helping and serving others, you will automatically attract spirit of like mind who will lovingly come to help and serve. Those who sit with the intention of 'wanting' are in danger of attracting lower spirit entities or blocking an open flow of energy in the room. It's important to leave any desires for specific outcomes outside the séance room door.

This is something to bear in mind if you should choose to start by using a Ouija board or a table, for table movement[1]. Although they can be valid and useful tools for experienced sitters, in the wrong hands they can lead people down a dangerous path, especially if there is raw psychic energy present (particularly in teenagers) which can attract mischievous and even malevolent entities of the lower realms, who are closer to the earth vibration.

If you decide to sit without knowing who the medium is in your group, you need to sit with the right intention. That is to wish to contact with love, asking for those who come in love to protect you from harm.

True loved ones in spirit will always try their best to help, guide and encourage you along your path of life in unity with your own freewill. They will never tell you anything that will cause you to worry unduly. At the same time, do bear in mind that they cannot make any decisions for you as this would be against the natural law of progression.

Your spiritual progression may come about in many strange and unusual ways, for example, suffering any type of illness on the earth plane may enhance our compassion, healing and understanding for others in the same or even a different predicament – a unique experience of learning giving us the opportunity to share the true meaning of those in need. For example, how can a perfectly healthy person understand the real trauma of the sick and disabled?

Primarily, although we do live in a material world, it helps to avoid the totally materialistic path. In this

---

1. Table movement is known as tiptology. It was much used in Victorian times and also by Mrs Osbourne Leonard with Sir Oliver Lodge (see *Raymond, or Life and Death*).

technological era, the pursuit of possessions, celebrity and wealth may take us over. Social media rules many lives and the overuse of such devices and platforms can interfere with our ability to respond to the quiet voice within, a quiet voice that is waiting to guide us in our spiritual development.

Never in my wildest dreams did I think that I would become an honorary member of the Stewart Alexander Home Circle; nor in my wildest dreams did I think that I would be giving talks and writing books. As it happened, it was to be my destiny. Yes, I did go astray at certain times as we all do. However, my spirit friends, acting like discreet signposts at an unclear junction, would patiently interact with my thoughts. This gave me a sense of direction, since it seemed they had the intention of placing me back on the right path – a path that I myself had to find and choose to walk.

I will always be indebted to them for their love, patience and service. I sincerely hope that the contents of this book have offered some insights as to what can be achieved if you search for it. I hope that your path will be, or has been, as adventurous and enjoyable as mine.

And, if you should discover and accept that the reality of life after physical death does in fact exist (if you haven't already), how will you live your life?

That may provide a radically different outlook towards the next stage of your own progression on this great school called earth.

It doesn't matter to which group we belong, what religion we choose to follow or even if we are agnostic. What is important is our quality of love, caring and compassion for others, while we are here.

Isn't this what progression is all about, to become at one with the united whole for the greater good of mankind?

Finding your true spiritual path with sincere meaning can bring an element of greater understanding and contentment. Wherever we choose to walk, it is always wise to be alert of any possible hitches, but don't let these put you off a meaningful and uplifting adventure that is rightfully yours.

It is a way of life and a beautiful journey.

I hope your personal quest for truth will always be successful as you walk your own path of life. It will be different from mine, as no two paths are the same, but one thing is for sure: however long or short the venture, all paths lead to a taste of the "real" world that is to come.

Lightning Source UK Ltd.
Milton Keynes UK
UKHW021150190123
415622UK00014B/897